No More
Silence

DAVID WHELAN

WITH MARION SCOTT AND JIM MCBETH

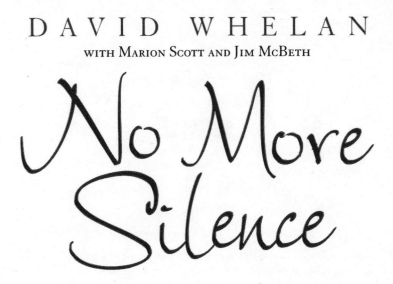

No More Silence

He thought he'd got away with it. But one day
little David would find the strength to speak out.

HARPER
element

HarperElement
An Imprint of HarperCollins*Publishers*
77–85 Fulham Palace Road,
Hammersmith, London W6 8JB

www.harpercollins.co.uk

and *HarperElement* are trademarks
of HarperCollins*Publishers* Ltd

First published by HarperElement 2010

1 3 5 7 9 10 8 6 4 2

A catalogue record of this book is
available from the British Library

ISBN 978-0-00-738890-5

Printed and bound in Great Britain by
Clays Ltd, St Ives plc

Mixed Sources
Product group from well-managed
forests and other controlled sources
www.fsc.org Cert no. SW-COC-001806
© 1996 Forest Stewardship Council

FSC is a non-profit international organisation established to promote the
responsible management of the world's forests. Products carrying the FSC
label are independently certified to assure consumers that they come
from forests that are managed to meet the social, economic and
ecological needs of present and future generations.

Find out more about HarperCollins and the environment at
www.harpercollins.co.uk/green

To 'Robbie' for unswerving commitment, and to my brothers and sisters, Johnny, Jeanette, Jimmy and Irene. You are always in my heart.

Acknowledgements

To Marion Scott and Jim McBeth, both superb journalists. My story was trapped inside me. They liberated it. Their commitment and guidance carried it from conception to completion. It was an emotional journey and without them there would be no book.

To our literary agent, Clare Hulton, for making it happen, and Vicky McGeown at HarperCollins.

To Finola McCann and family for sharing their lives, and in memory of Fay, who passed away in 2010.

To my psychologist Dr Kathy for bringing me back from the brink.

To Mary and Oliver Burke for all your support over the years and making me so welcome.

To Ian, a thousand thanks for fighting the good fight, and to Jeremy Kidd, who gives his time so freely to the cause.

To Sylvia for your friendship and help in my hour of need.

To Annie, Isaac and the Speakup team for support.

To all the friends who guided me from the dark.
To Strathclyde Police for pursuing justice.
To Michael McMahon MSP for action and not just words.
To lawyer Cameron Fyfe, for taking on the system.
To survivors everywhere … You are not alone.

Contents

Prologue

We had arrived. I had fallen asleep on the journey to a new life that promised peace, security and safety. I awoke with a start, in time to see the words spelled out in flowers – 'Suffer the little children.' My first sight of and welcome to Quarriers Children's Village. I did not realise then that the ancient words, spoken by Jesus in the New Testament, which were displayed so beautifully in a floral arrangement by the entrance, would be corrupted before I was much older. Nestling in the Renfrewshire countryside, this was a place far from the grime and unpredictability of life in an inner-city slum.

My sister Irene sat next to me in the back of the social worker's car, her eyes luminous with uncertainty. I shrugged off sleep and wiped moisture from the car window. My first sight of the bell tower. It rose high above what I would later learn was known as the Children's Cathedral. I had never seen anything so breathtaking. My world had been the drab, monotonous, utilitarian architecture of a sink housing estate, where no one looked up. Heaven was such a hard place to find. Structures such as the Children's Cathedral dominated only places where there was hope. The soaring steeple pointed to Heaven, but I would soon find it was pointing the way to Hell. He would see to that. The bell tower was where he took me, its impenetrable walls stifling my screams as he stole my innocence and planted the seeds of my own destruction, which would come many years later, when I was an adult and believed that I had left the past behind.

His name was John Porteous. He is at the heart of this story, but there will be few mentions of his given name. I once called him 'Uncle John', but I was a child then and trusting. I had yet to be betrayed by the man whose duty it was to protect me, to keep me safe. Therefore he is for ever the Beast – it is how I have referred to him in my mind ever since. For three decades it took all of my strength to block out the unspeakable things he did to me over my time at the children's home. A single phone call, 30 years after I escaped his clutches, proved to me that my entire existence was an edifice built on sand. In a matter of a few seconds, the façade that masked the pain of a lost childhood and a misguided sense of shame was torn away. I was forced to stop running in a race that I could not win, a race away from my past. This time, this time justice had to prevail and I had to play my part. The phone call placed me at the centre of Operation Orbona, the biggest police investigation into systematic sexual and physical abuse at a children's home. Eight of the abusers would be convicted, and I would witness the Beast going to jail.

I thought then it was over. I was wrong. It was just the beginning. Before I could reach the light, everything in my life would be taken from me. I would lose my successful career, the millionaire lifestyle and everything I had so carefully created as a shield against my secret pain. This is the story of how I fought back.

No More
Silence

Chapter 1

Born Into a World Beyond Poverty

I am searching for memories. I am four years old. I think I am alone. I am still hungry, but I force myself to save some food, the remains of lunch. Mother, a tall, fragrant woman with a kind face and a ready smile, is in another room. Father, big, bluff, reassuring, is out of the house, but I don't know where. He left with a cheery wave, ruffling my hair with large, clean hands.

I am in the drawing room, a generously proportioned space that is little used. The ceiling, with its ornate, elaborate cornicing, seems very high above me. Light floods in through the tall window, which looks out onto a broad expanse of lawn, running into the distance towards a destination that is as yet unknown to me. Mother's dog – a Cairn terrier? Misty? – is trying desperately to attract my attention, begging for what I have in my hand. The dog dances at my feet, but I reject the animal's overture. This is about survival.

I glance around the room, searching for prying eyes, before I unwrap the food from the napkin in which it is hidden. I am safe. I can hear the sound of clinking crockery coming from the kitchen. Dishes are being washed in a sink. Margaret, the middle-aged woman who seems to be part of the family while simultaneously distant from us, does the washing and cleaning for Mother.

Mother is elsewhere, entertaining two of her friends, regular visitors to the salubrious detached Victorian villa in one of the most exclusive suburbs on the Southside of Glasgow. I have already been wheeled out to be touched and poked affectionately by my mother's companions.

'Such a lovely boy,' says one.

'Such big eyes,' says the other, in a voice that tinkles like glass.

They smell so nice, better than the women in the place where I was before, a crowded, noisy, dismal barracks inhabited by a legion of nobody's children, all of them like me, all clamouring for attention. This strange new world is very different. I have not inhabited it for long. I don't know precisely how long. Time has yet to develop any meaning.

I am alone, though, with the food from lunch, which I push down under the cushions on the huge sofa. Even if someone sits down, they won't be able to see it. My hidden treasure now lies beside what remained of breakfast. I ensure once again that no one has discovered my secret place. If they don't give me any more food, I won't starve.

I was born into a world beyond poverty, the youngest of five children – the son of a brutish father, who was a drunkard and a rapist, and a mother who was emotionally and mentally unhinged. Naturally, I have no recollection of the period. I rely on my eldest sister, Jeanette, for information, and on the sparse notations in my social-work file, which record the time before

I awakened to the world and was able to remember. This document, the story of my life, runs to just two typewritten pages.

My first true memories are of these recently acquired 'parents' – two Glasgow doctors who fostered me from a children's home. I cannot even remember now which children's home it was. I was in so many homes that my memory of them is fragmented. They have merged in my mind as little more than a vague recollection. That day, when I hid the food – was it in 1961? – represents my first clear memory. Whatever instincts of survival I had acquired clearly still prevailed. I would learn later that it is commonplace for children who spend their first years in care to secrete food. It is also accepted that such children tend to steal the food of others. It's a survival mechanism – who knows when you will be fed again? Here, in this privileged place of sweet-smelling women and benign men, there appeared to be no shortages. What little experience I had gained, however, had taught me to hedge my bets.

The history of my family in so far as I know it stretches back no further than my natural parents – John Whelan and Evelyn Wolfries. I know nothing of my grandparents or great-grandparents. If they were anything like my parents, perhaps it is just as well I don't know. My birth certificate records that I was born in Stobhill Hospital, Glasgow, at 8.45 p.m. on 27 September 1957. My mother was 26 years old and already had four children. My father was 34 and is described as a builder's labourer. I doubt whether, in the course of his 75 years, he ever undertook any work as honourable as honest labouring. He was a drunken hoodlum, a man who employed casual violence to take what he wanted, when he wanted. In the incestuous netherworld that he inhabited, in the environs of 22 Kennedy Street, in the Townhead area of the city, my father was notorious. He considered himself a street fighter, but he couldn't compete with the real hard men, who fought each other on equal terms and disdained any man who lifted his hand to a woman or a child. My father had no such compunction. He was a monster who beat his wife and children, with the exception of me.

By the time of my birth, he already had 24 convictions and had been jailed for crimes of dishonesty and violence and neglecting his children. I escaped being abused only because I was too young. I don't believe I hate my father. That would require emotion. I have none for him. As for my mother – Ma – I recognise her now for what she was, a poor soul, weak and ineffectual, and every bit as much a victim as I would become.

The bottom line, however, is that for whatever reason they failed their children miserably, setting in motion a set of circumstances that would lead to the premature deaths of three of my siblings. The oldest, Johnny, took his own life at the age of 27. Jimmy, the third oldest, was tortured by mental illness until his death at the age of 46. My sister Irene died a broken woman, deeply traumatised by abuse in childhood, and passed away just after her 49th birthday. The banners proclaiming 'Happy Birthday!' were taken down only a few weeks before she died.

Ma also died young. The years of chain-smoking Senior Service cigarettes and swallowing the handfuls of pills that dulled the pain of her existence caught up with her before she was 50.

Only Jeanette and I survive. Thank God for Jeanette. In the course of this story, she will emerge as the rock upon which my life was built. My father lies un-mourned by us in a pauper's grave somewhere in London, in an untended, nameless plot of ground, as far as I am aware. There is an old saying where I come from that your life may be measured by the number of people who shed tears at your funeral. I don't know how many people cried at his. I wasn't there. None of us were.

My parents abnegated their responsibility for their children. My mother, this weak and irresponsible individual with no real notion of the concept of care, deserted my brothers and sisters even before I was born. It was in effect an act of self-defence. She was escaping the brutality of what we might mockingly describe as a challenging home life. My father beat her. He also beat his children. John Whelan had a perverse sadistic streak. One of his favourite pastimes was to sit his oldest two sons at the table and place a pile of pennies in front of them. If they failed to grab the coins before he did, they were punched. If they grabbed the pennies before he did, they were punched. It was a game with only one winner.

As my brothers grew up, they were challenged to fight. 'Are you as tough as your old da?' he would demand, flecking their faces with his spittle, preening himself over his street name, the 'Little Bull', earned because of his pugnacious nature. 'Put 'em up,' he would say, ordering Johnny and Jimmy to raise their fists. Da was usually drunk, swaying back and forward, as he adopted the same pugilistic stance. 'Show your old man what you've got,' he would shout, adding, 'Hit me!' When my brothers, who were little more than skin and bone, did hit him, they were pummelled into submission and thrown against the walls of the one-room flat in which we lived.

My mother was incapable of protecting them. She had long since been cowed into submission herself. All she could do was hide the bruises on their malnourished bodies from the neighbours. Da ensured Ma's compliance by trying to father a child during each year of their marriage. However, my mother would eventually seek to escape and ran away in January 1956. It was that year the family first came to the attention of social workers. Within days my father had put us into care. He could not be bothered to assume responsibility for his own children.

Like most battered wives, my mother returned, in November 1956. My brothers and sisters came home, and I was the inevitable result of Ma and Da's ill-fated reconciliation. Ma was not equipped to look after herself, never mind the rest of us, in such an atmosphere of fear and brutality. Explaining my mother's fractured state of mind is probably beyond my descriptive powers. Ma was an enigma. She apparently rarely spoke of her own childhood, hence my ignorance of my forebears. It appears that she had been badly injured as a child in a bizarre accident – a horse, which belonged to a rag-and-bone man, kicked her on the head. It could explain a lot – for example, why Ma spent long spells in a mental hospital and why she never had a proper education. She could barely read or write. I have long suspected that she was mildly brain-damaged, which could have led to her deteriorating mental state and the bouts of debilitating depression. It was a combination that made her easy prey for my brutish father. He 'owned' her. There were, mercifully, moments of respite from his drunken and abusive rages; he spent a lot of time in jail.

Ma had two brothers, Charlie and Davie, who would appear occasionally to threaten my father with violence if he laid a hand on their sister. Davie had lost one of his legs in a childhood accident. Generations of children played a game known as 'taking a hudgie'. I don't know where the word 'hudgie' comes from, but the game involved hitching a ride on the back of a moving vehicle, an extremely dangerous escapade. Davie had fallen from the tailgate of a municipal dustcart and been dragged under its wheels. The absence of one of his limbs did not, however, diminish his fighting skills. Ma and my siblings would apparently cower in the corner while he and my father swapped blows. My father was subdued by such encounters, but there was a dreadful inevitability about what would happen when Davie left; my mother would take another beating.

If Ma's brothers had really wanted to help, they would have physically removed her from Kennedy Street, which would have given her the chance to break free from my father's tyranny. This was not to be, however, and my uncles soon tired of coming to their sister's rescue. That suited my father. With no one to protect her, he could continue to use her as a punch bag.

It may seem strange to say such a thing, but according to my sister Jeanette the daily assaults on my mother and siblings were perhaps not the worst form of abuse my father inflicted. Psychological scars run much deeper than physical wounds. Jeanette told me, 'He brought home women and had sex with them on a camp bed in front of us and Ma! He would roar, "Turn your faces to the wall," before having loud, uninhibited sex, as we huddled in the bed recess. What kind of woman would consent to undress and have sex in front of a mother and her frightened children? It beggars belief.'

I should explain that this coupling was taking place in a tenement 'single-end'. Anyone who has not lived in one of these one-room dwellings, so common to the inner cities of the period, cannot appreciate the intimacy of such living conditions. Parents and children shared the same bed, which was in a recess in the wall. If you had delusions of grandeur, you put up a curtain, which was drawn across the area during daytime.

We lived 'up a close' – a vernacular term for the common entrance to a tenement, which was used to describe the entire building. Our tenement was four storeys high. There were at least three families on each floor, sharing an outside toilet, which was located on the landing between the staircases. Audiences around the world have laughed at Billy Connolly's description of life up a close – children crowded into bed with their parents, sleeping under winter coats instead of blankets or duvets – but there was nothing remotely amusing about the reality of such a life.

There was no such thing as privacy, but tenement etiquette demanded that you mind your own business. When my father was beating his family or having sex with trollops, every person in the building would have heard it, but nobody ever interfered – rules of the close.

Jeanette remembers a particularly harrowing episode when the two combined. She said, 'Da arrived, rolling drunk, with his fancy woman in tow. His floosy was drunk too, giggling foolishly, hanging on his arm. We didn't know women like this. The women we knew were mothers, grannies. These creatures were from another world. Even street walkers, women who sold their bodies, would not have sunk so low. Whenever Da entered a room, it was filled suddenly with angry noise, bellowing his orders for us to look away. Heaven knows why he felt the need to tell us to look away – he was inches from us! We did our best to hide in the bed recess. Ma shut her eyes tight. Her sense of worthlessness must have been reinforced by these appalling scenes.

'On one particular occasion, one of his women showed some compassion. Our distress was so evident to her that she left. Dad was enraged – "You can't even keep those brats quiet!" he shouted. Ma tried to reason with him, but it only served to inflame him. He began beating her. She begged him to stop, but he rained down ever more vicious blows on her, punching her as hard as he could in the stomach. To this day, I am convinced Ma lost an unborn child that night. She was bleeding, the frightening red stain spreading across the bed, increasing our terror. Eventually, he stopped, collapsing onto the bed in a drunken stupor. Even then, Ma would not allow me to go for help for fear of waking him. When she heard him snoring, she relented.'

Jeanette, who was only around six years old at the time, has spent the rest of her life haunted by this episode. Terrified that our mother was dying, she fled from the house and encountered a neighbour in the street. The man ran to a public telephone box and called an ambulance, and the police. They arrived simultaneously. As the ambulance took my mother away, the police dragged my father from the house and threw him into their van. He was still so drunk he didn't know what he had done. I'm certain that Jeanette saved Ma's life that night. My sister has no recollection of who looked after us until Ma was released from hospital several days later. By then, Da had returned. With no cooperating witness, the charges against him had been dropped.

It would not be long, however, before the police were back, with a far more serious charge – rape. It was a time to rejoice in the close as a dozen burly policemen bounced him down every stair and off every wall to the 'paddywagon'. Neighbours cheered and jeered. Women hung out of the windows on every floor, resting on their big, beefy arms, enjoying the spectacle of their hated neighbour being 'huckled'. No one enjoyed it more than the police, who knew him for the monster he was. He had picked up the woman in a pub and raped her in an alleyway.

I was a babe in arms and too young to be aware of this momentous event in our lives. It was October 1958 and Da was about to be sent to jail for eight years. He was gone – it would only be a matter of weeks before Ma was gone, too. If she had the strength of character of a normal mother, she would have used this respite to take us far away from my monster of a father. Instead, she deserted us, leaving us to heaven knows what fate.

Jeanette vividly remembers the day she left. My sister was sitting in the street outside the tenement, watching the trams trundle past. She heard Ma's high heels clattering down the stairs. Jeanette looked up and Ma appeared, all dressed up. Her hair was carefully coiffed, piled high in an elaborate beehive. Her lips were a gash of pillarbox-red lipstick, which exactly matched the colour of her coat. She wore black patent-leather stilettos – a sure sign that she was going somewhere special.

'Where you going all dolled up, Ma?' Jeanette asked.

'Mind your own business,' Ma said sharply. She tottered off on her high heels, looking over her shoulder long enough to say, 'Look after the children for a while.'

My sister tried to follow Ma, but she boarded a tram heading into the city centre. Even at such a young age, Jeanette knew she couldn't leave us alone long enough to establish where Ma was going. None of us would see her again for eight years, until the family was brought together in a short-lived and ill-advised reunion. I would learn years later that she had gone to Banstead, in Surrey. God knows why she went there. I can only reason that she wanted to put as much distance as possible between herself and our monstrous father, or perhaps she just didn't want to bring up five children on her own.

When Ma left, I was still in a pram, Johnny was seven, Jeanette was six, Jimmy was four, and Irene was barely two. Under normal circumstances, one might have expected Johnny to take the lead because he was oldest. It was, however, Jeanette who kept us alive when Ma left. Picture this child, knocking on neighbours' doors, begging for pennies to feed us. Even at that age, she covered up the fact that Ma was gone.

'Where's your ma?' they would demand to know.

'She's in her bed,' Jeanette would lie.

Somehow, she managed to scrape enough money together to buy bread and milk. Jeanette coaxed us to eat with what little food there was in the flat. The cupboards were soon bare except for stale bread and a handful of cereal. Jeanette remembers us crying with hunger. Even the etiquette of tenement life could not allow such a situation to continue. It became apparent to the women in the close that my incessant crying – coupled with my older brothers knocking on their doors begging for food – meant something was terribly wrong.

The 'cruelty man' – from the Royal Scottish Society for the Prevention of Cruelty to Children (RSSPCC) – did not come a moment too soon. When he arrived in the house, I was trapped under my upturned pram. My brothers and sisters were so desperate for food they had climbed onto the pram, in an attempt to reach the high cupboards, and tipped it over. I could easily have died. Once again, the neighbours were out in force, to see the final departure of the Whelan clan from Kennedy Street. No one cheered or jeered this time.

We were taken to a children's home the name of which I do not remember. At Glasgow Sheriff Court, on Wednesday, 28 January 1959, the RSSPCC was granted a Section 66 petition, which allowed Glasgow Corporation to commit us into care. Five months later, it was decided to send my four brothers and sisters to a foster home on the Outer Hebridean island of North Uist. It was also decided that I would not go with them. I remained behind, in the children's home. I only learned many years later that the authorities wanted to put as much distance as they could between my siblings and our brutal father. My older brothers were bruised and covered with welts from a belt. And they believed that my sisters and I would also be at risk if he had access to us. Irene was just a tot and I was a babe in arms. But it was thought that five children, including two babies, would be too much for a foster couple. They went. I stayed. And so my brothers and sisters disappeared from my life, along with my infantile memories of them and my parents.

It is a strange fact of my life that childhood memories elude me, especially those from my infancy. It is as if I have suppressed many of them. Perhaps the influence of my father, a man I effectively did not know, is stronger than I imagine. Whereas most children would enjoy fairly precise memories of their formative years – from about the age of three to four – I struggle to reclaim mine. Consequently, I have only the vaguest recollection of the two people who arrived at the children's home one day and talked soothingly to me of becoming my new mummy and daddy – their words. I do not even remember their names. They will be written down somewhere, but I have no access to those records.

By the time I was ensconced with the two doctors in their big house in Newton Mearns, just outside Glasgow, I believed I was alone in the world. Nobody thought to tell me otherwise. Even behind the scenes, however, the mother I didn't even know existed was manipulating my future. I learned later that the doctors wanted to adopt me, to give me their name and offer me a stable home and opportunities that someone from my background could only ever have dreamed of, but Ma refused to sign the adoption papers. God knows why. It was clear from her actions that she had not wanted me or any of her children. The doctors had treated me as their son for nearly two years, a period during which apparently they exhausted every avenue in an attempt to keep me, but ultimately, when it became clear that they could not be assured that I would be allowed to stay with them, they decided they could not live with that uncertainty.

On the day I left them, they were distraught. They stood by the door of that big house, watching me as I walked down the path flanked by two social workers.

Before I reached the garden gate and the waiting car, I pulled away and ran back to them. 'Was it because I stole the food?' I asked.

CHAPTER 2

Paradise Found

Paradise was 17 miles long by 13 miles wide. I took the measure of it on 6 August 1964. North Uist, in the Outer Hebrides, a place as remote as it is beautiful. My new home. I was seven years old, and an extended island family of 2,205 hardy souls who lived on the western fringe of Europe were waiting to welcome me to the next stage of my young and not uneventful life. Four of them would be the brothers and sisters who, until that momentous day, I did not know existed.

'I have something to tell you, Davie,' said the social worker, as we rode in a taxi from the tiny airport at Benbecula across an alien landscape beneath an endless sky.

I felt very small. The incredible excitement of the journey from Glasgow to the airport, and then the wonderful adventure of the flight, had subsumed any questions that had been forming in my mind. It had only been a few hours since I had left the doctors' house. My innocent enquiry about the food had sent them fleeing indoors, with tears streaming down their faces. I was confused. As I was ushered into the car, I heard from behind me a terrible howl of anguish, which I could not understand. They wanted me to go away, didn't they? There was no time to think about it now. I would think about it later. Now there was only space and wind and blue sky.

The social worker sensed that I had come back down to earth physically and metaphorically. It was time for answers. She placed her arm around my shoulder, drawing me closer to her in the back of the car, enveloping me in comforting warmth. I was too young and damaged to recognise such an action as intimacy, which had played little part in my life so far. However, I sensed she wanted to share something special with me.

'Do you know you have brothers and sisters, Davie? Did you know that?' she asked.

I was not sure what having brothers and sisters meant. The concept was unclear. My life had been a pretty solitary affair until that time, usually me and whichever adults had charge over my care. I looked for inspiration at the back of the silent driver's head and beyond, to his view of the astonishing landscape spreading before us. Neither he nor the cloudless sky offered any explanation.

'They went away when you were still a tiny baby,' the social worker continued. 'While you've been in one place, they've been in another – here,' she added, her hand indicating what seemed like a vast plain beyond the safety and seclusion of the old car, which was now rattling along a rutted track. 'But now,' she said, 'you'll all be together.' She looked towards the front, beyond the driver, to the ribbon of road lying ahead. 'We're nearly at Knockintorran – look!' she said.

The blue 'reek' of peat smoke was a thin, almost transparent column leaking into the sky from the chimney of an isolated single-storey cottage that was dwarfed by the landscape. I could sense the rough texture of the grey walls, which, from this distance, looked as cold as the feeling in my stomach. I was still grappling with this brothers-and-sisters problem.

It would soon be resolved. They were lined up against the wall of the croft house, an honour guard for the new arrival. They would soon have names: Johnny, Jeanette, Jimmy and Irene. Ranging in age from 9 to 13, they, too, had spent a significant portion of their lives separated from me, but they had the advantage of memory. A man and woman were standing behind the children, a tentative smile playing on their kind and ruddy country faces. These were folk outwith my experience, dressed in rough-and-ready clothes, with a quiet stateliness that I would come to realise was the hallmark of those who live in wild places. It is hard to describe. They had a dignity that belied their appearance. Morag and Willie MacDonald were my new mother and father.

I learned later that I was here because my natural mother had refused to agree to me being adopted by two childless doctors in Glasgow, despite not being able to care for me herself. Unbeknown to me, while I had been in and out of children's homes and foster care, my brothers and sisters had been staying with Willie and Morag. Ma's demand, which reunited me with my siblings, was arguably the only true act of compassion she had ever shown her children. The social worker gently pushed me out of the car and into my new life. The woman behind the children waved my brothers and sisters forward. It was an awkward moment.

Someone, I can't remember who, said, 'Hello, Davie!'

I had come home.

I still do not know what possessed social workers to despatch a gaggle of poverty-bred street kids from Glasgow to an island where English was the second language, but I bless them still for it. I would discover that my brothers and sisters were much changed from the urchins who had left the city so many years before. They formed a circle round me, and standing in the centre I suddenly had the feeling that I was where I was meant to be. Maybe that was what this brothers-and-sisters thing meant.

They were clearly fascinated by me, this small stranger who had without ceremony been added to their number. They looked from me to my new parents, asking questions in an unfamiliar tongue; they had acquired Gaelic. Children learn by osmosis and it would not be long before that incomprehensible and musical language would morph into words and phrases that I could understand.

I brushed aside the clouds of insects that had formed around my head – midges. Those familiar with the west of Scotland will know the scourge of these minuscule and annoying creatures.

Morag and Willie MacDonald took me into the warmth of their home, warmth that was as emotional as it was physical. Heat emanated from a large open fire beside an Aga, upon which a great black kettle was coming to the boil. I would discover that this kettle boiled from dawn till bedtime. Morag walked into a wall of steam. To this day I remember her in a halo of cloud. She never strayed far from that cooker and its huge pots of potatoes and stew, which took two hands to carry to the wooden deal table in the middle of her kitchen. It was the heart of the home.

My first – and erroneous – impression of the croft house was that it seemed sparse and bleak, but it was soon lit up by the bright, if stern, Morag. In retrospect, I realise Morag had none of the vanities of the city women I had known. Her looks were unprepossessing. Make-up and hair-styling were dismissed as the work of the Devil. Morag was a devout Christian. Her uniform of shapeless dress, cross-over white pinny and men's socks, rising out of sturdy shoes that would not have looked out of place on a man's feet, was good enough, thank you very much.

Willie was her soul mate, a silent, strong, hard-working man with cool blue eyes that took in everything but gave little away. He, too, wore a uniform – dungarees under a suit jacket and wellington boots. The sleeves of his collarless shirt were invariably rolled up to reveal bulging biceps. The ensemble was completed by a 'caidie' – a bunnet, or flat cap – which was removed from his head only at the dinner table or to wipe the sweat from his brow.

Their home reflected the couple. The term 'modern amenities' would have meant little to them. The toilet was in a shed at the back of the small garden. It was a treacherous journey in the dark. There was no electricity. The soft glow of light in the three-bedroom croft was generated by paraffin lamp, and while the world had long since been seduced by the age of television, it was an apparatus that Morag regarded as an abomination and an affront to the Good Lord. An ancient battery-powered radio, which broadcast the mournful Gaelic songs that became one of the soundtracks of my life, was sufficient for Morag and Willie. It would take me some time to come to terms with this strange new world of the Western Isles, a place with its own unique personality.

When I arrived on the island, the community survived on crofting. In English terms, crofters would be tenant farmers. My new parents had the lifelong tenancy of the croft, which had been passed down through generations of the family. Morag and Willie paid their rent to the 'laird', in this case the

Fifth Earl of Granville, a cousin of the Queen, who owned a 60,000-acre estate, part of which was divided into the small farms.

The Outer Hebrides are a bleakly beautiful collection of islands, stretching from the largest, Lewis, in the north, through Harris and the Uists to the butt of Barra, in the south. Separated from the mainland by the Sea of the Hebrides, it is a world apart in every sense. North Uist is flat, almost devoid of trees, and blasted by Atlantic winds that would soon cleanse me. Moorland extends as far as the eye can see in a landscape punctuated by croft-house chimneys and their plumes of peat-fuelled fire smoke. The adjoining crofting communities of North and South Uist, where Gaelic is the first language, are steeped in Highland history. When I eventually went to the local school there were children who had not spoken a word of English before they began their education.

This is the birthplace of heroines such as Flora MacDonald, the saviour of Bonnie Prince Charlie after the 1745 Jacobite Rebellion, which sought to restore the displaced Stuart dynasty to the thrones of Scotland and England. The romantic venture ended tragically with the defeat of the prince's ragtag Highland Army by a superior British force at the Battle of Culloden in 1746. To this day, however, the memory of how Flora spirited away the fugitive prince 'over the sea to Skye' is still strong in the minds of the inhabitants of the islands.

Memory and heritage are precious things in a spectacular and timeless landscape ruled by majestic red deer, which roam a land of lochans teeming with trout, beneath a sky that is the domain of eagles. I had never seen or experienced anything like it. Until I became part of it, my horizon was defined by the distance from the front door of my house to the end of the street. This was another world, where quiet folk spun cloth that was fashioned into the clothes they wore. The food on their table came from the land, the fruits of their own labour.

It was my first evening at Knockintorran and I was about to partake of those fruits. To a child raised on watery soup and insipid stews, the richness and quantity of Morag's fare would provoke the mother of all belly aches. All of us had somehow muddled through in the hours preceding dinner, operating in that self-conscious atmosphere in which much is thought but little is said. The social worker had long since departed. We were a guarded group as we gathered round the table, with the hatless Willie at its head. My brothers and sisters were subdued. There were obviously rules, which I knew nothing of, but I was street-smart enough to learn.

The table groaned under baskets of homemade bread and scones waiting to be smothered in butter, which had been churned by hand that day, and jam made from fruit grown in the garden. Morag emerged from her cloud of steam, bearing a large pot of potatoes, which she placed on the table. I reached out to take one and learned, somewhat painfully, the first rule of dining at Knockintorran. A wooden spoon tapped my knuckles.

'Now, young David,' said Morag, 'you don't snatch your food until we've thanked the Good Lord for what He's given us. I'll let you off this time because you don't know any better, coming from that heathen city you've grown up in, but you will go to your bed hungry if I see bad manners like that from you again. Got it?'

I got it.

Willie bowed his head. Morag and the children followed suit as he intoned words in Gaelic. Later, when my ear attuned to the language, I would learn that he said, 'Lord, for what we are about to receive, may we be truly thankful.'

When he finished the prayer, my new life began in earnest. Those who eat together become a family.

CHAPTER 3

Of Long Summer Days and Billy the Ram

Billy regarded me with solemn, unblinking eyes, lulling me into a false sense of security with his quiet dignity.

'Go on, Davie,' said a voice behind me. That was Johnny.

'Have a go!' This was Jimmy.

'I don't think you should,' cautioned Irene.

'You'll know all about it if you fall off,' warned Jeanette.

It had been several weeks since my arrival and I was settling nicely into my new life with my brothers and sisters, but I desperately wanted to be accepted. There was still a sense of distance between me and them. I knew that Billy, a ram of monstrous proportions, with great curling horns, might be the means to prove me worthy of their affection, but he petrified me. I was pretty scared of all the animals on the croft. If truth be told, I am still wary of anything on four legs. My knowledge of animals had been confined to the mangy cats and dogs that patrolled the streets of Glasgow.

Jimmy and Johnny were, however, well versed in the ways of the country. They thought it would be fun to introduce their newly found brother to Billy. I don't know what age Billy was, or whether he was suffering from some malaise, but his great shaggy coat looked as if it was in tatters.

'OK,' I said at last.

'Good man,' said Jimmy, who swung me onto the creature's back, while Johnny held its horns.

'Daaa-vie!' wailed Irene.

I was numb with fear.

'Ready?' said Johnny, letting go of Billy's horns without waiting for a reply.

Still robbed of speech, I nodded.

'GO!' shouted Jimmy, and I was off, like a National Hunt jockey heading for the sticks.

Someone was screaming in terror and I realised to my horror that it was my own voice. God Almighty could that beast run, round in circles, up and down, with me bouncing ever higher on his back. Johnny was already rolling on the ground, helpless with laughter, when the world went into slow motion and Billy came to a grinding halt, throwing me into the air over his head. I hit the ground and skidded through a muddy puddle. My shrieks had brought out the household and a bedraggled boy with a very sore bottom was gathered up by Jeanette.

She crooned, 'Davie, Davie, are you all right?'

I was speechless with shock as she carried me back to the adults, who were trying very hard, damn them, not to laugh at my discomfiture. The family gathered in the kitchen as I was deposited naked in the tin bath. My indignation was complete when Morag rolled her sleeves high up on her leg-of-mutton arms and began soaping me all over. Very soon I was respectable in clean shirt and shorts, and placed into the care of my siblings.

'Get off and play with your wee brother for a few minutes while we grown-ups have a talk,' said Morag, who added, 'And mind now, you've got jobs to do, so don't wear yourselves out.'

We all ran through the open door, out into the sunshine.

'Davie's a good sport,' said Johnny.

I was now officially one of them. I cried.

My brothers and sisters were soon revealing their individuality and personalities. Jeanette was five years older than me and she was the little mother, taking my hand and kissing me on the cheek, ruffling my hair and tickling me until I laughed out loud. She would whisper me to sleep in my bed.

I was closest to Irene. She was nearest to me in age. Irene was a serene girl. It quickly became apparent to me that Morag regarded her as special. I'm certain she loved us all in her own gruff way, but it was as if Irene were her own daughter. It was touching to watch the solemn child interacting with this child-less woman. It was new territory for them both. Irene and I would remain close until our teens, when she was abruptly removed from Quarriers after reporting that she had been physically beaten. Having to deal with our shared abuse and facing up to our abusers brought us close together, but for the moment we were safe from the future, distanced by geography and time from the bad days that lay ahead.

James, or Jimmy, was the joker, an incorrigible youth who enticed me into the barn one day to exhibit a country skill that I would have no problem in leaving behind me when I eventually left Uist.

'Look!' he said, holding out a pillowcase that was squirming alarmingly. 'I have something to show you.' He opened the bag to reveal a chicken. 'Watch,' he said, pulling the head off the chicken and throwing the quivering carcass at my feet.

I ran for my life, mouthing silent screams, to the echo of Jimmy's laughter. I believe Jimmy quite liked wringing chickens' necks, an everyday pursuit in the country, but a definite character flaw where we had come from.

Johnny was the oldest, older than me by six years. Poor Johnny had suffered, and it showed, God love him. He apparently took the worst of the beatings from our father and his sleep would be for ever broken by nightmares that caused him to wet the bed. He would be mortified and the usually sanguine Morag would be furious. Johnny would have to wash himself and his sheets in cold water from the pump at the side of the house. My brother never talked about it, but we could sense his pain, which resulted from the torment inflicted on him by my wicked father. He was, however, a good person. During the eerie night hours, when the world was filled by strange noises and animal songs, he would be the first to comfort me.

Life was good, but there were legacies from our old existence. My brothers and sisters were all afraid of the dark, thanks to our less than loving father. When we lived in Kennedy Street, he invariably chose to arrive late at night, when he was in a drunk and violent mood. He would rouse the boys from their sleep and challenge them to fight. Morag understood our distress and provided us with paraffin Tilley lamps. That light saved us from the darkness.

Morag was kindness personified, but even that good woman would not allow herself to be seen to be spoiling the Whelan brood with such fripperies as chocolate. I'm certain, however, that she had a deal going with soft-touch Willie. He would often call us into the barn and ceremoniously close the door after ensuring, somewhat theatrically, that his wife was out of earshot. Bars of Cadbury's Dairy Milk would appear as if by magic from his dungaree pocket. As he broke up the chocolate into equal shares, he would say, 'Wheesht now. Don't tell Morag. She'll have my guts if she finds out I've been spoiling you.' We would wolf down the chocolate, promising never to reveal our secret.

Soon after, I would be required to keep other secrets, terrible secrets, but I still delight in the ones we shared with Willie, a good and honest man.

Long before we returned to the bad times, the croft would echo to our laughter. We were content. Life was anything but easy. Morag and Willie were disciplinarians, insisting on the maintenance of Christian values that were adhered to strictly. The Sabbath is a big day in the Hebrides, the last bastion of Presbyterianism. No games were allowed, no playing, no washing on the line, no radio. Reading the Bible was the only recreation permitted. In spite of being nominally a Protestant, something in my Irish Catholic genes railed against the notion. I was content to go along with it, though.

On the Sabbath, we went to church three times. The Reverend Ian MacDonald had a particular talent for making scripture as unutterably boring as it could possibly be. Hollywood may have by that time injected high drama into the Old Testament tales of Moses and Samson, but the Reverend Ian could not. I recall there was much talk of heathens, hellfire and damnation.

The church was fashioned from grey stone as dull as his sermons. It was typically Protestant, devoid of decoration. There were no statues, paintings or stained glass to reflect a rainbow of colours that might have illuminated the Reverend Ian's dreary monologue. I prayed for the day the strong gusts of Atlantic wind might blow off the corrugated-iron roof. It was as cold inside as it was outside and our legs required to be swung to and fro to maintain circulation. This did not please Morag. 'Don't think God doesn't see you, Davie Whelan – playing instead of praying.'

There would be a brief, if welcome, respite for lunch before afternoon Sunday school. The final service at 6.30 p.m. was mercifully shorter than the morning version. I never worked out why God required our presence three times on a Sunday. Morag declared it to be representative of His love. God must have loved us an awful lot.

School was just as stern, although even our teacher, 'Corky' – more properly Miss McCorquodale – could show compassion to young boys. In one of my small acts of rebellion I was sucking a gobstopper during a lesson when it lodged in my throat and I began choking. The teacher was clearly not familiar with the subtleties of the Heimlich manoeuvre, so she bent me over and started beating me on the back. When that failed to dislodge the offending confection, she proceeded to stuff her fingers down my throat in an effort to make me sick. Blue in the face, I vomited the sweet and watched as the gobstopper, red and magnificent, clattered to the floor and smashed to smithereens. I had been so enjoying it.

'That'll teach you,' said Corky, rather unsympathetically, I thought.

There is little room in the island mentality for moral weakness or gobstoppers. I believe moral weakness was expected of us – we were the 'city slickers', for ever the outsiders, but we were strangers who were exotic and welcomed because of it. Even our surname set us apart among friends with names such as Mary McIntosh, Alistair McDougall, Donald Archie McKay, Susan McCluskey and the gloriously named Marina

Sherwood. There were also more MacDonalds than you could shake a stick at.

Many of the children arrived at the village school in boats, which fascinated me no end. It was Irene's job to ring the big hand bell that demanded they come to class, a task she performed with relish. Mr Blance, the headmaster, ruled with a rod of iron over the proceedings, and while the tawse – a leather belt used for corporal punishment – stayed in his desk drawer mostly, the threat of it was ever present.

My introduction to the Gaelic had already begun around Morag's great Aga, but it was reinforced every morning as I passed the wall chart that recorded the days of the week and numbers up to 10 in both languages. Despite our being different from these uncomplicated island folk, so secure in their heritage and place in the world, they welcomed us with their revered Highland hospitality. Long days passed in an atmosphere of kindness and laughter.

It wasn't all drifting along on fluffy white clouds, however. Youngsters of today could not conceive of children, from the youngest to the eldest, working in the fields – the back-breaking work of scything hay and cutting peat until the blisters on your hands are transformed into calluses. I can feel them still today.

If Morag ruled the home, Willie's domain was the fields. Willie was a typical crofter, forever mucking out, herding cattle and shearing sheep. His sheepdog, Tidy, would round up Billy and his ilk, answering Willie's every shrill whistle of command. When he was not tending animals, Willie would deploy his enormous strength to the crops. He could swing the scythe through hay as if he were cutting tissue paper. Willie appeared to work every daylight hour that God sent. When the Aga in the kitchen was not providing food, it was drying his outer clothes after a day in the elements.

He had one despicable bad habit that to this day makes me queasy. He would blow his nose and deposit the contents on the ground. Even a snotty-nosed 'keelie' from Glasgow had enough manners to know a hankie should be used. However, in the scheme of things, it was a forgivable fault. And for those with the experience, there is no finer feeling in the world than laying down your tools at the end of a hard day's work. What a glorious feeling to see the arrival of the tractor that would take you home to one of Morag's dinners. By now, my belly aches were a thing of the past. You may have all the money and possessions in the world, but there is nothing more precious than rest and filling yourself with good food.

Then there's the added joy of the bath. Bath time in the MacDonald household consisted of lining up with your towel beside the great tin bath, which Morag had filled with hot water from the contents of endless kettle runs. The pecking order was youngest to eldest, a happy position for me: I always washed in the cleanest water. Morag would dry us in front of the fire with a rough, if kindly, touch and make us squeal with laughter by hitching up her skirt and warming her legs by the fire. It was a favourite pastime, leading to what we Scots describe as 'corned-beef legs' – hot red patches on our traditionally pale skin. She would quickly return to decorum when the croft door, which was never locked, opened to admit a guest. Our childhood was populated by the people who congregated in our home, prattling away in Gaelic. Not a lot happened in such an isolated community, but they could gossip for hours.

The arrival of a visitor was the signal for the children to go out and play. Hide and seek among the hayricks was a favourite, but it was the sandy *machair* that became my adventure playground. *Machair* is a Gaelic word describing the extensive fertile plain that lies between the sea and the cultivated land. It is unique to the Western Isles and a world-class conservation site. We would roam far and wide, exploring fjord-like sea lochs that stretched to infinity and from which came the blustering Atlantic winds that had long since blown away the grime of the city from our life. We could hear Morag and Jeanette's voices in the distance, calling us in for our tea, but we would ignore them. Only when Morag's voice darkened with anger did we realise we had run to the end of our rope. Jeanette would then appear at the side of the croft, waving a white tea-towel – a flag of truce. To ignore that signal was to go to bed hungry. We invariably made it back in time for dinner, although Johnny did on one occasion run out of the invisible rope.

One of the great treats of childhood on the island was the frantic run home in time for the arrival of the big, green Co-operative Stores van, which motored between the crofts. Ian MacDonald drove the van and his wife, Ina, served. Their nod to corporate image was matching beige shop coats. This rolling Aladdin's cave could be seen for miles, your anticipation growing as it drew ever nearer. Ian and Ina brought wonderful treats – iced buns and glorious cakes with names such as Eiffel Towers. We were given first pick. On one occasion, this was not good enough for Johnny. He was sent to the van for a message and spent some of Morag's change on sweeties. She was furious: 'I'll not have any boy stealing in my house. Now get up to your bed and lie and think about what we will be eating tonight while you go hungry.'

The recalcitrant Johnny climbed out of the bedroom window in his bare feet and dropped down into the courtyard at the rear of the croft. He went to the barn, got on his bike and pedalled off across the fields to the shop in the village.

Alas, the dreary Reverend MacDonald saw him pedalling along, captured him and returned him to the croft. The minister had barely departed when Johnny was seriously cuffed about the ears. 'You've black affronted me, out in your bare feet,' said Morag, using the Scots phrase for being mortified.

Of course, his caring brothers and sisters thought long and hard about the nature of his wrongdoing and the justice of righteous punishment. How we laughed.

Laughter was a constant companion. It was such a joy for a little boy who was still in many ways the timid child in the corner, who could take fright at things that had no power over other children – such as Santa. Santa is rarely perceived to be ominous, but he scared the hell out of me on my first Christmas on the island. We trooped off to the laird's 'big house', Calarnais House, for the annual bash. The ground was thick with snow and we poured into the elegant surroundings of another way of life entirely. I occupied my usual position in the corner and waited for the arrival of this legendary figure. Father Christmas had not featured large in my life until that time. When he arrived with his great white beard and red coat, I ran for it, straight into the heavily decorated tree. I was trapped in the tree, tied up by tinsel, with only my legs visible as it slowly toppled. Poor Santa was only helping when he attempted to extricate me, but the sight of his big red face made me howl even louder.

Santa said, 'My, my, what a lot of noise from such a wee boy.' He rummaged in his sack and a brightly wrapped present materialised. 'Now, see what Santa's got for you,' he said kindly.

I bawled and refused the gift. My brothers and sisters pushed me forward, but Santa's smiling face served only to make matters worse. I bawled louder. I was led from the room, tear-stained and howling. The journey back to the croft seemed dark and terribly long. I got a few sore 'nips' in retribution from Jimmy and Johnny. They, too, were empty-handed, thanks to me. I had failed them. Never been a big fan of Santa ever since.

Not every trip to the big house was so fraught. Lord and Lady Granville would invite me and Jimmy there for a birthday party for one of their children, who were educated in England and did not speak Gaelic. There were few children on the island who spoke English as well as we did, so we were brought in to translate, and to keep the laird's children amused.

It would not be the only occasion when we would rub shoulders with the aristocracy and royalty. The Queen was a regular visitor in the summer, when the royal yacht *Britannia* sailed around the islands. Her Majesty would come ashore for the annual Agricultural Show and picnic with her cousin the earl and his family. In the year that I was there, Jeanette was chosen to present Her Majesty with a bunch of flowers when she came to open the show. Morag's ample bosom heaved with the pride of it all, the signal for Jeanette to be prodded, poked and decorated with a brand-new pink party dress that made her look like a fairy on a cake. She hated it with a vengeance.

'You will *not* embarrass me, lady,' said Morag, 'by wearing a tatty school uniform to meet the Queen. It's the new dress for you, whether you like it or not.'

Jeanette could never have been described as 'frilly' but frilly she was, in spades. Morag had looked out her catalogue – a Bible of delights that had to be ordered from the mainland: North Uist, like my sister, did not do frilly. When the dress arrived, Jeanette was hoisted onto the kitchen table for a fitting.

My poor sister, who was 14, declared, 'I feel like a pink blancmange! Why can't I wear my school uniform?'

'Do you want everyone to think you're a scruff?' Morag mumbled through a mouthful of pins. 'You'll not give us red faces, do you hear? This is a beautiful dress. If I'd had a dress like this when I was your age, I'd have thought I was the cat's pyjamas. Now, stop jumping around while I pin this hem. You don't want the Queen to see you with a squint hem, do you?'

Jeanette suffered for hours until Morag decided the dress was 'just right'. It was only the beginning of Jeanette's discomfiture. For weeks she had to practise how to greet Her Majesty with a proper curtsey. This was a joy to the rest of us. We howled with laughter. Poor Jeanette was never the lightest on her feet. She was ordered to curtsey very low and deferentially. Jeanette then had to take three steps, hand the Queen a bunch of flowers and say, 'Good morning, Your Majesty.' We practised with her, behind her back of course, stifling our giggles for fear of offending Morag's sense of decorum. Jimmy and Johnny could not curtsey if their lives depended on it and they would inevitably end up tumbling over each other, whereupon a fight would ensue.

On the big day, we all trooped along to the show, wearing our kilts. Jeanette waited for the arrival of Her Majesty, picking at her dress, an act that had Morag drawing daggers with her eyes. When the Queen arrived in a big Land Rover, she waved to the locals and offered a wonderfully benign smile. Morag was resplendent in her Sunday best, a navy-blue two-piece 'costume' suit that smelled disconcertingly of mothballs. Dear Morag looked glamorous … almost. Even Willie had escaped from his dungarees, replaced for the occasion by a suit and a heavily starched white shirt, which, as the day progressed, was intent on choking him to death. In the end,

Jeanette was perfect in words and actions. We stuffed our faces and returned home lit by the glow of it all.

We thought the good times would never end. How wrong we were. The only security in the lives of the Whelan children was the certainty of insecurity. The bombshell dropped when the MacDonalds were informed by the Social Work Department that our mother wanted us back and we were to be returned to Glasgow. For some godforsaken reason known only to the authorities, we would be prevented from maintaining contact with the only real parents we had known. There was no rhyme or reason to it, a casual and probably unintentional cruelty. It would be 20 years before we would see Morag again.

I had been on the island for little more than a year when we prepared to return to Glasgow and God knows what. The only thing we were certain of was that it would not be good. Paradise was about to be lost. The halcyon days would be left behind for a return to the slums and – worst of all – Quarriers beckoned.

CHAPTER 4

Paradise Lost

I had cried myself to exhaustion. As the aircraft carrying us away from North Uist arced out of Benbecula into an endless blue sky, my heart and stomach lurched. The feeling was more than physical. The Whelan siblings were surrounded by people embarking on journeys. We were in a sea of smiling faces, but we could not share the excitement that was so evident in our fellow passengers. They had something to look forward to on their journey. We did not, and we were terribly alone with our thoughts and the uncertainty of the future.

I was too young to fully appreciate what had been going on, but I had nonetheless begun putting together the pieces of a jigsaw that had been puzzling me for days: Willie's grim-faced stoicism and Morag's demeanour, so withdrawn, shedding tears at the slightest provocation. He had evidently been strug-gling under a dreadful burden, bearing a secret he could not share. Whatever was going on, Jeanette had been fretting about it, too, and it had transmitted to Irene, who had been abjectly miserable. It would be some time before I learned of the secret meetings in the barn between Willie and Jeanette when our future – or lack of it – was laid out before my eldest sister. Somewhere above my young head, the most recent chapter in our lives was closing and the next sad episode was in the process of being written. Our world was coming to an end. We would soon be leaving the island and we would not be returning. I was not party to the knowledge that we were going back to Glasgow to live permanently, but I knew, some-how I knew. I had been experiencing a dreadful sense of loss without quite knowing why. I wasn't certain any more of what lay ahead.

Later, as we sat on the aircraft, our geographical destination was Glasgow. From the vantage point of adulthood, I am aware now that the distance between what had been and what would be was measured in more than mere miles. The clues had been there, but I was too naïve to identify them. The atmosphere at the croft had changed dramatically in the early part of May 1966, like the temperature in a room dropping suddenly. I could not, however, see the complete picture, only glimpses of a mysterious canvas. As I said, Morag had begun to cry at the smallest thing and she clung to us as if she would never see us again. She wouldn't for a very long time. It would be many years before my sister Jeanette turned up on her door-step, as a grown woman and the mother of three children. It would be even longer before we would be reunited with the only mother we had ever truly known. In the days before our departure, Morag had clung to us, a particular mystery to me because she was hardly the most demonstrative of women. Willie would take himself off to the barn, seemingly unable to hear me when I shouted a greeting at him. I knew instinctively I wasn't being ignored; he was preoccupied.

What I did not know was that Willie had taken Jeanette to the barn because he had news for her. Jeanette revealed to me much later that this big, strong man was weeping unashamedly when he told her that Morag was broken-hearted because our real mother had demanded that we return to Glasgow, to start over 'as a family'. He swore Jeanette to secrecy, which must have been a dreadful burden on her. I was playing in the early-summer sunshine, throwing a ball for Willie's sheepdog – even working dogs were allowed a little fun in their life. Boy and dog were having a wonderful time, but our innocent game wasn't quite managing to dispel the gloom of misery hanging over Willie as he headed into the barn. He beckoned to Jeanette. Something was amiss. I played on, oblivious to the life-changing events that were unfolding. Willie's bright, open face, creased by sun and biting wind, had somehow crumpled. It was sorrow. I had seen enough of it in my life to recognise that mask. Jeanette also knew Willie was distressed, and within a few moments she knew why.

'Lass, I have something to tell you,' he said in a faltering voice. 'This is the hardest thing for me, but I have to tell you.'

'What?' said Jeanette, alarmed.

Willie took a deep breath. 'You're all going back to Glasgow.'

Jeanette was dumbfounded. Tears sprang into her eyes. 'Why?' she whispered in a voice that was not her own. 'We're all so happy here. Why do we need to go back?' she pleaded. 'Don't you want us?'

Willie had promised himself he would be brave, but he was lost. It was his turn to plead. 'No, no, no, lass! We love you like you are our own. You know that, don't you? We've never made any difference between any of you. I hope you know that?'

Jeanette was blinded by tears. 'Is it because we were bad?' she asked, falling into the trap that has snared unloved children from the beginning of time – believing it's your fault when things go wrong. My sister grabbed Willie's hand and said, 'Please, Willie, it was just a joke. We were only having fun.' Jeanette's mind was swimming. She believed that it was the recent prank she and Jimmy had played on Willie and one of our neighbours.

The two of them had found a tin of paint in the shed and had deemed it a great jape to paint the lambs all over – in blue! They hadn't realised that colour patches were daubed on the animals so each crofter could identify his own beasts. Willie had been really angry with Jimmy and Jeanette and had berated them, but he hadn't realised I had been watching, and when they were out of sight he'd laughed out loud to himself.

'No, lass! This isn't about the sheep,' he told Jeanette.

She wrung her hands. 'It's about the postie's van, then, isn't it?' Another jape. Johnny and Jimmy had seen the post-office van parked in a lane with the keys inside. The postman had been having a cup of tea with a crofter and hadn't reckoned on the arrival of two unmitigated scallywags. They took the van for a joy ride and crashed it into a hedge, by virtue of losing control of the vehicle because Johnny's feet didn't quite reach the pedals. No harm had been done to the vehicle or its drivers, but Morag had been incandescent with rage. She'd bellowed at them, 'You've black affronted me, you two. How can I hold my head up in church with everyone knowing I can't control you boys?'

Willie reassured Jeanette, 'It's not about the postie's van. That was just a bit of nonsense.' For a few moments, Willie was lost for words, and when he found his voice, he said, 'This is something we can't fix. Your mum has demanded the social workers take you all back to Glasgow, to be a family again. We've tried arguing with them, but they say your mum has rights. We've loved you all from the moment you came. We've tried to give you everything we would have given our own children if God had granted us the blessing of having any. No matter what happens now, we'll still always love you, no matter where you are. I'm so sorry.' The cruelty of the moment was heightened when Willie revealed the worst of it: 'They've told us that we can't even stay in touch with you – no birthday cards, no Christmas cards, nothing.'

Jeanette was inconsolable.

Willie added, 'You have to promise me not to tell the others. Not yet. It would only upset everyone more. We're waiting to hear when the social worker is coming to collect you. We just want your last days here to be happy. We want you all to have good memories of us.'

Willie recovered a dog-eared letter from the pocket of his dungarees and handed it to Jeanette. It had come from Jenny, our mother's sister. Jeanette told me later that Jenny had written to Willie and Morag, telling them she was sorry that we were all being taken away from the only loving home we had ever known. She apparently thanked the MacDonalds for looking after us all so well, far more than her sister had ever done for her own children.

My sister's face was ashen when she came out of the barn and suddenly I lost interest in throwing the ball for Tidy. From that moment, everything in the croft changed. Heaven knows how Jeanette kept the secret and endured that deeply troubled period.

A few days later, the beginning of the end was heralded by a perfect early summer's day – 25 May 1966, a date etched in my memory. People who have led normal lives recall the good days in their lives. The disadvantaged and abused remember the bad times. We were told we were 'going on a trip'. In any other child's mind, embarking on trips would be anticipated with fun, a sense of adventure, but I wasn't like any other child and this was going to be like no other trip I had ever been on. Morag told us to get washed and to dress in our Sunday best. I kept asking why. We were only going to school, weren't we?

She was distraught, struggling to appear as if it was just another day, exhorting us to get ready quickly. 'Because I told you, Davie – and remember to wash behind those ears!' The woman could not see for tears.

The household was silent, except for her sobs. I was crushed on her behalf. I had never seen her like this before. She was the sort of woman who would have faced up to the Devil. We were soon all ready and had to endure a silent inspection by Morag and Willie. Even in their grief, they were privately determined that if this was the last time anyone saw us, we would at least be looking our best.

We left the house and trooped down to the school. We didn't know it yet, but we were going to say goodbye. When we arrived, our classmates were subdued. They knew what was happening. The headmaster and our beloved Corky could not speak. We were each presented with a white leather-bound Bible with embossed gold script. Our names had been carefully inscribed inside the cover in precise copperplate writing. It felt cold in my hand. One associates the Bible with spiritual and emotional comfort. There was no solace in this sad, if beautiful, little edition of the Good Book.

Our school chums shifted uneasily, unable to make eye contact with us. They had been told they would not be allowed to know where we were going, so friendships formed and the bonds created were being severed for ever. We suddenly realised what was happening. We were going. Everything we had known, everything that had seemed so safe and permanent, was being removed.

It was a long, silent walk on leaden feet back to the croft house. We plucked at the hedgerows, as if we could keep a tiny bit of Uist alive in our hearts and minds by gathering these tawdry little souvenirs of the times when we were happy and safe from harm. The taxi was waiting for us. Like condemned men being rushed from a death cell to the gallows room, we were ushered towards the vehicle by the social worker. We all suffered the same moment of panic, looking for a way out, like prisoners confronted by bars who attempt to make a final bid for freedom.

Jeanette was trying but failing to keep us calm, promising us we were safe, that we were together and she would look after us. Irene, poor Irene was howling like a wounded animal. I had only heard such anguish in a human voice once before – when I left the doctors' house in Glasgow. Irene had to be prised physically from Morag's bosom.

We left our island life with the clothes we stood in. Our toys and other belongings remained inside the croft, where Morag would turn them into a shrine to the children she loved and lost. I started to cry and I did not stop.

Normality is a majority concept. I thought my life was normal because it was my experience and that of those I knew and loved. Only later, when I was able to make comparisons, did I realise how abnormal our lives were. When people who live normal lives are on the threshold of something new, they describe it as looking forward. Up until that juncture in my short and troubled life, I had never been conscious of looking forward to anything. Such an emotion implies that there is hope, the promise of something, anything. Peace?

Contentment? Love? I had never entertained the possibility of finding anything other than the next episode of uncertainty. My time on Uist had taken the edge off that emotion, but it was ever present. My view of the world had never truly been elevated above ground zero and the horizon was an alien, unreachable destination. It did not, however, prevent me from yearning. My dilemma was that I wasn't sure what to yearn for. I knew, somehow, that I wanted, needed something that had not yet visited me, but without having a means of comparisons or terms of reference by which to judge, it remained an imponderable mystery.

I had been on Uist for less than two years, but such was the influence it had on me that even when I thought very hard about it I could not conjure up a vision of what had gone before. The past was a film running in my mind, but it was an old movie, sepia-toned, blurred and moving far too quickly to make any sense.

By now, I knew that we were being reunited with Ma, a mythical creature, with her long, lustrous hair, dark eyes and faded glamour. I knew her only through what I had been told. If the knowledge that I had brothers and sisters had been a surprise, the fact that I had a mother was a revelation. I had thought I was an orphan. For as long as I could remember I had no real sense of having a mother, merely a succession of female figures who, to a greater or lesser degree, offered me security and care. Morag had come closest to fulfilling the role. However, very soon, I, and my brothers and sisters, would be reunited with the woman who, in spite of her manifold problems, clung to some notion of keeping a family together. I am still not sure why, and I don't think she was either. I don't believe she could have articulated her reasons, but I cling to the belief that there existed within her some degree of mothering instinct that would not allow her, no matter how bad things were, to relinquish her brood.

On that day, in the aircraft, when the sun sat high above the clouds in a place that is for ever summer, I could not know how bad things were going to get. I was travelling towards yet more uncertainty, an uncertainty that would characterise my life until the blessed moment when, many years hence, I would escape the horrors that it bred. As the aircraft made its descent through the white clouds and back into the more familiar grey world of my experience, a scintilla of hope began to form in my mind. It would, as always, be extinguished before too long, but in that moment I was comforted by the knowledge that she was waiting for us. Our mother. And from somewhere deep inside me a kind of love for her was dragged to the surface. Can one ever not love one's mother, no matter how neglectful or remote or cruel? Many good women had looked after me, but this woman was my mother, and my mother wanted me.

It was 1966, and many of the inhabitants of the great industrial metropolis of Glasgow had been transplanted from their deprived and dirty inner-city ghettos into the vast new council housing estates on the periphery of the old city. The city's fathers had burst with pride when they created the housing schemes in the countryside, into which a beleaguered population could escape, with the promise of a new life far from the slums. It was a time of hope. Who was I to swim against the tide? I ran forward to meet my mother. I should have known that hope always comes with an expiry date.

CHAPTER 5

'Give Your Ma a Kiss'

'It would seem that Mrs Whelan is basically a weak, inadequate individual almost wholly unable to cope … There has been a serious and consistent deterioration in the already weak family structure'   SOCIAL WORK REPORT

'Davie, give your ma a kiss.' The dark, exotic stranger, with her red lips and raven-black hair piled on her head in a beehive, offered me a pale powdered cheek. Morag's condemnation of cosmetics as the wiles of the Devil flew into my mind. 'I've been waiting for this moment for a long, long time,' she said in an accent that was pure Glasgow but underscored by the softer tone of Middle England, where she had apparently been living for several years.

She had come back to the city with an impractical and naïve dream of reuniting her family. I would learn soon that the novelty of being reunited with that family would last little more than a few weeks, presumably far less time than her anticipation of this reunion.

From somewhere behind her, the strains of 'Nobody's Child' were emanating from one of the as yet unknown rooms in this strange and too modern dwelling to which we had been brought. The song is a mawkishly sentimental ditty that began life as a country-and-western song. It had been espoused by a much-loved Scottish singing duo known as the Alexander Brothers. Ma was of a maudlin disposition. As an adult, the irony of that particular song playing is not lost on me. She favoured these sad songs by performers such as Jim Reeves about tribulation, heartache and the odd dog dying. In Glasgow, they are described as songs that 'make the blood run oot the record player!'

'I've never stopped thinking about you all,' said this creature I had no memory of. 'We'll be one big, happy family now. We'll muck in together. It's all going to be all right, you'll see.' She was dressed in a two-piece pale-blue suit – what used to be referred to as a 'costume' – and she wore black leather stilettos.

Where are her wellies? I thought.

As she bent low to cuddle me, it felt so awkward, angular and unnatural. The mask of white powder and rouge seemed to hide more than her face. My thoughts returned, as they would do for some time, to Morag, until the months and years eventually distanced me from her. When Morag clasped you in one of her fierce embraces, there was warmth in it. This woman, who smelled of smoke curling from the burning Senior Service cigarette in her hand, had no maternal love in her. I kissed a stranger.

We were all awkward with her, but especially Irene. She refused to go near Ma and hid behind Jeanette. Irene had been devastated by leaving Uist. I would learn her resentment towards Ma was all-encompassing. To her dying day she blamed our mother for us being put in care. Irene could not and would not bond with Ma. She would also blame Ma for the cruelty and abuse we suffered at Quarriers. They had a difficult and fractured relationship, which would endure until Ma's death, in 1980, when she was just 49.

When Irene set eyes on Ma and our new home, she began wailing loudly, burying her face in Jeanette's skirt, resisting all attempts by our mother to comfort her. Johnny and Jimmy, who were older and had clearer memories of Ma, were less awkward and hid behind bravado.

The social worker, who had escorted us from Glasgow Airport, broke the tension. 'Right, I'll put the kettle on,' she said. 'This has been a big journey for you all.' It was an understatement of massive proportions.

Ma gave up on Irene and took Jeanette, with Irene still clinging to her, into the bedroom where the two sisters were to share a double bed. Johnny, Jimmy and I were to sleep in a second bedroom. As the oldest, Johnny had the privilege of a single bed, while Jimmy and I would share a double.

Our address was 34 Katewell Avenue, Drumchapel, Glasgow. This was the neighbourhood of the young Billy Connolly, who would go on to make a living from his ability to translate the barren existence of life on estates such as these into a hugely successful comedy career. The Hollywood actor James McAvoy, a star of such films as *Atonement*, *The Last King of Scotland* and *The Chronicles of Narnia: The Lion, the Witch and the Wardrobe*, had yet to be born into this often troubled place. The comedian and the actor represent nuggets of gold in a mountain of dross. The vast majority of the rest of us would be shovelled through lives characterised by want and unfulfilled potential. There would be few escapees. Good people lived here, but good chances were few. Kinship and community spirit were their armour.

We had four rooms on the top floor of a three-storey tenement overlooking green fields and fresh hopes. Ma showed us around the flat. There were no carpets on the floors. Patched linoleum struggled to cover bare wooden boards. The furniture was utilitarian and mismatched, all of it second-hand, courtesy of the Social Work Department. The living room was crowded with a hard nylon-covered three-piece suite, which left marks on your legs if you sat on it for too long. By the window were a table and four chairs. The only heat source in the entire house was a minuscule coal fire in the living room, which heated the water in a back-boiler. Ask any child of their memories of growing up in such a house and they will tell you about awakening on winter mornings and scraping ice from the windows on the inside of the glass.

The kitchen was equally sparse. A large white ceramic sink perched on cast-iron legs. The larder – a food cupboard – stood floor to ceiling, dominating a small Formica-topped table in a corner. A four-ring electric cooker completed the ensemble. Refrigerators were still a distant dream from such houses. You kept milk fresh by standing the bottle in a sink half filled with cold water.

Ma's brothers, Charlie and Davie, had provided us with a temperamental old television set that worked only when it had a mind to. Often it sat dormant in the corner, mocking us, usually because Ma had not put enough shillings in the coin-operated electricity meter. The world being plunged into darkness was a common feature of childhood in such places. It was inevitable when a finite supply of shillings competed with an infinite appetite for cigarettes. Ma would put Senior Service on the mantelpiece before she put food on the table.

So this was what poverty looked like? I'm reminded of a line from one of Billy Connolly's performances when he said that he didn't know he was deprived until a social worker told him so. I know exactly what he meant by that. However, my life would be characterised by more than mere poverty. You can be poor but emotionally stable. You can have little but be rich in love. There may be material things you cannot have, but there is often that bedrock of emotional security that protects you. This was the way of life enjoyed by the vast majority of our neighbours. We lived somewhere else entirely. Abuse comes in many forms and we would be victims of it. It was a different kind of abuse from that which I would suffer in Quarriers. It wasn't governed by malice or sexual deviance. This abuse would be born of ignorance and living in an emotional vacuum.

My mother was not morally reprehensible. It is an overused phrase, but she, too, was a victim. Her notion of love, her sense of compassion and the mothering instinct had long since been beaten out of her by her monster of a husband. Even today, far removed from that time, I find it difficult to allude to him as 'my father'. However, the combination of conditioning and weakness conspired to make my mother anything but a mother in the sense that most people would understand. This is, of course, the analysis of an adult looking back on the past, which someone once famously and accurately described as a foreign country.

As a child, when I first saw the empty shell of 34 Katewell Avenue – and the rouged face of a woman I didn't know – I was encompassed by a sudden and inexplicable sense of loss. It went beyond leaving Uist. It was more than losing Morag. It was a different emotion from leaving behind the life I had known. I know now that it was the loss of me. That sense of loss, hidden from me in any intellectual sense, would manifest in many ways. I developed what they describe today as 'behavioural problems'. Doctors have since found a name for it – encopresis – an indicator of the effects of extreme stress and emotional abuse. The medical profession demand that the words they use carry a certain gravitas. It wouldn't do to describe a situation merely as a nightmare, which would be my interpretation of encopresis.

My only comfort was acquiring 'gold stars'. They were my prize for showing signs of 'recovery'. How I longed for those gold stars. People of a certain age will remember how, when they were at school, their efforts were rewarded with such stars. If you were competent at reading, arithmetic or whatever, you received a small paper star, which was attached to the work. It was something to run home and show Mum and Dad, a badge of honour. I did get gold stars, but not for academic achievement. They were for not shitting in my pants. One of the many manifestations of my encopresis was what they described delicately as a 'hygiene problem'. I soiled myself, frequently. Perhaps some of you may be able to dredge up a memory of a kid like me – isolated, alone, looking out with dead eyes on the others, who view him with a mixture of pity and disgust. It is the loneliest corner in the landscape of childhood. To her credit, my teacher did not condemn, but worked out an incentive scheme to encourage me to combat this problem. I was given a book. My underpants were checked regularly, and if I was clean I received stars of varying colours. I coveted the gold stars above all others and took to 'wearing' my pants in my jacket. I took them off and hid them in my pocket. That way, they remained clean. The teacher would applaud me and fix another star in my book. I was inordinately proud of them. I craved the attention, the applause, if you will, of achieving something, anything. More than anything I craved love.

Ma was not big on love. Where Morag had been a home-maker, Ma was the opposite. Cooking, cleaning and washing could have been cities in China as far as Ma was concerned. She was so wrapped up in her own troubled mind there was little hope of that changing. The role of a mother would be assumed by Jeanette, who was by now 14.

However, with the blissful ignorance of those who do not know any better, we were all getting on with what approximated to a life. Johnny, my oldest brother, was 15 and had just left school. He was supposed to get a job, but there was too much of Ma in him. It isn't a surprise that Johnny was Ma's favourite. 'I only ever wanted Johnny. I didn't want the rest of you,' she used to say.

Johnny favoured drinking and betting over industry. That being said, he was a sweet soul, kind and good-natured. When he had money, he brought it into the house to supplement the meagre state benefits, which were our sole source of income.

Jimmy was 12, but the family dynamic demanded that he act a lot older than his years. He was a different personality from Johnny, less good-natured and, God love him, a thief who regularly stole money from Ma's purse and watched as others were blamed. Irene, who was 10, once took a terrible smacking from Ma, who accused her of stealing a 10-shilling note, a huge amount of money then, the difference between eating or going hungry. Irene had seen Jimmy take the money, but he was such an accomplished liar that he brazened it out. Ma looked for any excuse to condemn Irene – she had never forgiven her for rejecting her – and Irene was blamed.

In his defence, Jimmy was the family clown and made us laugh. When he was in trouble, he turned on the charm and swam out of hot water. Jimmy was once on the hook for some infraction and he escaped censure in the most remarkable way

– he became Shirley Bassey! She was one of Ma's favourite singers and when Jimmy appeared dressed as the diva, wearing Ma's make-up, with two oranges stuffed down the front of her good frock and singing 'Hey, Big Spender', it diverted her wrath.

Jimmy wasn't always so lucky, but his escapades were redeemed by a hilarious sense of the bizarre. He once shoplifted a can of lager and was soon to be found in the close half drunk and loudly singing a Sandie Shaw pop song: 'I wonder if one day that you'll say that you care.'

When he sneaked into the house, Ma was waiting behind the door. She thumped him round the ear and sang back, 'I wonder if one day that you'll do what you're bloody well told!'

Jimmy and Johnny were a handful, but they endeared themselves to Ma – unlike Irene, who never forgave her for taking her away from Morag. Jeanette, as always, was the rock. We were a troubled crew. It was apparent to those around us that the Whelans were different. It was often the mundane that brought those differences so sharply into focus. I can still laugh at one episode when I brought a pal home from school. We were in the kitchen and I had just poured milk into the tea and raised the drink to my lips.

'Why are you drinking out of a jam jar?' he asked.

'What?' I replied.

'A jam jar. That's a jam jar!' My companion, a boy from the other end of the street, was sitting opposite me at the table.

'What?' I repeated.

'It's a jam jar. You keep jam in it. Where're your cups?'

'Don't have any. They're broken,' I said.

'Can't you get new ones?'

I shrugged. Explaining the vagaries of day-to-day existence in the Whelan household was becoming part of life in this brave new world of Drumchapel, where those around us seemed to have things we did not – like proper cups.

My pal extrapolated the theme. 'You don't have many clothes either.'

I shrugged again. As a nine-year-old, I was unsure of the point he was trying to make. By now, we were developing a reputation – the children of the mother who seemed to spend most of her time sleeping, the family with too few clothes.

'You don't have much,' said my companion, looking around the spartan interior of our home. 'Why don't you have carpets?' he asked.

'We do!' I said.

'No, you don't. Those are doormats.'

I looked down at the disparate collection of mats on the floor, laid together in the impression of a carpet. Johnny had been busy. He stole them from the front doors of our neighbours. My companion was rendered silent by this strange household he had entered. He took another broken biscuit from the plate. They were Woolies' finest. We would all wander to the nearest shops and ended up pinching broken biscuits from Woolworths. We were hungry.

Drumchapel was the antithesis of Uist. The only legacy of that idyllic place, the memory of which was diminishing rapidly, was that the Whelan children who were still at school had developed an oddball reputation as the only family in Drumchapel who could sing in Gaelic. Soon after our arrival we were invited to an open day at the local Kingsridge Secondary School, where we performed like a bizarre, deprived version of the von Trapp family from *The Sound of Music*. Jimmy and Jeanette were at the school, while Irene and I attended Cleddens Primary School. The teacher's attempt to make us feel special by exhibiting our language skills may have been with the best of intentions, but it backfired. In the world of a poor Glasgow childhood, anything that sets you apart from the herd presents you as a potential victim. We took more than a few beatings for being different.

The school Irene and I went to was opposite the flat and we could see it from the windows. Being so close to home gave me a certain sense of security. I felt that when things were at their worst I was never far from safety, whatever that meant in my case. Home at least was a place of refuge.

In those days, Drumchapel was not a community. It was a collection of tribes gathered from all over the city, who brought with them their religious and social prejudices, as well as a territorial imperative harking back to where they came from. The rigidly designed new streets with their Eastern European aspect became mere extensions of the city districts lately deserted by their new inhabitants. Tribalism brought conflict, particularly of a sectarian nature. In the Glasgow of those days, you were a 'Billy' or a 'Tim' – a Protestant or a Catholic, a supporter of Rangers or of Celtic. It was not an option not to pick a side. We were Billies – Protestants. The religious divide in Glasgow, while wide, is nowhere near as lunatic as that of Northern Ireland, where the conflict had originated and been transferred to Scotland in the late 19th and early 20th century by an influx of immigrants. In the main, apart from a hard-core minority, it took the form of friendly rivalry rather than enmity.

Whatever tensions existed, however, were exacerbated by the great flaw of the Glasgow housing schemes of the mid-1950s and early 1960s – a lack of basic services. They had the atmosphere of internment camps as opposed to communities. The bus service was almost non-existent, and there were too few shops. Residents couldn't call 'the scheme' home because it had no high street, no heart. If you asked someone where they came from, they did not reply Drumchapel. They said Partick or Govan or Dennistoun, or whichever part of the inner city from which they had originated. In spite of it all, there was still a sense of newness, the beginnings of hope, but the newly planted trees would have to grow much higher before there was any true sense of community.

The day-to-day problems of the Whelan family were less philosophical than actual. The cracks were beginning to show in Ma's resolve. Her ambition to be a family once more was foundering on the rocks of reality. Her first words to us – 'We'll be one big, happy family now. We'll muck in together' – had not come to pass. Within weeks of our arrival she had begun to take handfuls of pills. Ma spent a lot of time in bed, leaving us to fend for ourselves in a hand-to-mouth existence. A mother's duty fell to Jeanette, and it was she who tried to hold us together. Ma didn't even dress us or put shoes on our feet. That was the role of social workers, who would trail us to Glasgow city centre for new clothes. The use of the word 'new' is a misnomer: I never owned an item of new clothing during childhood, apart from a school uniform. The Welfare dressed me as a child. Our 'department store' was a vast warehouse in John Street, where the clothes racks marched in serried ranks to apparent infinity. For some reason, I was always excited by the place. I still don't know why. The smell was the first thing you noticed, a mixture of mothballs and sweat. It was the smell of poverty. You carried it everywhere you went. It singled you out.

In the so-called working classes of Scotland there exists a pecking order. We were technically working class, but we were physically and culturally separated from families where dads worked and mothers acted as homemakers. To my knowledge, the man I hesitate to call my father never worked a day in his life. He was a wastrel who lived by his wits and thievery. Proper working-class Scottish families are, in English terms, lower middle class – hard-working, if unskilled to any degree. Below that stratum was the 'poor folk' – families in which the dad might not work and the mum might be less than house-proud. Somewhere several levels beneath were families like mine – dysfunctional, deprived hostages to a different kind of poverty that was as much emotional as physical. I would emerge from the John Street warehouse with clothes that no amount of washing could freshen and my 'sannies' – thin, black canvas plimsolls that were worn winter and summer as the ultimate badge of deprivation. Ironic, isn't it, that those flimsy little shoes have become so fashionable today.

The daily third-of-a-pint ration of milk at Cleddens Primary School and free school dinners were the only real sustenance we were enjoying by this time, and even school dinners were an indicator of your status. Privilege came in a different colour from poverty. Blue dinner tickets were full price – 2 shillings, or 10p – paid for by those from the good working-class homes who could afford them. Pink dinner tickets were cheaper, for those who could afford to pay only part of the cost. My dinner ticket was brown – a free dinner and yet another stigma. This sense of disenfranchisement was heightened because the free dinner tickets were allocated last. We had to stand in line, in front of the class, while those who paid got their tickets first. Then the poorest children were dealt with. Even at that age I was conscious it was a humiliating procedure. It seemed an intentional part of the system – as if we had to be kept in our place. Perhaps they believed that it would have been inappropriate to offer us any hope of another way of life. There was, however, no one to champion us against these injustices.

By now, my mother had truly lost her way. Our first family Christmas was a bleak, almost Dickensian affair. On Christmas morning I stood with my nose pressed against the window of the living room, looking out at my peers racing up and down the street on their new bikes and scooters, their squeals of laughter echoing against the glass. I couldn't be part of their world. I had a *Beano* album and an orange. Our Christmas dinner would be fish fingers and tinned creamed rice. I turned from the window to a room devoid of festive decoration and my heart sank. Naturally, I told a very different story of our Christmas when I returned to school after the holidays. I regaled my friends with tales of all the great presents I had received. They, of course, knew the truth.

Chapter 6

'Where's Yer Whore of a Mother?'

'Despite considerable casework and support to this family, there has been a serious and consistent deterioration. In order to bring some measure of stability to the two youngest members of the family, it is proposed to ask Quarriers Homes to admit them into care'   SOCIAL WORK REPORT

'Ma! Ma! Maaammy! Please wake up!' I pulled her, heaving at her shoulders, pleading with her to come back from whatever dark place she had gone. I was sure Ma was dead. I was 11 years old, small for my age and terrified. I couldn't rouse her. A loud, long and insistent wail came from somewhere deep within me, summoning Irene. My sister, barely two years older than me and every bit as scared, flew into the room.

'She's dead! Ma's dead!' I told her. Even at that young age Irene was infinitely more practical than me. She applied her hand to Ma's face. 'She's warm, Davie. Stop greetin',' she said. 'She's not dead.'

I followed Irene's line of vision to the bedside table, where a scattering of pale-blue capsules lay spilled from the open top of a small brown bottle. 'She's taken too many of her pills,' explained Irene, still matter-of-fact. 'Ma! Ma! Get up,' shouted Irene, dragging Ma up from the pillows. She still refused to be roused. 'Davie, quick, water!'

I leaped from the bed to the kitchen and filled a jam jar, spilling half of its contents on the floor as I dashed back to the bedroom. Irene tried to force some of the water into Ma's mouth, but it dribbled from her lips onto her nightdress.

I had lost all hope when, like the sound of a trumpet blast from the cavalry riding to the rescue, Jeanette's voice called from the front door, 'Irene! Davie!' By some miracle, known only to the forces that protected our mother, Jeanette had come to visit. Jeanette always knew what to do! We had missed Jeanette's presence and influence on life at Katewell Avenue. Just a few weeks before, she had moved out of the family home for reasons I'll explain.

Jeanette, however, hadn't abandoned us. She knew that Ma was a terrible mother and she returned often to ensure that we were being looked after. This was one of those visits, and I have never been so glad to see Jeanette as I was on that dreadful morning. She took charge immediately. It was in the days before telephones in the home were commonplace, so Irene was despatched to the police station and I was told to dry my tears and go to the living room. I sat on the sofa, rocking, wrapped in my own arms, listening to Jeanette's entreaties. Suddenly, there was a groan. It was Ma! Jeanette's voice, soothing and authoritative, was bringing her back. The groans grew louder, drowned now by the sound of an approaching siren. Within minutes, the house was filled with big men in uniforms. Irene had by now returned, and Jeanette emerged from the bedroom. We three sat together on the sofa as Ma was carried from the house on a stretcher.

'It's OK, Davie,' said Jeanette. 'It's OK.'

The three of us moved to the window, in time to see Ma being carried from the building into the back of the ambulance. Her eyes were open, but she saw nothing. The vehicle drove off quickly and disappeared round the corner of Katewell Avenue. It was 10 a.m. on 4 January 1969, and, unknown to us, it was the beginning of the end for us as a family. The hospital doctors would pump her stomach of the tranquillisers, but she would be transferred to a psychiatric hospital and kept there for almost a year. I wouldn't see her again until she visited me at Quarriers.

For the moment, the Social Work Department's immediate task was to ensure the welfare of her two youngest children. Jeanette was of course settled in her own place. For reasons I'll soon explain, Jimmy and Johnny were no longer in the picture. Irene and I were the problem. The solution was to put us with a foster family until the officials decided on our long-term care. Ma's short journey to hospital that day would be the catalyst for our much longer journey ... to Hell. Irene and I would soon be on our way to Quarriers.

When I look back, I realise that Ma's overdose had been a long time coming, the result of a combination of heartache, weakness and her inability to cope with the family dysfunction she created. As I said, Jimmy and Johnny had gone by the time Ma was taken to hospital. Their departure – to approved schools for delinquents – had been the final blow to her fragile psyche. Jimmy had been breaking into the homes of our neighbours, stealing shillings from their electricity meters. It had been a bitter-cold winter, and with Ma's home-economic skills our money had, as usual, been spent on other things. Jimmy was not unlike his father in character, a smoker and a bit of gambler, but there was enough good in him to bring home some of the stolen shillings to put in our meter. During that winter of 1968 we were kept warm with 'stolen' electricity. The house was a lot colder when Jimmy went away on what Ma described to us rather quaintly as a 'long holiday'.

Jimmy's departure had been a blow, but it was the loss of Ma's beloved Johnny that had tipped her over the edge. He had eventually been caught stealing the doormats that masqueraded as carpet in our home. Johnny might have been a thief, but you could not fault his sense of honour. He gave himself up to the police after his friend and partner-in-crime was arrested. Poor Johnny ... all he wanted was to make our home more comfortable. He was sent to a particularly tough approved school. That experience, added to what our father had done to him, affected Johnny for the rest of his life. He would never speak of those days, even when he was an adult. It was years later, after I had emerged from my own nightmare at Quarriers, that I realised Johnny had probably suffered as I had. We shared the same haunted look, claimed the same dark secret. We differed only in one respect: I survived. Poor Johnny didn't.

The last days of Johnny's tragic life will find their proper place later in this story, but for now, when I recall Ma's overdose, I realise it was arguably one of the most defining days of my life. I remember that look in Ma's eyes as she was being taken away in the ambulance. There was no light in them. They were unfocused, looking at something only she could see. They were certainly not looking in our direction. If truth be told, I know now that Ma hadn't been looking in our direction in any meaningful way for a long time. If she had been a normal mother, putting our needs first, she might have recognised that her actions were placing us on a dangerous path. If she had cared, how different might our lives have been? If only … if only … but what can you say? If she had realised her shortcomings, she wouldn't have been our ma.

Ma had deserted us before, when we were tiny children living in Townhead. While Da was in prison, she was in Surrey, flitting in and out of mental hospitals. During one of her lucid periods, she began a relationship with a Scotsman living in England, a single man, who gave Ma the impression that he would marry her, absorb her family and we would all live happily ever after. It was this that had given her the confidence to come back to Glasgow and demand the return of her children. The social workers had agreed, promising Ma a new home for her and us, with the proviso that she divorce our father. Ma filed for divorce and the die was cast. It's never failed to amaze me how our lives are washed back and forth on the tides of the whims of others. How many lives were affected, and in some cases ruined, by Ma's belief in the empty promises of a person who is described in our Social Work reports as her 'paramour'?

If I've learned one thing, it is that one should not cling to a notion of what might have been but deal only with what is. However, today, I am haunted still by the pain caused to Morag and Willie by our departure from their care. They had taken us into their lives and the heart of their community. What might have been had we stayed? Even before Morag and Willie, there had been the two doctors who had wanted to adopt me. What might have been then? Alas, you play with the cards you are dealt, and right now we were dealing with life at 34 Katewell Avenue. Let the heartache begin …

* * *

The Dansette record player throbbed to the sound of Long John Baldry singing that very song. I can't think of a time in my childhood when Ma's Valium-fuelled taste in music did not reflect the reality of our lives. It was bizarre, as if we had been conjoined to a weird country-and-western parallel universe. From the safety of adulthood, there are moments when it makes me almost laugh out loud. If I could release the laughter, there would be no joy in it. It would be the sound of someone witnessing the blackest of black comedy. Ma lived in a world of her own, where social workers and any figure of authority were the enemy. A knock at the door froze us, like gazelles sensing the approach of a stalking lion. The most feared visitor was the 'tally man' – a Glasgow term for an illegal money lender. 'Tally' is vernacular for counting money – for example, 'Tally up what I owe you.' Ma loved new things, but she was too impatient and profligate to save for what she wanted; she wanted everything immediately. The tally man was only too happy to oblige – at a massive rate of interest. He also had no scruples about breaking your legs if you didn't pay in time, even if the legs belonged to a woman. In those days, normal kids were driven behind the sofa by the monsters on *Dr Who*. In our case it was a big man with cropped hair, a scarred face and a brass knuckle-duster, and you thought Daleks were tough?

The result of Ma's profligacy was that she was constantly in debt. Hiding from money lenders, the rent man and even the little man who ran the corner shop became a way of life. Ma owed everyone. We would be sent on errands with no money to pay for her cigarettes or other 'messages'. Ma reckoned shopkeepers would feel uncomfortable turning a child away. She was often correct in that assertion, but when they refused you turned away with a sense of embarrassment that gnawed at you all the way home.

Perhaps my sense of embarrassment indicated my growing isolation from those around me. I don't know why, but I was never part of what psychologists would now describe as my peer group. I never became 'pure Drumchapel'. I remained a novice in terms of street-smarts. It was arguably caused by the time I spent with the middle-class doctors, followed by the otherworldliness of Uist, which had left me with the aptitude of a much younger child. This was exemplified one day by a visit from the dreaded tally man. I was in the kitchen when I heard a knock at the door. This was an angry knock, an attempt to remove the door from its hinges rather the signal for the arrival of a visitor. The rest of the family scattered as I walked into the hall and opened the front door.

'Where's yer fuckin' ma?' said the biggest man I had ever seen. I was dumbstruck. 'Tell 'er I'm here,' he said.

'Tell her yourself,' I replied. 'She's behind the sofa with my brothers and sisters.' I led Godzilla down the hallway into the living room, where Ma, somewhat red-faced, and my siblings emerged from behind the sofa wearing a look of sheer panic.

'Oh, Davie,' said Ma, 'you've found us – now it's your turn to hide.'

'What?' I said, having absolutely no idea what she was talking about.

'It's your turn to hide now – *hide and seek*, remember?'

While I was still pondering this, Godzilla snatched up Ma's handbag and spilled the contents onto the table at the window. He turned to Ma. 'You think I'm a fuckin' idiot, missus?' The big man didn't wait for an answer. He opened Ma's purse and pulled out the banknotes, discarding the loose change.

'Don't take it all,' begged Ma. 'We won't eat!'

'It's the money or your legs,' he said.

Ma was silent.

We didn't eat that day or the next, apart from the broken biscuits we had filched from Woolies. Ma had proved yet again that she could offer us no defence against the world.

As time went on in Drumchapel, her behaviour became increasingly erratic. When she wasn't in a drugged fugue or lying in her bed, she was screaming like a banshee. The repercussions were enormous. I was lost in a dreadful period when I was soiling myself and being bullied at school as a result. The gold stars could no longer make up for that. The result was that I was sent to a series of meetings with child psychologists. Ma refused to attend the consultations. My Social Work reports record that 'David's mother is too busy arranging her divorce.' When I returned from the meetings, Ma was relentless in the pursuit of establishing what had been said about our home life.

'They asked me what I had to eat,' I told her.

'What did you tell them?' she demanded to know.

'I told them I ate potato peelings,' I said.

Ma's anger at my childish fib was palpable and it reinforced her determination not to take part in this unwanted inquisition into her mothering skills. Medical opinion on my psychological state was divided. One of the doctors decreed that I was hyperactive and anxious. He prescribed Ritalin, then a relatively new and controversial drug, which turned me into a zombie. When Ma kicked up a fuss, I was sent to another doctor. I spent an hour with him, arranging square and round pegs into the appropriate holes. I told him any idiot knew you couldn't put a square peg in a round hole. His opinion was that I was not so much ill as suffering from a malaise that was well known in the city of my birth; I was diagnosed as a 'cheeky wee bastard'.

There were, however, darker clouds on the horizon. Irene was living in a daze, clinging to Jeanette, crying herself to sleep every night. The only time Irene was galvanised was when she was defending me from playground bullies. She would lash out, fighting like a boy. Meanwhile, Jeanette, who hadn't yet left home, was still the rock, placed under tremendous pressure and forced to assume the role of a mother. It was she who cooked – when there was food. She got Irene and me up in the morning for school, fed us 'jeely pieces' – jam sandwiches – the staple diet of poverty-stricken Glasgow children of the period. We would be delivered to our school before she went on to her own. When she returned in the evening, she would wash our clothes by hand in the kitchen sink and hang them up to dry on a pulley washing line, which hung from the ceiling. We often went to school wearing damp clothes. Jeanette did her best, but the house was often so cold that our clothes would not dry properly.

By now, Ma had abnegated all responsibility. The mask she had worn for the social workers during the ill-conceived campaign to get her children back had slipped dramatically. In retrospect, I am reminded of the character of Blanche Dubois in Tennessee Williams's *A Streetcar Named Desire*. Ma wasn't a typical Glasgow 'keelie'; she wasn't the least bit coarse. Perhaps if she had been, she would have handled life better. Under normal circumstances she spoke softly in a well-modulated voice. She dressed elegantly. None of *her* clothes came from the dank Aladdin's cave that was the John Street warehouse. And like Blanche, she inhabited her own fey world in which the cold reality of life failed to intrude. She was possessed of a psyche that was, to say the least, brittle. The arrival, out of the blue, of the man who bore the title of my father would shatter it.

Although my father's name on the street was the 'Little Bull' – a very apt *nom de guerre*, as it turned out, Ma called him the 'ratbag'. She wasn't big on swearing, but she could introduce real venom into that colourful little word. He was never referred to as 'your father' or 'my husband' – only as the 'ratbag'. It is probably why I never conceived the notion of having a father. I never heard the word spoken in the house.

I was only months old when he was arrested and removed from our lives. Consequently, I met him properly for the first time 10 years later, in the summer of 1968, when he turned up at our door. He had found our address on Ma's divorce papers. I was confronted by a short man, with a barrel chest and long, muscular arms.

'Who the fuck are you?' demanded this stranger, reeking of whisky and beer, his eyes inflamed by anger and alcohol. Glasgow hard men tend to get to the point.

'I-I'm David Whelan,' I stammered.

His face softened momentarily and a new look came into his eyes. 'Fuck me! Wee Davie!' he roared. He bent low, hands on hips, surrounding me with drink fumes, and said, 'Son! Say hello to yer da! Now, where's yer whore of a mother?' The softness in his demeanour disappeared as quickly as it had come and the eyes were once more cold, hard pebbles. I was swept aside. This was not a man to get in the way of, and right now he was angry. Very angry.

'You, come here!' he shouted at Ma. 'Don't think these fuckin' brats will save you. You're *my* wife. Fuck do you think you're doin' with this divorce shite?' He may have been a small man but he filled the room with his anger. 'You'll do what I say. You're nothing but a useless whore!'

My mother shook from head to toe. I had never seen her so terrified. Even Jimmy and Johnny, who were no slouches in the fighting stakes, became silent statues in the face of this force of nature. And then, suddenly, there was our Jeanette.

She emerged from behind the sofa – and the look in her eyes! I know she will not take this the wrong way, but in that moment she was John Whelan's daughter. They were nose to nose. The atmosphere was electric, but no words passed between them. He could have swatted her like a fly, but there was something in Jeanette's eyes that day. My father was reduced to muttering vile threats as he turned on his heel and left. Jeanette remained standing, unflinching, until he was gone. Then she seemed to deflate, subsiding onto the floor and sobbing.

It would be 35 years before I laid eyes on John Whelan again, but my sister taught me a singular lesson that day: don't ever let the bully see the fear. Da may have gone, but the effect of his explosive visit did something to Ma. She began to unravel. Ma had never been much of a drinker, but Jeanette suspects she began to drink in secret, developing a fondness for white rum mixed with cola. Her fanciful notion of us all being one big, happy family had long since been abandoned. My father's visit seemed to rob her of any lingering hope of such a proposition.

She began disappearing, sometimes for days on end. We knew when it was coming. Ma lived in a padded dressing gown, but it would be discarded when she 'dressed up to the nines'. Make-up was applied with great care, to the accompaniment of Patsy Cline on the Dansette. The Barrowland Ballroom beckoned. The famous dance hall in the East End of Glasgow was an institution, a favourite haunt of predatory men and lonely women. It was also, at the time, the hunting ground for the serial killer known as 'Bible John'. John picked up three young mothers in the ballroom. They were later found murdered and posed ritualistically. He was never caught and so became the bogeyman of the city. Every time Ma left

the house and didn't come home for several days, Jeanette
agonised over her fear she had become Bible John's next
victim. On a more prosaic level, there was also the fear that the
social workers would find out we had been abandoned. It
could mean us being taken into care again. Life wasn't great.

At least we were together, but we were fast reaching the
point where Jeanette would be forced to leave us. Jeanette was
harbouring a secret. She had left school, to take a job as a
seamstress, and she had met a young man, an apprentice in the
shipyards, who would become her first husband. The secret
was that she was pregnant. Jeanette's pregnancy changed
everything. Ma's skivvy would soon be creating a family of her
own.

Ma raged at the thought. Jeanette was a 'whore', a 'prostitute'.
In retrospect, it was incredible Ma should occupy the moral
high ground – Jeanette and Johnny had been conceived out of
wedlock. Jeanette's pregnancy caused such furious rows that
the involvement of the dreaded social workers was inevitable.
They tried to pressure Jeanette into giving up her child for
adoption, claiming she would not cope. There is a bitter irony
in that contention. Jeanette had been functioning as a mother
for years; it was a role she first played as a six-year-old when
our father was sent to prison and Ma deserted us. The relationship between Ma and Jeanette became so acrimonious that the
social workers found my sister a place of her own.

Jeanette's departure from the house unloosened the few
remaining screws in the fragile machinery of our lives. We
were now hurtling towards Ma's overdose and our final abandonment. Without Jeanette's stabilising influence, Ma could
not control Jimmy. He was disruptive and began drinking and
gambling. His heart of gold hardened. God love him, though,
his rebellions usually backfired spectacularly and often to

hilarious effect. On one occasion, in an attempt to get Jimmy on side, Ma bought him an expensive watch, which he pawned and used the money to buy a ticket to a Rangers versus Celtic game. 'Old Firm' matches in Glasgow are the biggest games in British football, more fiercely contested even than the derbies of Manchester, London and Tyneside. The lure proved too strong for Jimmy. But again the black comedy that was the life of the Whelans prevailed. On one of the few occasions when our dilapidated television worked, it transmitted the match. As the BBC cameras roamed over the grandstands of Ibrox Park, there, revealed in flickering black and white, was the hapless figure of Jimmy. He was waving his Rangers scarf above his head and his arms revealed the singular absence of a watch. When he walked through the door that evening, he was disappointed not just by a Rangers defeat but the mighty thump with which he was greeted.

'What time is it, Jimmy?' Ma asked.

Jimmy made a great show of looking for the now non-existent watch. 'I … I … I –' An empty milk bottle bouncing off his head ended the thought.

An hour later, Jimmy was presented at the A&E department of the Western Infirmary.

'How did this happen?' the doctor asked.

A well-rehearsed Jimmy replied, 'Someone threw a bottle out of a multi just as I was passing.'

As far as the records of the Western Infirmary are concerned, walking beneath the windows of multi-storey flats in Glasgow can be a dangerous business.

Ma, however, was so wracked with guilt that she went into debt again to buy Jimmy a bike. Jimmy pawned it to back a horse, which, given his luck, fell at the first hurdle. Ma found the betting slip in his pocket. Some people never learn.

As it was, Jimmy's nefarious activities would soon take him out of the picture and into that approved school. Which left Johnny. He, too, would soon be on his way, after being caught stealing those infamous doormats.

While my older brothers exasperated my poor demented mother to the point where she lifted her hands to them, Ma always regarded me as the baby of the family and never once hit me. I saw her mood swings, but I never saw her strike anyone. However, I was by now old enough to realise that Ma's ersatz fantasy of a family life was doomed. It couldn't go on, and it wouldn't. As we approached the Christmas of 1968, it would be the last festive season we would spend together.

Our last Christmas was ironically almost normal. Despite living away from our home, Jeanette had used her wages to buy Christmas decorations for the house at Katewell Avenue. Ma's estranged boyfriend, the famous Scotsman still living in England, arrived laden with gifts. I was soon the proud possessor of a train set and a Johnny Seven gun. For the first time, I was not ashamed to join my pals in the street. I had, at last, something to show off.

I should have remembered that expiry date on hope and happiness. Within days of Christmas, Johnny and Jimmy were gone. Ma and her 'paramour' disappeared over the festive period on a party binge, leaving me and Irene with 'friends'. Jeanette had gone back to her own life, unaware that we had been abandoned. Days later, Jeanette found us in the street, begging for food from a van that sold fish and chips. We were filthy and my head was crawling with lice. Jeanette believed she had no option but to call the Social Work Department. It was, she thought, the only right thing to do. It was a decision that has haunted Jeanette all of her life, but how could she know what was to come?

The social workers located Ma and she was ordered to come home. However, when confronted by reality, Ma acted true to form and on that January day she took the overdose of pills. The social workers decided this destructive cycle of dysfunction had to be broken. We went into the foster-care system for four weeks, until social workers arrived to tell me and Irene that we were being sent to Quarriers. It was, they said, for our own good. No one, not the social workers, not my selfish and self-centred mother nor my estranged father, would realise that their actions were about to deliver me into the hands of a paedophile.

CHAPTER 7

A Very Special Place

'Admitted to Cottage 31. Clean and tidy. Appears uncertain about his surroundings. Poor appetite, rather pale. Of slim build'

FIRST WORDS WRITTEN ABOUT DAVID
BY HIS HOUSE FATHER WILLIAM DRENNAN,
ON ARRIVAL AT QUARRIERS

'This is a very special place, Davie,' the social worker had told me. The words came back to me now as a hollow echo from a great distance. It was pitch black, night-time. The corners of the shed were not visible. Beneath my bare feet, the uneven concrete floor was cold, hard and damp. I was in an outhouse. Movement in any direction was to be engulfed in a miasma of spiders' webs. I was rooted to the spot. Like so many other occasions in my life, I was utterly alone, physically as well as emotionally. I was being punished. Banishment to the shed at the back of the cottage during night hours was commonplace. A child thus censured would return to the cottage in the grey dawn light, shaking, broken in spirit and more amenable to the harsh regime in a Quarriers cottage.

In my case, I had been accused by my house father of 'insubordination'. The word meant nothing to me. I would learn much later of its military connotation, indicating the grave offence of refusing to obey the orders of a superior officer. In the months ahead, I would realise just how apt the use of that word was in the system that prevailed. My defiance had been to refuse to eat creamed rice. The only creamed rice I had ever eaten came from a can – it was called Ambrosia and it was absolutely delicious, probably the only culinary treat I enjoyed in Drumchapel. The glutinous, pale, sugarless concoction that had been in my bowl that day was rice in name only. The thought of eating the soggy mess had turned my stomach.

'I can't eat it,' I told my house father.

'You will, you ungrateful wretch,' he barked. 'There are children starving in the world today who would love to be sitting where you are, David Whelan.'

'I can't!' I said.

For my sins, I was consigned to the outhouse. I was frightened now, very frightened. I was a child of the city. The sharpness of the memories of my life on Uist had been dulled by my return to Glasgow and living in Drumchapel. Two years is an eternity in the life of a child. I had once more grown used to the city's clamour. The quietness of this place was oppressive, as if I was being suffocated by silence. The screech of owls and the yelp of foxes were now alien and unsettling. Only the nocturnal cries of these animals reminded me that I was not alone in the world, but their moans heightened my fear. What if they came in?

When this was over, I would eat the rice. The system ensured compliance. The same portion would be presented to me in the days that followed, until I capitulated. It was grey and solidified by then. I surrendered because I didn't want to go back to the outhouse.

It was, I would find, a forlorn hope. There would be many more acts of insubordination. Shoes not burnished to a military shine; an imprecise knot in a tie; shoe laces undone.

'This is a very special place, Davie,' the social worker had told me. She had been right. It was. But not the kind of special I had been promised …

My head, held in the vice-like grip of the woman's hand, was pushed forward to a position where pain radiated from my neck to my backbone. 'This won't hurt,' she had said in a not unkind voice, as she dragged the nit comb through my thick, tangled hair. She lied. It was the first of many lies. Foul-smelling liquid had already been applied to my scalp. An infestation of lice couldn't be tolerated. They were ensuring that Irene and I, as the new arrivals, were not bringing with us any unwanted guests.

Monday, 10 March 1969, our first day at Quarriers. The first thing they did was to separate me from Irene, a casual act of cruelty that by the standards of today would be appalling. Then, it was normal. But what did I know about normal? I felt only the pain, yet another ache, overlaying all the others that had accrued from the many dramatic changes in my life so far. Even at the age of 11, I was emotionally jaded enough to know that new beginnings, however hopeful, would end badly.

Events in childhood inform who we are, moulding us for good or ill. If you enjoy a normal upbringing, few of these events can be said to haunt you. I wasn't yet aware that this new episode in my life would be infinitely worse than anything that had gone before. And I *am* haunted. From the moment I wake until the moment I sleep. Sometimes, even sleep offers no escape.

Irene was absorbed into a crowd of children. Before she was lost to my sight, I witnessed her speaking words I couldn't hear, but I knew instinctively they were entreaties to stay with her brother. I cried. Every new beginning began – and ended – in tears for the Whelan children.

'Where's she going?' I asked, fearful that I would never see her again.

'Cottage 7,' I was told. 'You're going to Cottage 31.'

I tried to count between 7 and 31 and lost my way at 22. The distance between the numbers seemed so great. In reality, the two cottages would be a short walk from each other. I use the word 'cottage' to describe the 'family' homes, but it is a misnomer. They were in fact large Victorian villas, each of them architecturally distinct from the other. William Quarrier, the Victorian philanthropist and founder of the Village, had decreed that each child should have a 'different door to go through'. Some of the houses resembled baronial castles; others had the look of the homes built in Glasgow by wealthy Victorian tobacco barons. The houses were constructed of huge blocks of red and dull grey stone, and all of them were hugely impressive. Quarrier said his children should have the best possible start in life.

Surrounded by the rolling Renfrewshire uplands, and dominated by the magnificent Mount Zion Church, the Village was truly a beautiful place, built with wonderful intentions. A bed of flowers in front of the church spelled out the words 'Have faith in God.' The entire Village had been created by one man's faith and it was in every sense a self-contained community.

Dairy produce was provided by the Village's own herd of cows at Hattrick Farm. The milk churns for each cottage arrived in the morning in the back of a van. It would become one of my jobs to polish the squat aluminium cans to a mirror finish. Bizarrely, the house parents of each cottage vied with each other to have the shiniest churn. Large wicker baskets, each painted with a cottage number, were delivered daily from the massive village store – a supermarket where no money changed hands. Quarriers girls laboured in the laundry room for pocket money. The tuck shop was the favourite haunt of all the children. There was a workshop and garage for a fleet of vehicles, where one of my other chores would be polishing duties. Children attended Quarriers' own primary and second-ary school, although in the future I would be one of the first children to go to an 'outside' school. At one time, the Village even had a fire brigade. The Beast, who would rob me of my childhood, was the fire officer. When he returned from his day job, he became a house father to the children in the cottage run by his wife, Helen.

The ethos of Quarriers was to prepare children for the world, rather than produce academic high achievers. There was great emphasis on the practical. In many respects, it was a progressive and enlightened system, managed – mostly – by good people who were motivated by the best of intentions. Many of the children who arrived at Quarriers were devoid of hope, stigmatised by their appalling backgrounds. These young lives were directed towards opportunities they would probably never have had. A large proportion of the girls would go on to frontline occupations, such as nursing. The mechani-cal and woodworking training in the workshops guided many of the boys towards skilled trades and the merchant navy. Quarriers' own army cadet force launched many careers in the military. I could not have followed this career path – I didn't have the temperament to slavishly follow orders, although after the rice-pudding incident I was more amenable. It has to be said that the majority of children passed through Quarriers happily enough. I was not one of them.

His default expression was a scowl. A smile was a stranger on the face of William Drennan, my new house father. His wife, a singularly unattractive woman with a shock of ginger hair, stood half a step behind him, clearly subservient. I would learn very quickly that these people had been plucked from a bygone era – 20th-century Victorians who demanded that children be seen and not heard, required to do as they were told immediately and silently. Drennan was ex-army. It was as if he had never left. The swagger stick, which he no doubt carried during his years of service, had been translated into a thick walking stick. It resided in the corner of the hallway, suggesting a threat, which, on occasion, became a dreadful reality. Mrs Drennan wore a white doctor-style coat, which added to the clinical atmosphere. The house parents of Cottage 31 were not people who would encourage laughter.

I absorbed this scene through the unsophisticated eyes of a child, and accepted it. What was normality to me? I had no concept of it. In the course of my life, I had gone from the vague recollection of children's homes, the clearer memory of a spacious suburban house, a paradise that was North Uist and the squalor of a city slum. This was just one more step on the journey.

'So you're David,' said Drennan in a voice bereft of emotion.

His wife smiled without warmth. I had at least come to recognise a genuine smile, when the emotion of the expression is reflected in the eyes. Mrs Drennan's smile didn't make it that far. I stood with head bowed, unsure of how to react to these people. I had arrived at lunchtime and could see children sitting at the tables in the dining area, which smelled of boiled cabbage. The children ignored me until one of the older boys was ordered to show me around.

I was suddenly hungry. The journey from Glasgow in the social worker's car had seemed endless. Excitement and fear had curbed my appetite, until now. I found my voice and asked if I could get something to eat.

'Certainly not!' said Drennan. 'There are proper mealtimes in this house. You'll learn, boy. We have rules here and we stick to them. You'll eat at teatime with everyone else.'

I accompanied the older boy up the stairs and he showed me the dormitory where I would sleep. I carried no baggage. My only possessions were the clothes I wore.

'You have to put your shoes in the cloakroom at the back of the house,' the older boy said. 'Dirty shoes are not allowed in here.'

The beds in the dormitory marched in a regimented file towards the windows of the big, airy room, each covered by a bright-orange candlewick spread. They were stretched tightly, tucked in military fashion with hospital corners. There were no toys or any paraphernalia that hinted that the occupants of this room were children. My heart sank. It wasn't just austere; it was sterile.

I was led back down the stairs and shown into what the boy called the playroom – a contradiction in terms.

'You have to keep your toys in here,' he said. I didn't have any toys. 'This is the staff sitting room,' he added, indicating another room behind a closed door. 'You don't go in there unless you're asked,' he warned. I sensed from the way he spoke that it was not a good thing to be invited into this room.

Mrs Drennan appeared again, still wearing the white coat and the facial rictus that passed for a smile. She ordered me to follow her to the drapery. The drapery turned out to be a smaller version of the John Street Welfare warehouse from my previous life, filled with second-hand clothes. I was assailed by that familiar smell.

CHAPTER 8

Who Was William Quarrier?

I still wonder what the great William Quarrier would have made of that second-hand smell of poverty. He had been driven by faith and compassion to create the haven that bore his name. In the long and illustrious history of his creation, his name would be associated honourably with many, many good deeds. He demanded only the best for his 'special' children. Others would not always live up to his standards.

William Quarrier was a Scottish contemporary of the perhaps more famous Dr Thomas John Barnardo. Both were motivated by a desire to alleviate the suffering of Victorian Britain's lost children, but while the Dublin-born Barnardo unashamedly courted public support, his Scottish counterpart never actively sought a donation. Barnardo was a pragmatist; Quarrier believed God would provide. Perhaps that is why there is an entry for Barnardo in the *Chambers Biographical Dictionary* and no mention of Quarrier.

However, in London and Glasgow, the wealthy philanthropists shared a similar vision, although Quarrier was ahead of Barnardo in revolutionising the concept of childcare. In Victorian Britain, the young were the biggest casualties of deprivation and poverty. Quarrier and Barnardo believed the future of society lay in the hands of those children. They had to be saved.

Barnardo, who was born in 1845, started his good works in 1866, when he began founding homes for street children. By the time he died, in 1905, his organisation had rescued 60,000. Like Quarrier, Dr Barnardo was a committed Christian and his first ambition was to be a foreign medical missionary. However, he saw dreadful deprivation far closer to home and concentrated on alleviating the suffering of the poor in the East End of London. In 1867, Barnardo set up the Ragged School, for abused, vulnerable and neglected children. His first home was opened in Stepney in 1870. By the time he died, there were 112 such places.

The realisation of Quarrier's vision would be smaller, but no less influential. The wealthy Glasgow shoemaker had experienced poverty in his own childhood and was appalled that children were sleeping rough on the streets of Glasgow, the second city of the Empire. In spite of his piety and goodness, he had a grandiloquent streak and likened his mission to that of the prophet Moses. 'Like Moses of old, I had a strong desire to go down to my brethren, the children of the streets, and endeavour to lead them from a life of misery and shame to one of usefulness and honour,' he said.

Quarrier was born in Greenock, Renfrewshire, in 1829, the son of a ship's carpenter, who died from cholera when Quarrier was five years old. Quarrier's mother, Annie, was left with three children. There was no future for them in the Clydeside town, which was the industrial heartland of the shipbuilding industry. The family moved to Glasgow. Mrs Quarrier took in sewing, and her son became the main breadwinner at the age of 7 by earning a shilling a week from his job in a factory, working 12 hours a day, 6 days a week. A year later, he was apprenticed to a shoemaker. 'I remember standing in the High Street in Glasgow, barefooted, bare-headed, cold and hungry, having tasted no food for a day and a half,' he would recall later.

From there, he moved to a shoemaker in the neighbouring town of Paisley, walking the 10 miles between home and work twice a day, ironically with no shoes on his feet. By the age of 12, he was a journeyman shoemaker and had found a better job in a shoe shop in Argyle Street, a fashionable establishment where the good-looking youth would eventually catch the eye of the owner's daughter, Isabella. She would become his wife in 1856.

Long before that, Mrs Hunter, his future mother-in-law, had introduced him to religion. The young man soon developed a strong sense of commitment during weekly worship at the Blackfriars Street Baptist Church in Glasgow. At the age of 17, he declared, 'For the first time I heard the great truth of the Gospel.' Faith would be the cornerstone of Quarrier's life and good works from then on. Around the same time, he began courting Isabella, whom he married 10 years later.

In the interim, he had opened his own shop at 243 Argyle Street. Quarrier had taken the first step to wealth and privilege. He would soon own a chain of shops and by the age of 34 he was a rich man.

His life changed for ever on a cold winter night in December 1864 when he walked from his office to his palatial home in Kingston Place, on the south side of the River Clyde. He came upon a little boy who was selling matches, a common occupation of poverty-stricken children. The child was sobbing inconsolably. Quarrier enquired why. An older boy had stolen the child's earnings and stock, he was told. The wealthy businessman knew that the robbery had effectively condemned the child to die in the gutter. And there were so many such children on the relatively short journey he made every evening. He gave the child money to replenish his stock. Quarrier saved the life of the child that evening and for ever changed the course of his own. He realised that giving a child a few pennies was only a temporary solution, allowing the waif to survive. What the boy needed more than anything else was shelter, education, a trade, a Christian faith and hope.

Quarrier set about making it a reality. He began by rescuing shoeblacks – children who polished shoes in the street for a ha'penny a pair. He organised them into a brigade, an early form of trade union that offered mutual support. His brigade wore a uniform, a cap and a navy-blue flannel jacket, trimmed with red, with a red badge on the arm. However, some members of the grandly entitled Shoeblack Brigade of Glasgow clearly found it difficult at times to leave aside their early life survival mechanism. Quarrier invited 40 of them to his home in Kingston Place for tea and sandwiches, and when the motley crew left Mrs Quarrier informed her husband that most of the ornaments in her home had departed with them.

Quarrier was not dissuaded from his philanthropic path by this obvious ingratitude. He forged ahead with his vision. His brigade of boys were allowed to keep 8 pence out of each shilling they earned, with the remainder going into a central fund, which was used to pay for their lodgings and education. At a stroke, Quarrier had found a way to take children off the street. They now had security as well as hope.

Quarrier's strong Christian values prevailed. The boys' first lessons in reading and writing were drawn from biblical themes and they were required to attend Sunday worship. He soon extended the brigade model to boys who sold newspapers and delivered parcels. Quarrier was, by now, a father to four children of his own.

The shoemaker was beginning to hear great things about his philanthropic contemporary in London, Dr Barnardo, who was creating the children's homes. In 1871, Quarrier followed suit by opening a night refuge in Renfrew Lane, and his good work soon began to attract unsolicited donations from all over Britain. He used the money to build another night refuge and two children's homes, one in the city centre and the other in Govan Road, on the Southside of Glasgow.

He believed, however, that having so many children under the same roof was not the ideal way forward and he began to develop his 'great vision' of a children's village, far from the industrial grime. 'It is my ambition,' he said, 'to deprive the poorhouse of as many children as possible.'

Quarrier was four years ahead of Barnardo in pioneering the concept of 'cottage homes', where a 'family' of 20 children would live in the care of two house parents. Like any community, it would be self-sufficient in skills and the provision of food, healthcare, education and, of course, godliness.

He identified a suitable piece of land, a 40-acre site near the village of Bridge of Weir, in Renfrewshire, almost 20 miles from the city. Nestling among rolling hills, it was a world far removed from any that children bred to poverty had ever known. He needed the enormous sum of £20,000 to fund the project, and slowly but surely the money began to roll in.

Quarrier paid £3,560 for the site at Nittingshill Farm and began building the first cottages. By the early 1890s, there were

34 cottages, a school, a church, a farm, a dairy, a hospital and a fire station within Quarriers Village, which was soon home to 800 children.

Dr Thomas Barnardo was the guest of honour when the Village was officially opened on 17 September 1878. Quarrier told a gathering of dignitaries, 'I am here to testify that God has not failed me at any time.' By then, he had attracted donations of £34,000 and used the money to rescue hundreds of children.

At its height, Quarriers Village would accommodate 1,500 children at any given time. Such was the reputation of the project that middle-class Victorians and Edwardians would take special excursion trains from St Enoch's Station, in Glasgow, to visit the 'wondrous' Children's Village.

It was indeed a haven. The main street of the village was called Love Avenue. At its heart lay Mount Zion Church, which became known as the Children's Cathedral. The church and its 120-foot bell tower were built in 1888 with a donation of £5,000 from an anonymous benefactor. Mount Zion could easily accommodate 1,000 worshippers, and several times a day Quarriers children would be seen marching, side by side, up streets named Faith, Hope, Peace and Love, with their Bibles clasped under their arms.

The village was a model of Victorian discipline and organisation. The children rose at 5 a.m. to work. The youngest of them would clean cutlery and boots, while the older children performed domestic duties in the cottages and worked in neighbouring fields. Once their chores were completed, they marched in military fashion to school, where education was compulsory for every child between the ages of 5 and 13. It would be years later before society as a whole adopted Quarrier's education model. However, as I said, it was a model of *Victorian* discipline, which could at times be very harsh by the standards of today. Children were compelled to embrace Christianity and the regime was uncompromising. Families were often separated, with children growing up unaware that their natural brothers and sisters were living in adjacent cottages. And of course corporal punishment was commonplace. Extreme forms of corporal punishment had become such a concern by 1937 that Dr James Kelly, the chairman of Quarriers, felt compelled to write to house parents warning them that nothing could be achieved by 'severe thrashings', a practice he described as 'loathsome and unnecessary, producing defiance rather than penitence'. Two women of my acquaintance, Christine Miller and Jan Gordon, were children at Quarriers in the 1940s. They talk of being beaten 'in the name of God'. Both women still bear the emotional scars of the harsh regime.

However, over the years, perhaps the greatest ignominy was the transportation of 7,000 children to Australia and Canada. They were effectively sold into slavery to work in factories and farms. The practice was not confined to Quarriers, but was a British Government initiative that, as recently as 2010, elicited an 'unreserved' apology from the then prime minister, Gordon Brown. Australia's prime minister also proffered a similar apology to the 'migrant children'.

Mercifully, those days are gone, and on balance it must be admitted that, within the limits of its time and place in history, Quarriers arguably did more good than harm. However, society began to change in the 1970s and 1980s, when more enlightened Social Work Department policies decreed that Quarrier's – and Barnardo's – philosophy of childcare was no longer in tune with modern thinking.

From 1878 until then, Quarriers had cared for more than 30,000 children, and it remains the third largest charity in

Scotland. Nowadays, it provides care and support for disadvantaged teenagers, people with disabilities, the homeless and sufferers of epilepsy. The majority of the original cottages in the Village have been sold as private homes, and Mount Zion Church has been redeveloped as luxury flats. I often wonder if the people who now live in them hear the echo of so many troubled and painful pasts.

However, in spite of what I and others suffered there, few of us would argue with the words on the plaque that adorned William Quarrier's coffin after his death on 16 October 1903. The memorial declares that in his lifetime he had been 'a friend to the poor and needy'. Unfortunately, those words cannot be attributed to some of those who came after him and so signally failed to embrace his philosophy of care for the vulnerable.

CHAPTER 9

The Intimate Stranger

With seconds left, Irene threw the ball with unerring accuracy towards the hoop. It clipped the ring, hung tantalisingly and dropped through the net. The crowd went wild. Irene had carried Quarriers to supremacy in the netball league. She was rewarded with a medal. I was condemned to three years of sexual abuse. My sister carried the guilt until she died …

The fateful netball game that for ever changed my life by inadvertently delivering me into the hands of the Beast was still some way off and life continued in this 'very special place'. Living with the Drennans had turned out to be all that I had feared it would be. I had already felt the weight of Drennan's dreaded walking stick and I was by now intimate with the cloying darkness of the outhouse. Care and compassion played little part in the repressive regime that was life in Cottage 31.

The couple were relentless in their pursuit of the 'perfect' children. This moulding process was predicated on 'discipline'.

I was, however, becoming inured to what, by any standard, would be classified today as wanton cruelty. The mind and body become conditioned to corporal punishment. You develop an emotional and physical shield. You shut down. Even the outhouse held fewer terrors for me than it had on my first visit. The night-time sounds no longer had any power over me. Now it was merely cold and miserable. I armoured myself by retreating into the 'quiet place'. It is a facility that endures to this day. When I am troubled, or need to think something through, I take myself to another room and sit quietly on my own. The difference is that nowadays the surroundings are more pleasant and I am in a place of my own choosing.

Before I joined Irene and the Porteouses in Cottage 7 – a direct result of my sister's sporting prowess – there would be other landmarks in our lives. The first was the arrival of Ma. She had re-emerged from yet another period of rehabilitation in Woodilee Mental Hospital. It was June, three months after our arrival, when she turned up with Jeanette on a clear, blue summer's day. I was sitting on a grass verge outside the cottage as she approached. The sun was at her back and her face was cast in shadow. At first glimpse I didn't recognise her. It was an almost mystical experience. Her features were dark and indistinct, obscured by a halo of light. Then Jeanette emerged from behind the mystery Madonna. I had been receiving letters from my sister, so my connection to her was still strong.

Jeanette swept me up in a fierce embrace, lifting my feet off the ground. 'How are you, little man?' she crooned.

She released me from the bear hug and I turned to Ma – this intimate stranger. Ma was ill at ease. I was, however, delighted to see her, even if her arrival threw me into a state of confusion that would translate later to despair when she left without me. Ma. Poor Ma. From this distance in time, and decades after her passing, I still find it almost impossible to express the nature of my feelings for her. There is, I am certain, a doctorate to be gained by writing a thesis on the relationship, or the lack of it, depending on your point of view, between such mothers and sons. The 'baby' of any household usually occupies a privileged place in the family dynamic. Ma had by now finally broken free of my father and the dreadful abuse he inflicted, but, while I was the last-born of Ma's children, I was also evidence of their final and ill-fated attempt at reconciliation. As a result, I don't believe my mother was capable of truly loving me. The price was too high for her to pay. Who knows?

Her visit, however, offered a merciful, if brief, respite from the colourless existence we were leading. When Ma arrived, I was wearing my 'new' clothes from the drapery – a grey school uniform. I was fiddling with my blue and black striped tie when I heard her voice.

'Davie,' she said softly.

No one had called me by my pet name for a long time apart from Irene. In this place I was 'David' or, more commonly, 'David Whelan!' spoken in an accusatory tone. For some reason, my thoughts flew back to that first day in Drumchapel, when I ostensibly met my mother for the first time and her words to me were, 'Davie, give your ma a kiss.' I instinctively put my arms around her. She bent low and kissed my head.

'You're thinner,' she said, producing a bag of sweets from her pocket.

It wasn't surprising that I had lost weight. I wasn't eating. I got hungry, but my stomach was now too easily filled. The huge meals that I had once wolfed down in North Uist were a dim and distant memory of a life to which I could no longer relate. Food had not been plentiful during the desperate, deprived years in Drumchapel. I had lost my appetite for food as well as life, and these days I was also working very hard. There were no passengers in Quarriers. Chores were a necessity, a part of life – and often a punishment. A childhood slip of the tongue, perceived by the Drennans to be insolence, was a cardinal sin. I used a swear word once and was condemned to clean the uncleanable Aga that was blackened by decades of use. My fingers were bleeding from scrubbing with steel wool when I was ordered to stop. The Aga was, of course, still not clean enough for Drennan, but it was long past bedtime.

My least favourite job was manhandling the manually operated floor polisher, a huge, cumbersome device that was almost as heavy as me. It dispensed orange-coloured liquid, which burnished the linoleum to a deep shine. Later, when the Beast violated me, the mirror shine on those floors would assume a new and dreadful aspect. I would see the reflection of his face behind me. But for the moment, polishing the floor was just a task that had to be performed after every evening meal. The floors of Buckingham Palace did not receive so much attention.

'I'm fine, Ma,' I lied.

Ma stayed for two hours with me and Irene, a period characterised by stilted, largely meaningless conversation. None of us truly knew what to say to each other. What was there to say? We were all carrying the memories of too many bad times. I watched Ma and Jeanette leave with a sense of longing, but for heaven knows what. However, on some level her visit had cheered me up and there was a fresh spring, almost a swagger, in my step.

It was probably this new-found bravado that gave me the confidence to stand up to Brian, a much bigger boy. Bad mistake. It almost resulted in the beating of my life – over my ability to read better than he did. Brian didn't like me and I certainly didn't like him. The teacher had praised me for my reading and in the cruel world of childhood any applause from authority is rewarded with taunts from your peers. I was, according to Brian, the teacher's pet. I took exception and challenged him. Brian attacked. Picture David and Goliath but without the traditional happy ending. I was enveloped in his arms, my feet lost contact with the earth, and he was trying his best to squeeze the life out of me. A dreadful hammering would surely follow. Enter Irene. She flew across the playground, her hair flowing in the wind, her face set in a determined mask. Was this what Boadicea looked like when she took on the Romans? Irene cuffed Brian on the back of the head and I dropped from his grasp. I would play no further part in this confrontation, not that Irene needed my pathetic help. A crowd had gathered. Fights attract an audience. Irene's underdog status earned her the sympathy vote and cheers. Apparently, I wasn't the only one who didn't like Brian. Irene's fists hammered like pistons into his face and body. He subsided slowly like a felled tree, begging her to stop. Brian received another two or three thumps for good measure. Of course, I was still on the ground and I felt my body shudder from the impact of Brian's heavy landing. Ever the 'cheeky wee bastard', I looked up at Irene and said, 'I couldae done that!'

Irene hoisted me to my feet and declared, 'Next time, fight your own battles.' She had not escaped unscathed. An angry red mark was blossoming on her forehead. Brian was less fortunate. He was left to mourn his wrecked credibility and the end of his reign as a tough guy. The badge of courage on Irene's forehead would fade as quickly as it had arrived, but her reputation endured. From that day, no one messed with my more than capable tomboy sister, and by default I basked in the glow of her invincibility. Happy days. Almost.

This ersatz impression of happiness was to continue. I was, I was told, to go on holiday, whatever that meant. This unknown concept was introduced to me by Drennan: 'Get everything packed up. We're going away,' he ordered.

Where? Why? The notion of going somewhere – and then actually coming back – was alien. When I moved, it was usually permanent. Sort of. I learned now that we were to travel to Aberdeen, spend two weeks by the sea and then return to Quarriers. My first holiday holds no particularly fond memories. Same regime, different scenery. I was, unbelievably, more excited about returning to Quarriers. I had learned that I was to be one of the first Quarriers boys to attend a school outside the Village. There had been a shift in thinking about the children's education. It was felt that, to promote better integration into society, some of us should be exposed to children from normal backgrounds in a mainstream school. I was enrolled at a school in the nearby village of Linwood.

There was more good news. I was to be transferred from Cottage 31 to Cottage 7, to be reunited with Irene. They had at last listened to my entreaties to live with her. Cottage 7 was run by two spinster sisters, the Misses Davidson, who had a reputation for managing their cottage like a family home rather than a barracks. Two birds, one stone. Alas, this was to be a short-lived sojourn, which would end badly thanks to my liberation from the repressive Drennan regime, my frustration, Irene's anger and a potato peeler. More of that later.

I packed my bags and made the short journey between the cottages. The first few days were heaven. However, it became clear very quickly that the allegedly benign Misses Davidson could be every bit as cruel as the Drennans. It just manifested in different ways. Their outhouse was still a nocturnal prison and Irene was a regular detainee. Corporal punishment remained a way of life. Silence was also used as a psychological weapon. Irene suffered badly from this tactic. The sisters would not acknowledge her when she spoke. She was blamed for starting quarrels even when she was not present. My sister's enmity towards the spinsters led to her being examined by a psychologist, who in a report concluded that Irene 'has been put in the shed often and another girl was put there with her and her bed brought down. Miss Davidson struck [Irene] across the face with a belt and it sounds as if she and her brother have been treated quite harshly. [Irene] is ignored by the assistants even when she asks them something. Irene seemed a likeable, pleasant girl who expressed herself well verbally. I did not feel that she was making up stories. She had the kind of [facial] expression that could look impudent and sulky and this possibly irritates the sisters.'

Everything irritated the sisters. They were paranoid about the house being burgled. Children being children, we took advantage of their fear: at night, we stole from our beds to unlock the doors and rattle the handles. The sisters would run down the stairs in a state of fear and alarm. From our hiding place, we thought this was hilarious. Chaos reigned. I hesitate to say anything positive about the Drennans, but to use the vernacular, they kept 'a lid on it'. We ran riot in Cottage 7, playing pranks and sending the Davidsons into ranting rages. I became 'unmanageable' and I loved it. I should explain how a child in care learns to play the system – every bit as much as the system plays the child. The threat of serious punishment was of course ever-present, but you had to push the Davidsons so much further.

The other dynamic of life in care is the constant sense of injustice, not just for you but for others. Many of the transgressions of house parents were sins of omission, a lack of understanding, a lack of care. One poor girl who twitched uncontrollably while in church was physically punished by one of the house parents. I knew instinctively that her disability was not bad behaviour: she was physically incapable of controlling her legs. Even so she was smacked. I jumped up and ran to the end of the pew to comfort her, driven by some natural desire to protect. It would be many years before I recognised the twitching girl's symptoms as Tourette's syndrome. When I returned to my seat, the Davidsons were incandescent and Irene was angry because they blamed her for the disruption to the service. This episode would have far-reaching effects. After we left the church, Irene's frustration, which had been mounting, boiled over and she physically beat me. I was astonished. Irene had always been my shield.

'That was your fault! Don't I have enough problems!' she shouted into my face.

Her words stung harder than her fists. The Davidsons' punishment for my 'disruptive' behaviour in church was less traumatic, but the consequences would be far greater in the long run. I was ordered to peel a mountain of potatoes. I was given a potato peeler and ordered into the kitchen.

As I struggled with blistered fingers, the sisters kept coming into the room to goad me: 'Are you not finished yet, David Whelan? It's nearly dinnertime!'

At the tenth jibe, I broke, exploded. With an angry roar, I leaped to my feet and chased one of the sisters. I can't remember which one it was. She fled screeching, running up the stairs to seek refuge in the bathroom. I had long since dropped the peeler as I raged at the bolted door, beating on it with my fists.

The commotion attracted every child in the house, and the other Miss Davidson. My time at Cottage 7 was over.

A few minutes later, I was looking into the hard eyes of William Drennan. I was back where I started – only the cottage had changed to number 11, as the Drennans had by this time moved house. I could not know it, but time was running out for me. My outburst had placed me firmly on the road towards my abuser. I would never be the same again. After that, there were few occasions for me to be able to spend time with Irene. Our time at school was busy, and we had so many chores to do when we arrived back at the cottage that there was little chance for us to get together.

Quarriers always encouraged children to be competitive, especially in sports. This provided Irene and me with one of the most incredible episodes in our lives – a reunion with our brother Jimmy, who had disappeared from Drumchapel for that 'long holiday'.

We were watching Quarriers boys playing football against a team from the Gryffe, a home for delinquent boys. Jimmy was playing for the opposition. We couldn't believe our eyes.

'It's Jimmy!' shouted Irene.

'Where?' I asked.

'There,' she said, and bawled, 'JIMMY! JIMMY! It's us!'

Gryffe's flying winger paused to look in our direction. Jimmy's look of recognition made Irene and me hug. When the game was over, Jimmy ran over and we had a group hug at the side of the pitch.

'Where have you been?' Irene demanded, her arms around Jimmy's neck.

Our brother had not changed. 'I'm doing my time at the Gryffe,' he said.

'Ma said you were on holiday,' I said, ever the naïve one.

Jimmy laughed. 'They caught me for doing the meters. The Gryffe's hellish, but I'll be out soon. I can't believe Ma never told you where I was. I'm only two miles up the road. What are you doing here, anyway? Where's Ma? Where's Johnny and Jeanette?'

Irene and I looked at each other.

'Ma disappeared and we were brought here,' said Irene. 'She just left us. Jeanette's been to see us, so has Ma. They say we've got to stay here for now.'

The Drennans were less than happy about the impromptu family reunion. 'You, boy, back to the cottage,' Drennan barked at me. 'Don't fraternise with undesirables.'

I protested that Jimmy was my brother, not an undesirable, but we were soon being dragged away. I wouldn't see or hear of Jimmy again until the funeral of our brother, Johnny, in 1978.

My memory of the relatively short period before I was sexually abused is shrouded in darkness. It seems to me now that the years spent blacking out the terror of the Beast have snatched at the edges of other memories before the abuse began. I have to rely on the Quarriers children's records to fill in gaps.

There is no doubt that after I returned to the Drennans my behaviour changed for the worse. Today, in our more enlightened age, such a rapid deterioration would attract the attention of child psychologists and elicit a willingness to investigate what was going wrong. It is clear from my school reports that I was a capable and intelligent child, but my Quarriers file records, 'David has been very insolent of late. He requires firm handling and constant supervision. David is cheeky towards staff and insolent.'

In a bid to bring me into line, Drennan demanded I join the army cadet force, which he ran as if he was still in the grown-up army. I hated it. The less-than-glowing reports continued: 'Easily led into trouble and bad company.'

I began absconding. My first time 'under the wire' was spent hiding with another boy in the garage adjacent to Cottage 36. We were discovered by Joseph Nicholson, the house father of Cottage 42. Years later, he would be convicted and jailed for the sexual abuse of a 13-year-old girl in his care at Quarriers.

My short-lived escape was the first in a series. Another notation written by my house parents, on 24 February 1971, in my Quarriers' records, states: 'David decided to walk out this evening. Before going, he stated he hated the cottage staff and everything in it. "School was also rotten. No one here is any good." This boy resents any form of discipline or correction.' My punishment on this occasion was the withdrawal of privileges for a week. I have yet to work out in my mind the precise nature of these 'privileges'. I felt anything but privileged. I had got their attention, though, and there was talk of another transfer.

The final straw for the Drennans came on 28 February 1971. My record states, 'Resents punishment period imposed on him. Causes upset in the cottage during lunch, becomes abusive, insolent and defensive, using filthy language towards house mother when reprimanded for his conduct and behaviour.'

Within days, I was out, heading back to Cottage 7. The Davidson sisters had given up the ghost and moved on, to where I do not know. John Porteous – the Beast – and his wife, Helen, were now in charge. Irene was, of course, already there and by now she had become a fine all-round sportswoman. The Porteouses loved having high achievers in any field in their cottage. They basked in the reflected glory. The couple were willing to take me, in order to keep Irene happy. My sister had, through no fault of her own, taken me to the edge of a nightmare that would endure for the rest of my life.

I arrived in Cottage 7 on 3 March 1971. There was no escape now.

CHAPTER 10

I Lose My Shield

I am in my own bed, with the special secret, our secret. Helen has returned and he is gone. He showed me the forbidden books, but if I tell anyone, he will send me to a borstal. The tears have dried on my face and I am too tired now to cry any more. My face is pressed into the pillow and my fingers grasp the candlewick. I can breathe again, but there lingers the memory of the pressure of his heavy body. His words are still in my head. I wonder why my mother does not love me. My threadbare dressing gown, with its rope cord, is wrapped around me. It is some comfort. I am quiet. I did make some noise earlier, but he cuffed me into silence. The smell of the hair lotion is still strong. Before he left, he made me put on the special underpants, the ones I think of as girlie. For the moment, I am safe. But it won't last long. I am helpless.

Irene had protected me. Big Brian was not the only threat that she had nullified, but she was gone now. Within weeks of her departure, the abuse had begun. It was not until much later that I realised the Beast had engineered her departure. When I look back on it, it was, of course, the only way he could ensure that he had unfettered access to me. Irene had many qualities and one of the greatest was her lack of fear. She was wilful, recalcitrant and indomitable. My Irene would have stood up to the Devil. On reflection, that is what she did during our time at Quarriers. If she had stayed at Cottage 7, my sister would have been a shield against the Beast, but while she remained she represented a great and ever-present threat to that which the Beast most cherished – his respectability. He wrapped it around himself like a cloak.

To the world at large, he played the part of a man dedicated to the poor mites who had nothing in life and no one to care for them, a kindly 'uncle' devoted to their needs. In reality, he was a poisonous, perverted bastard. The title of 'uncle' is an honourable one, describing a special relationship between a child and a man who is freed from the constraints and demands of fatherhood. Uncles buy you presents, cut you slack. They are the good guys when your dad is ... being a dad. The Beast perverted the concept beyond belief, but he hid it so well. The man was a superb actor who played the part to perfection. And to get at me, he had to be rid of Irene.

The pair of us had only been in Cottage 7 for five weeks before she was forced to leave after a campaign of confrontation engineered by the Beast. At first, it was fairly low-key: finding faults with everything she did. Later, the confrontations would become violent. There was no badness in us, but we were recalcitrant children, for ever trying to escape. We were confused, pained, emotionally drained and afraid. It was the hallmark of our lives.

I believe – and I hope and pray – that modern childcare has moved on from the casual cruelty of the past, when fear rather than love governed the interaction between the carer and the allegedly cared for. In those days, every infringement was met with disapprobation, recrimination, threats.

On one occasion, Irene was using a typewriter, clattering out words on a piece of paper and no doubt dreaming of the day when she would become a shorthand typist, a profession that represented the zenith of ambition for many a girl of our generation.

'Write dirty words!' demanded her silly little brother.

She looked at me askance. This was serious work. There was no room for frippery. 'Go away!' she said.

'Go on,' I pleaded.

I could see the smile twitching on Irene's lips. The serious-minded shorthand-typist was falling into one of the great traps of childhood – a fascination with the forbidden. Consider your own childhood. On the first occasion when you were handed a dictionary, did you look up word 'onomatopoeic'? You probably looked up something more basic and entirely rude. Irene had been holding out, but I could see she was weakening.

'Go on. Go on,' I said.

Irene capitulated and with a throaty chuckle she began typing some wholly innocuous words such as 'bum' and 'tits'. The Beast's wife, Auntie Helen, caught us. I believe that, today, such a misdemeanour would be greeted with a wry smile and a stern rebuke delivered in a voice hovering on the edge of mirth. That was not Helen's way. Her face suffused with anger and she turned on Irene and shouted at her. Eager to protect me, Irene never let on that I had put her up to it.

Having Irene in the cottage after my period of isolation was like heaven to me. Irene was a real tomboy and much better at fighting my battles than I ever was. If anyone dared threaten her wee brother, she would roll up her sleeves and wade in with fists flying, landing punches on any target that presented itself. She was a better street fighter than I was and, damn her, a much better footballer. Irene made me feel safe. The Beast did not like that. I had seen him looking at me when I first arrived in the cottage, but the expression in his eyes, which would have been identified so easily by an adult, meant nothing to me. He did not look at Irene in the same way – or the other children in the cottage. It was a special look for when we were alone. The arrival of Irene made him look twice, and not with the same expression. My sister would not just win battles for me outside the cottage; she stood up for me within it. Irene was pugnacious, to use that beautiful old word. She was a warrior. If the Beast or his wife were down on me, she would leap to my defence. The Beast became increasingly anxious to be rid of her.

The rows began on any pretext. A favourite ploy was to complain about her clothes. We were barely out of the 1960s, the decade that teenagers and cool fashion found each other. Irene was like any normal teenage girl. She liked to look attractive and modern. The Beast and Helen took exception to this ambition for reasons known only to them. There was really no point in arguing; house parents were imbued with a godlike power.

Inevitably, the tension caused Irene to run away. We both did on occasion, but we were always brought back with our tail between our legs, usually in the company of a member of the local constabulary. After a particularly nasty confrontation in October 1970, Irene absconded for three weeks. In a report written by the house parents, they claimed there was no apparent reason for Irene's disappearance. I knew differently. But there was no mention of the Beast's brutality in the official papers, which followed you wherever you went. Someone once said that history is written by the victors. It's true. It was inevitable then that the conflict between the Beast and Irene would have to reach some kind of conclusion and it would almost certainly not be in her favour. No doubt with that in mind, he pushed her relentlessly.

There was a youth club at Quarriers. It was only a few yards from our cottage and the older children went there to listen to music and hang out. It represented a semblance of normality for kids who were perennial outsiders. However, the Beast and his wife hated the kids from Cottage 7 going anywhere near anything unless it was associated with the church. Irene was defiant and would not attend such activities. She wanted to be normal.

Things came to a head one evening while I was downstairs playing on my own. I was alerted by raised voices and a terrible commotion upstairs. I could hear Irene and the Beast shouting at each other. I rushed to find out what was going on. I could hear him shouting, 'Get washed, girl!' and her saying, 'Not just now! Not just now!' There was a crashing sound, but before I could run up the stairs to see what had happened, my sister was already running down them with blood gushing from her nose. Her face was bright red and she was crying. The Beast was a few steps behind, calling her to come back, but before the brute could catch her she had fled through the front door. It banged on its hinges with a rattle.

By now, I was distressed and crying. I followed Irene, but my skinny little legs couldn't catch up with my athletic sister. I realised she was on her way to the superintendent's office. The superintendent of the home was Joseph Mortimer, a grim and stern-faced individual. I saw Irene disappearing into the office, but I was too afraid to follow her. I paced up and down outside, wondering what was happening. After what seemed like an eternity, she re-emerged from the office with Mortimer at her side. Her entire body language screamed at me not to get involved and I trailed behind them at a safe distance. Irene was still wiping blood from her nose. My heart was beating hard with fear and anger.

Irene was taken into the cottage from which she had so recently escaped and I watched as Mortimer marched her up to the Beast and forced her to apologise to him. She mumbled incoherent words and fled to her bedroom. When I got there, she was crying with anger. The pain in her face had been subsumed by the pain of frustration. She was dabbing her bloody nose, which was bent out of shape.

She blurted out, 'They made me apologise to him, the bastard, the dirty bastard!' Irene claimed. 'He was the one who hit me and I have to apologise to him!'

'What did you say to Mortimer?' I asked.

She replied, 'I told him I wanted a report written. I wanted it on my records. I wanted Porteous done for what he did to me.'

'What did he say?'

'He said I was making a very serious allegation and that John could lose his job if I insisted on a report going in. He said that John and his family might have to move away and lose everything if I reported him. He said I had to think very carefully before he took things further and to come and see him again in a week. But he said if I insisted on making a report, I couldn't live here any more.'

My heart sank. The thought of being without Irene terri-fied me, a fear that would be realised within the following 24 hours.

Irene added, 'Mortimer said I would be going away to college soon, anyway.'

The next morning, Irene's face had swollen up like a foot-ball. Her eyes were black and blue, and her nose looked as if it was broken. As far as I am aware, she never saw a doctor or received medical treatment. I went to school, and when I arrived home that evening, my sister and all her belongings were gone. It was Wednesday, 7 April 1971, arguably one of the worst days in my life. I didn't have the chance to say goodbye. My protector was gone and I was alone. I was overwhelmed, confused. The sense of abandonment was unbearable. In the weeks ahead, I would cry myself to sleep every night. In the daytime, I would act up. They told me she had gone away to a commercial college, but I learned much later that she had been transferred to a hostel in the Dennistoun area of Glasgow. I would not see Irene again until January 1978, when I was 21 years old. And so the horror continued …

CHAPTER 11

'Are You Clean, David?'

I cannot breathe. I am face down on the bed, pinned to the candlewick cover. I am smothered by the pillow. His weight is so great I struggle, but I cannot move. I am alone. I am afraid. He is whispering in my ear in a dark voice so unlike his normal voice. The pain is excruciating, but the greatest pain he inflicts is with his whispering words that tell me my mother never loved me, never wanted me. The abuse begins.

The push-bolt on the bathroom door is too flimsy to keep him out for long. He always beats me for locking it, but I try in vain to keep him from me for just a few minutes more and lock it anyway. I have nowhere to run any more. The door rattles on its hinges. His fist is beating on it. There is anger in the sound … and something else.

'Are you clean yet?' he demands to know.

Sitting in the bath, with the water cooling around me, my arms embrace my skinny shoulders. I have realised now that I can never be clean enough for the Beast, but perhaps my silence can stave him off for a few moments more. He never enters the bathroom after the first ominous thump on the door. He waits, savouring the moment. I lean over the side of the bath and my face, pale and frightened, is reflected in the shiny linoleum. It is burnished daily to a high shine with a heavy buffer, which is dragged over blotches of polish that smell strongly of disinfectant and oranges. I know how much work goes into maintaining the shine; it had been one of my many tasks in other cottages.

The door rattles again. He is impatient. My dark-green checked dressing gown, with its flimsy cord, is hanging behind the door. The moth-eaten jacket, no doubt handed down from generations of Quarriers kids, may cover my body, but it offers no protection from him. It seems very far away at the moment.

The door rattles. 'Are you finished?' he repeats.

The bathroom is one of his favourite places to trap me. I am alone there, helpless, and from this distance in time I realise now that I have given up, fallen into submission. There was a point when I still had some fight in me, but it is increasingly difficult to overcome this tidal wave of fear. I am at the stage where I just hope and pray it will be over quickly. The pain inflicted on my young body is bad enough, but it is his cruel words that stab at me, and will do so long after the physical effects of his beatings and abuse have healed. The vile things he whispers in my ear are threats interspersed with endearments, a combination I do not have the capability to understand. It is like when a child falls down and a parent comforts and berates them simultaneously.

He tells me my mother never wanted me, never loved me, and I believe him. Being here is surely evidence of that? If Ma loved me, why would I be here? He tells me that I will end up in a borstal, just like my 'scum brothers', and I believe him. Children in care learn the meaning of not being safe. Our lives are defined by the stories and dreadful rumours of how bad it is in other places. They can always send you somewhere worse. It is a fact you have to weigh in your hands like balancing a scale. Above all, I am alone. That is the worst place of all. The Beast has seen to that by stripping away my last protective barrier – Irene. She is gone now. He made sure of that. The Beast engineered a row with her in order to get her out of the way. I am now like someone standing in the path of a charging bull with only a lace curtain to protect me.

The door rattles again. I can picture the Beast, his soft hands, his hard eyes. His shirt sleeves will be rolled up, revealing tattoos that represent his time in the military. He served in the Royal Air Force. It is a decoration that commemorates an honourable service, which by his actions he has long since dishonoured. I am assailed by the cloying, if phantom, smell of Silvikrin, the lotion with which he tames his unruly hair. For the rest of my days, I will be able to conjure that smell just by thinking of the Beast.

'Are you finished yet?' he demands, his voice strident now with anger. Then the door opens, as it always does. He offers a benign smile, but I know him now for the vicious, sadistic, perverted brute that he is. He looms over me. The silence of the house has followed him into the bathroom.

I look down at the bath water, but I feel compelled to lift my eyes to him – and beyond into the hallway, which is empty. There is no help for me there. By now, the other children in Cottage 7 are in bed, and his wife, Helen, must be out, probably looking after 'her girls' at some meeting or Bible study.

He only ever comes for me when she is absent. The Beast never takes chances, never lets his mask slip, particularly on a

Sunday, when he stands in church, his head bowed in pious prayer, shoulder to shoulder with normal people who are not attracted to the bodies of not yet fully grown boys. I am as alone as I have ever been in my life and suddenly very cold. In the recent past I have leaped from the bath, but my shins bear the marks of previous encounters such as this when I barked my legs in an attempt to escape. I have learned. It is not worth fighting. He is too strong.

'I wanted to check if you were clean,' he tells me, his eyes never leaving my body.

'I'm clean,' I reply in a very small voice.

I am barely in my teens and slightly built for my age. I have no defences against this big man. Behind his back, some of the older boys describe him as a 'Jessie' – the Scots word for a man who acts in an effeminate manner. Effeminate or not, he is still large and threatening and much too powerful for me.

'Let me see if you are,' he says, forcing me to stand up, naked and vulnerable. He takes too long looking over my body, as he usually does. The word to describe it is 'lingering', a word that may be as comfortably applied to a look of love. In my case, it has nothing to do with love.

I make a vain attempt to get out of the bath, pretending I don't know what is happening, and reach for the towel, in the hope that I might be able to cover myself. He stops me, placing a hand on my shoulder. The pressure is gentle, but it promises to become heavier if I resist.

'You're not nearly clean enough yet,' he says, with his tiger's smile. Still maintaining the pressure of his hand on my shoulder, he uses the other to reach down and scoop cold water up and douse me with it. I am suddenly embarrassed. It is, I know, a ridiculously silly understatement, but my fear has been subsumed by it momentarily. Only babies should be bathed by adults – not 'big boys'. However, the fear returns with a rush as he begins to lather my body with the soap. There is a roughness and an urgency in his hands.

I know that later he will show me the books he keeps secret from his wife. I close my eyes.

CHAPTER 12

The Strange World of the Beast

'If I thought John was guilty of sexually abusing any child, I would not fight for him ... but I would support him'

HELEN PORTEOUS,
SPEAKING IN AN INTERVIEW WITH THE BBC

John and Helen Porteous grew up in Quarriers Village. They married in Mount Zion Church in 1969. Orphans and waifs acted as flower girls and page boys. Helen's brother, Alexander 'Sandy' Wilson, was the Beast's best man. Thirty-five years after the wedding, Wilson, who was also a house parent at Quarriers, was sentenced at the High Court in Glasgow after being convicted of 15 charges of sexually abusing eight girls over a period of 19 years. Uncle Sandy's favourite expression was, 'Would one of you girls come up and switch out the light?' A victim recalled later how she and her 'sisters' would stand at the foot of the stairs in his cottage and decide whose turn it would be that night to keep Uncle Sandy 'happy'.

Helen was sitting in bed, propped up on pillows. The Beast was lying beside her. He and Helen may have been trying to create a normal family atmosphere in which children felt comfortable enough to visit them in their bedroom, to talk over whatever had happened that day, but I was a growing boy and I wasn't their child. It exemplified the almost schizophrenic atmosphere of Cottage 7, in which care and protection collided with abuse and cruelty.

The last time I had seen Helen she had been wearing a severe Girls' Brigade uniform and had been barking orders like a regimental sergeant-major. Heaven knows what those God-fearing Christian girls would have made of this scenario. Was it because of what the Beast had already done to me that made the scene so disconcerting? I was 13, albeit small and immature for my age, but here I was, confronted by a woman in her night clothes. There was no impropriety in her demeanour, but I was decidedly uncomfortable, given what her husband had been doing to me. I had to get out of there. I didn't really know why. Such confusion was the hallmark of life with the couple.

John and Helen Porteous had only a passing acquaintance with the outside world. He had been in the RAF, having swapped one regimented way of life for another. Helen had flirted briefly with a civilian job in an office before being drawn back to, in her own words, the 'magnet' that was Quarriers. When the Beast left the RAF, he worked for the fire service at Glasgow Airport, but his burgeoning relationship with the young Helen persuaded him to apply to become Quarrier Village's fire officer. When I arrived, that was his day job. In the evenings, he assumed the role of house father.

Cottage 7 was not so much a home as a fiefdom. The couple ruled it like feudal magnates. Any semblance of family life was an approximation of how things happened on the outside, no more than an illusion of normality. Their orders had to be obeyed instantly and their word was law. There was no appeal, no recourse to any higher authority other than one that invariably supported them.

The world of the Beast was one of extremes, in which amusement and abuse merged in a *melange* of carefree holidays and cruel beatings, treats and tantrums, days of laughter, nights of fear. He created a rollercoaster of emotional agitation in which you never knew whether to laugh or cry, smile or scowl. The Beast was vain, arrogant, prissy and incapable of passing a mirror without preening himself. His wife was short, pugnacious, a disciplinarian with a voice strident enough to freeze you on the spot.

Many years later, in an interview with a television reporter, she would declare, 'I confess that if a child was really naughty, I would smack them, but I think that was quite the norm in the 1960s; if a child misbehaved, they got a smack [*sic*] bottom or whatever. I smacked children.'

The Beast did more than smack. A smack does not cause blood to pour from your ears. The bleeding was occasioned by blows delivered by the Beast. The pain was excruciating. Later, when I told him I was in agony, I was sent back to bed. My Quarriers review report for 4 October 1972 records that my general health was 'good – apart from perforated eardrums'. It goes on to state, '[he has a] good relationship with staff – especially house father, with whom he very much identifies'. I've already mentioned that history is written by the victors. I had gone into Quarriers with perforated eardrums. What the report does not reveal is that my ear problem was exacerbated by a beating during one of my all-too-rare moments of defiance. I had wriggled out of his grasp as he sexually abused me and, in my anger, threatened to tell. He went insane, his face purple with rage, as he punched me repeatedly on the sides of the head. He was still sane and conniving enough to know that he could not leave a mark on my face. My ears took the brunt. The next morning, the pillow was red with my blood.

The Beast was determined to use any means to keep 'our secret'. Bizarrely, on the one occasion when he believed that he had been exposed, he *pretended* to punish me. Helen had caught me and another boy 'showing each other our willies' – a not uncommon practice among pubescent boys, I understand. She was enraged. 'Wait until your house father comes home! He'll deal with you.' I was banished to the dormitory and remained there until the Beast arrived to be confronted by Helen. I could hear the sound, angry and declamatory, but not her words. Then I heard, 'David Whelan, come and tell your house father what dirty things you have been up to!'

By the time I came downstairs, the Beast's face was ashen, his eyes hot with anger and ... what was it? ... fear? Before I could speak, he was dragging me to the bathroom, where Helen could not hear his words.

'What have you said?' he hissed. 'Have you told her?'

I stuttered a reply that I had said nothing, and then, to my utter amazement, he administered a series of painless 'baby' slaps to my bottom. It was one of the few occasions in my young life that I was grateful for the proximity of Helen Porteous.

The Beast was down on his knees. We huddled around him, taking turns at a board game. It was one of the *good* evenings. I hesitate to concede that there were any happy times in Cottage 7, but by then I had become part of this schizophrenic world and was somehow able to place the different areas of my life into compartments. Yes, he was abusing me horribly; yes, he was causing me to live in a state of fear; but somehow, with a child's ability to adapt, I could still sit beside him, playing a game of Monopoly or Snakes and Ladders. The bad would never be overtaken by the good, but, some of the time, it was tolerable, and, like all abused children, I was so *desperate* to please.

The Beast and Helen truly regarded themselves as a 'Mr and Mrs Quarrier', fancying they were steeped in tradition, the inheritors of a great man's vision to care for children. There were others who felt the same and as a result cottage life was competitive, but the children of Cottage 7 had to be the best at everything, from winning prizes for cleanliness to excelling at the annual sports day. I was not particularly good at anything, except satisfying the Beast's perverted lust. His wife may just have been a woman of her time, believing that corporal punishment was acceptable, but her husband was a sexual predator in the perfect position to prey on the young. He had unfettered access to children. In the evenings, he would take boys on various excursions and organise camping expeditions for the Village's Boys' Brigade.

In hindsight, it is curious to me now that I was oblivious to the possibility that he may have been abusing others. I don't know if it even occurred to me that anyone else was 'special' to him. He would eventually be convicted on my evidence, and that of another abused child, but if someone had asked me at the time I would have claimed to have been his only victim. His mask of respectability was impenetrable, so there were the games of rounders, the board games in the evening and the wholly innocent pastimes of a 'father' with his children.

In 1982, long after I had escaped his abuse, he was accused of similar offences by another boy in the Village. The accusation could not be proved and he was allowed to remain an employee until 1998 – only four years before my evidence helped put him behind bars, when the trial judge, Lord Hardie, had, at last, torn off the mask that the Beast had worn for so long, and never allowed to slip.

Astonishingly, as late as 1996, I later learned, the Beast was the chairman of a children's panel advisory council. And, at one point, he was a governor of a local school. The Beast even ran an association of former Quarriers boys and girls, set up within the Village, although it was not an official Quarriers' organisation. He too, it would seem, had the ability to separate the two roles he played. On one hand, he was the children's saviour; on the other, the sexual predator. I believe that he had truly convinced himself he was a good man. Such is the nature of the depraved.

The good man was rarely in evidence when I was a satellite in his orbit. He identified the victim in me and his first task was to break my spirit. Physical punishment was meted out regularly; being deprived of meals for minor infractions was commonplace. I was, at times, guilty of indiscipline, within the terms of reference applied by the Beast, but my moments of rebellion had so far been few and pathetic. For most of the time I lived as quietly as I could, occupying my place in the pecking order in the cottage, which was fashioned on a pyramid of privilege.

The house parents, the kings of the mountain, were at the apex. Their 'Quarrier children', the waifs and strays from the slums and broken homes, were far below, in the valley. It always appeared to me that the natural children of many of the house parents were privileged in comparison to us. Childhood is a cruel country and in this landscape they seemed to be the ruling class. It was not they who suffered abuse, or were given toothbrushes and ordered to clean the outhouse. They wore better clothes – new clothes. They often went to 'proper' schools, where they were given the opportunity to prepare for jobs that would propel them into the middle classes. This led to a sense of superiority, which was probably inevitable. Along with their parents, they were often a law unto themselves. In 2005, William Gilmore, then 48, and the son of house parents, was convicted of sexual offences against three Quarriers children while he was a teenager. For many of us, life was a constant battle, a corruption of William Quarrier's vision, but proof, if it was needed, of Darwin's contention of survival of the fittest. It was an atmosphere in which no true friendships could be forged.

Many years later, as an adult, I saw the Hollywood film *Spartacus*. I'm reminded of a scene in which the titular character attempts to introduce himself to one of the other slaves in the gladiator school, where they had been taken to be trained to fight in the ring. Spartacus' companion tells him, 'I don't want to know your name – I might have to kill you.' Melodramatic, I know, but I understand what he meant. It took me a long time, long after I had left Quarriers, before I learned how to trust.

For now, we, the children no one wanted, sat at our tables of six. We looked forward to wearing fancy dress on dark Halloween nights; the egg-and-spoon races on sports days; the relief of rare bright summer holidays outwith the confines of a largely dark world. We constructed karts from orange boxes and pram wheels and raced them down the long hill behind the Elise Hospital. We looked after the pets – I had a rabbit, which I fed on porridge oats and carrot peelings. Quarriers even allowed me to go on a school cruise. I looked forward to small privileges, such as being allowed to sit up later than the others to watch grown-up television – until it became a precursor of abuse, on the evenings when Helen was not at home and unaware of what was going on. I had by then decided that I might like to be a chef and sometimes I was encouraged to cook.

What I am trying to say is that I – we – endured and suffered the abuse in silence. Why didn't I tell someone? Why didn't I run away and never come back? Who was I to tell? Where was I to go? How far could I run from Uncle John? I didn't know there was a world out there in which children did not have to fold their clothes over a chair in a precise way. I didn't know there were children whose names were not sewn into their underpants. I didn't know there were 'uncles' who didn't bathe children as old as me. I didn't know there were uncles who didn't take children into dark places to perform unspeakable acts. Ordinary, normal children of my generation will remember how they did not come home and tell their parents when they had been punished at school by their teachers. They feared it might provoke additional punishment. Then, unlike now, figures of authority were always given the benefit of the doubt. Consider what happened to my sister Irene when she told. She was effectively made to disappear. Even on the rare occasions when Ma and Jeanette came to visit, it never occurred to me to blow the whistle. A child of today probably would. I said nothing.

Ironically, Jeanette was inadvertently responsible for a change in my behaviour that prompted me to small, if ineffectual, acts of rebellion. She had asked the Quarriers authorities if I could visit her in Glasgow. It was a red-letter day. I was permitted to spend the weekend with my sister and her husband at their flat in Hyndland Street, in the West End of Glasgow. They took me to the shops and bought me my first pair of long trousers. When I returned, the Beast was not happy and took them away from me.

This casual act of cruelty was followed by another incident that transformed my frustration into anger. I refused to eat pineapple at dinner. It was a scenario similar to the one I had suffered in my early days with the Davidsons in Cottage 7. I hated pineapple, and this wet and too-yellow circle of fruit rested on a slab of pink rubber that was masquerading as gammon steak. The pineapple – and only the pineapple – was placed in front of me at breakfast next day and then again at lunch. I snapped. I hurled my dinner plate against the wall. I was in another place. I heard Helen's voice from somewhere very far away as I ransacked kitchen cupboards, spilling dishes onto the floor. She shouted for the Beast. He appeared like a raging bull, dragging me by the hair to the shed. I was beaten and spent another night in the outhouse.

It is said that no matter what suffering a person endures, the human flame cannot be fully extinguished. I had enough spirit left to run away. As usual, I did not get far. I was found eventually by the police, who returned me to the Village. A kindly senior officer had asked me if anything was troubling me. I looked up into his eyes and for a moment, just a moment, the floodgate almost opened. I almost told him about the flimsy bolt on the bathroom door. I almost told him of the loud knocking, the demands to know if I was clean. I almost told him about sitting on the sofa, watching television and looking at the Beast's secret books. But I didn't. The silence continued. I especially did not tell him about Sunday mornings in the bell tower.

CHAPTER 13

The Beast of the Bell Tower

Beneath my feet, the well-worn stairs are scuffed almost white by the passage of generations of small boys and men trudging towards Heaven to ring the bell and call the faithful to prayer. For the moment, the bell is silent. He is leading me, alone and helpless, on the seemingly endless climb towards the tower. The bell rings out every Sunday morning for a period of 15 minutes – no more, no less – before the beginning of the service at 11 a.m. In that so brief quarter of an hour, he does things to me. And then he goes back down the stairs to his prayers.

The opening line of the longest psalm in the Bible reads, 'Happy are those whose way is perfect.' I am of course less than perfect – as he is so willing to tell me. I am the bad seed, not fit for the company of normal people, a failing boy separated from the failed adult only by the passage of time. I will get there soon enough, he has told me. In the interim, I am to be beaten and terrified, and no one is coming to help me because no one loves me enough to care. The Beast has chipped at my defences for ages now, violating me in soul, mind and body.

I take comfort, however, from the opening line of Psalm 119, with its hefty 176 verses, each one of which I have been ordered to write out by the Beast. It is my punishment for being a disruptive influence – and it has bought me some time. I decided that if I were to escape the Beast, I would have to do wrong in the eyes of a good man, the minister of Mount Zion Church, Reverend Arthur Fraser. I am disappointed that I have fallen on the wrong side of this good man, but for as long as I am barred from the church by my scribe duties, I am free, for a time, from a bad man. It means one fewer climb up those stairs to the bell tower, where I am alone with the Beast. It means one fewer episode of stumbling back down, confused and empty. If I write slowly, I still have 20 verses to copy. Another week of grace perhaps, please God.

The Beast has a special treat for his 'favourite' boy. I am taken up the stairs to the bell tower on a Sabbath morning. As we climb, the faithful have yet to arrive, dressed in their Sunday best and carrying the special Quarriers Sankey hymnals, which contain the wisdom of the ages and the word of God. The words offer comfort and salvation to all but me as I climb the stairs to the bell tower. The bell has a huge wheel. The strength of an adult is required to wind the mechanism that enables the bell to ring. The tower is a cold, austere place high above the ground and those below, who are too far away to know what is going on. A small stool sits adjacent to a series of levers rather like organ stops. A reference of instructions indicate which levers to pull in order to activate the different chimes of the bell.

'Can you feel it?' he says – not in reference to the sound of the bell.

I remain silent, trying to ignore him and what he is doing. My body is alive with the sensation of a million needles pricking my skin. I am wearing my Quarriers Sunday best – a kilt beneath a green jacket, the uniform of the Sabbath.

The Beast is fussing over me. 'You aren't dressed right,' he says.

No matter where I am, I am never dressed right or clean enough. My back is to him and he is 'adjusting' my kilt.

'Do you feel it?' he asks again.

Again, I ignore him. I don't know why I remain silent. Fear, probably. I squirm, but he holds me still. However, no matter how afraid you are, a survival mechanism kicks in when you are under attack and suddenly I am struggling. It is to no avail. My struggles only serve to anger him.

He grabs me, shakes me until my teeth rattle. 'Be still or I'll see you're sent to a remand home like your hoodlum brothers,' he hisses.

I stare resolutely at the wall until he is finished.

His voice is calmer now, less tense. 'There,' he said. 'You do want to look your best, don't you?'

CHAPTER 14

Public Applause, Private Degradation

*The bell has stopped ringing and he has returned from the tower
to take his place among the congregation. My body aches, but no
one sees my pain. No one ever sees my pain. If they do, my
punishment will be severe. His eyes have lost their hardness now.
His hands clutch the hymnal. His head is bowed in deference to
God. His voice offers no threats. He is singing to high Heaven.*

The first incident in the bell tower set a pattern that would last
almost until I left that dreadful place at the age of 16. My sense
of helplessness was total. If I told, who would they believe, the
boy from the sink estate or a pillar of the community? You
might also be forgiven for thinking that a teenaged boy might
eventually be a match for any man, particularly one who is
causing him so much pain. I have replayed that particular one
in my mind many times over the years. I have yet to find the
answer. I can only liken it to a variation on Stockholm
syndrome.

In psychology, Stockholm syndrome is a term used to describe a paradoxical psychological phenomenon whereby hostages express adulation for and have positive feelings towards their captors. It is of course irrational, in light of the danger or risk endured by the victims, but research by the FBI showed that more than a quarter of victims display signs of the syndrome, which was given a name after a raid on the Kreditbanken, in Stockholm, in August 1973. The robbers held bank employees hostage for five days, during which the victims became emotionally attached to their captors and even defended them after they were freed from the ordeal. If that can happen in the course of five days, how much greater must the symptoms of indoctrination be when it occurs over a period of weeks, months and even years? I was, remember, the child no one wanted – worthless, alone, afraid and terrified of the unknown. I could have made a run for it – and sometimes I did – but experience had taught me that there was always a reckoning, always the road back to where I 'belonged', and more abuse. So I would put out the Bibles in the pews and arrange the cushions and allow myself to be led up the stairs to the bell tower.

Abusers play a clever game. The horror is interspersed by kindnesses for which you become grateful. It is a perversion of a normal relationship, but to a thirsty man even a few drops of water are precious. Given the nature of how we lived at Quarriers, it was impossible to avoid the company of the Beast. I could no more avoid him than a child of the outside world could avoid his or her father in a normal home. He wanted always to be near me, and in the beginning there was comfort in being 'liked'. I could not know there was a sinister motivation behind it all. And I liked having a 'father', and being the centre of attention. I did not see through the façade. I had nothing to compare it to. My natural father was a stranger to me. Choices? No choices. Do as I was told or take a beating. This was, after all, 'normal' to me. It was a situation beyond questioning. My only inclination that it was not proper was the hint of alarm bells ringing somewhere deep in my psyche, a gene memory of what constituted acceptable behaviour.

The emotions raised by being, at times, honoured or privileged by his non-sexual attention only served to add to my confusion. The Beast would give me special responsibilities. I was treated like a grown-up at times, which made me feel special. We would watch television in the staff sitting room like adults. He also knew I wanted to be a chef and he would encourage me to cook. I would make a cheese soufflé for the Beast and his wife, and he would tell everyone I was wonderful. Public applause, private degradation. I basked in the glow of the moments of kindness that were no more than pinpricks of light in the darkness. As I said, thirsty men crave drops of water.

I would try to find ways to be as far from him as possible. I would stay out of the house, but there are only so many excuses you can make to stay away from home. He would simply wait until I returned to the cottage and get me on my own. His moves became bolder. He had slowly but surely introduced the other, darker elements. 'Do you know about the birds and bees?' he would ask. Then he would show me the secret books, the ones he kept hidden from others, particularly his wife. He always sat close to me, too close, when he talked about the books on adults and sex. I did not want to hear the words. They mortified me. I wanted to move, but I was in a vice. Then the touching began. Then he would take my hand. The Beast was telling me he was teaching me. He said I had to learn. It did not matter that I was crying, or that I was in pain, or that I did not want to do the vile things he was forcing upon me.

Worst of all, I could not understand why my body was responding. Later, he would tell me that my reaction meant I was like him. It would be many years before I learned that the body is governed by its own rules. The first time it happened, the inner conflict was worse than any physical pain. My response pleased the Beast. He would smile his sly smile. Nowadays, they describe it as grooming, but what did I know then? All I knew then was my hand was being grabbed and I was being forced to do these terrible things.

'Do it, boy,' he would growl. 'Do it or I'll see to it that you are sent away.'

I knew he had the power. He had made my sister disappear. And it was difficult to think straight when he grabbed my ears and punched me into submission. I never knew when it would happen and I was never free of the dreadful anticipation. It haunted my sleep. And some nights when I awoke in the dark, I knew he was there, standing over me. I would close my eyes tight, feigning sleep, but my heart was beating so fast and so loud it seemed that he could tell I was pretending. Sometimes, he would do no more than stand there. I tried not to look at what he was doing. On other occasions, that was not enough. His hands would come under the covers. I would turn onto my stomach and lock my legs, desperate to keep him from me. It was no defence. He would not stop until he was satisfied.

This abuse would happen two, three, four times a week. When the Beast's wife went into hospital to have the first of their two children, the attacks intensified. The birth had been difficult and Helen was required to stay in hospital a bit longer than was usual. With her away, the coast was clear. He would call me into the staffroom. 'David, make sure all the others are in their beds and come back in here. I have something to show you,' he said.

I would move with the slow, tired tread of one walking knee-deep in water. I knew what he wanted to show me.

Today, no doubt an eagle-eyed social worker would see the signs – recognise them for what they were. In those days, showing defiance ended in being beaten. No one ever asked if anything was wrong. I didn't exist. It is ironic that, by the standards of the day, Quarriers was in many ways a progressive establishment dedicated to the care of the young. For example, they introduced an allowance, which permitted the teenagers to buy their own clothes. The Beast would even hijack that enlightened example of social care to further his own perverted agenda. He would accompany me on the shopping trips to Glasgow, which to a kid like me was a great adventure. I could not understand why it was he who chose the underwear I was to buy. I remember they were exclusive to Arnott's, an upmarket store in Argyle Street, which was part of the Harrods group. I could have bought much less expensive underwear at Marks & Spencer, but the Beast was insistent. I remember being horribly confused and embarrassed on our return home when he asked me to put on the underwear and parade around in front of him.

'I'm just checking to see if it fits,' he would say, as he made me walk around the room. All the time he was touching himself. I could not bear to look at him in case I caught his eye. I was aware the pants were strange and girlie, and I remember being embarrassed when I changed for PE in front of the other boys. They whispered among themselves. I didn't know why they were nudging each other and wearing sly smiles. What do I know? This is the way I live.

CHAPTER 15
Hope and Awakening

'David Whelan!' a voice roared from the other side of the playing field. 'Even your sister is better than you! You have no future as a football player. Find another career!'

Loath as I am to admit it, dear Mr Cooke was on the money. I had been bounding around the pitch, displaying my all too apparent lack of physical coordination. I did not, however, see it quite in those terms. In my mind's eye, I was moving swiftly, silkily, into my opponents' half. A vociferous if imaginary crowd of spectators held its breath. I envisaged the ball leaving my boot and sailing straight as an arrow into the top corner of the net. The reality? Well, I have to admit it fell somewhat short of the ambition. I think they are probably still trying to locate that ball. Much as I desired the possibility, David Whelan was never going to share the same team sheet with the likes of David Beckham or Wayne Rooney. Such is life. I had long since given up fighting the war against disappointment, disapprobation and a sense of loss. I was just glad for the moments when there were no tears or fear.

I arrived, breathless and chastened, but still in this philosophical state of mind, to pause in front of one of the biggest men I have ever met in my life. Mr Cooke, the former police officer, was sports master at Quarriers. He stood four-square, as tall and solid as an ancient oak, regarding me with a look that encompassed weariness, disdain and, bless his memory, more than a little compassion.

He teased me. 'What do you want to be when you grow up, David Whelan, apart from a very bad footballer?' he demanded to know in his customary gruff voice.

I thought for a moment before replying, hesitantly, 'A chef … I think … sir.'

'Good choice, David Whelan! Now get changed and go and find some pots and pans,' he said, dismissing me from the field of play with the lightest cuff to the back of my head.

I am still grateful to him to this day. I ran away, towards the changing room, with my unfulfilled dreams trailing in my wake and a smile playing on my lips. Mr Cooke's words, condemning me to a future without football, may not have been music to the ears of a 15-year-old boy, but I was grateful at least that this huge, burly man had the ability and the grace to say my name without investing it with accusation and blame. He was, of course, correct in his assertion that I would never make a footballer and, damn him, that Irene had been a superior physical specimen. I fell far short of my sister, a natural athlete, who was being used by Mr Cooke to bludgeon me in the kindest way imaginable. Irene had excelled at sports, but she was long gone now, having been driven away by the Beast.

I had not stopped mourning the departure of my sister, who had been the last line of defence against my abuser.

However, there were changes forming in my life. I could sense them like an animal smelling a new scent on the wind. I was reaching a place where I could dare to dream. I was growing up. The dreams were, of course, amorphous, but in recent months I had identified something new in myself, something indefinable and elusive, like a screen of smoke obscuring a significant event. They were encouraged by a growing knowledge that I wasn't doing too badly at the business of normality. As I've said before, I had no true terms of reference to define the word 'normal' or the assertion that I could achieve such a state. There had been too many Sundays in the bell tower – and nights without number, cowering behind that bathroom door with its flimsy bolt, which offered me no protection against the Beast. There would, indeed, be more such episodes behind locked doors, more Sundays in the tower, in the staff sitting room, on bath nights. There was still much to endure before my ordeal would be over. Nevertheless, I sensed, somehow, that the current chapter in my life was reaching its final paragraph and the next was about to be written.

I would of course carry the dreadful secrets of this time for more than three decades, but for now I was cushioned by a burgeoning sense of hope. I was, I knew instinctively, travelling in the direction of a different place from the one I had known. For the moment, it was merely emotional. I did not realise quite then that it would soon become a physical journey. In the meantime, life 'on the outside' was good enough to make my time 'behind the wire' seem more tolerable. Children in care, in homes or organisations such as Quarriers, develop the siege mentality, a particular way of thinking that is perhaps similar to that of prisoners of war or detainees in internment camps.

Quarriers did its best, I suppose, and was often far-thinking in its approach to childcare. Because my mother no longer wrote or bothered to visit, Quarriers organised a weekend 'step-family' for me in Glasgow. Jim and Jenny Sutherland had two teenage children and they welcomed me into their home. They are gone now, but I remain in touch with their children. I hope Jim and Jenny knew how much their kindness meant. They were good people and I could not bring the evil of the Beast into their lives. I should have told them, but I didn't. They held Quarriers in high regard and I did not want to destroy that. Their kindness helped me more than they ever knew, but when you are in care there is still the outside and there is the inside, where you live with the ambition and hope of defecting from one to the other permanently.

The Sutherlands, and school, especially a mainstream educational establishment, represented the staging post between the two, an opportunity to mix with the mundane, the usual, so-elusive 'normal'. And I had been doing pretty well at mixing. I was academically bright and heading towards success in my O-level exams. I had not been pretending when I told Mr Cooke that I had ambitions to be a chef. It was what I wanted to do. As it turned out, my career would veer off in another, if not unrelated, direction, but the desire to cook had been crystallising in my mind for some time, reinforced by the support of a very good cookery teacher at Linwood High, who had encouraged me to believe that I could pursue a career in the hotel and catering business. I just wasn't sure how I was going to do it, but I was beginning to believe that I could.

My childhood had been a sheltered affair; not sheltered in the sense that I was cosseted or protected in the usual way, but I had been in many respects denied access to the real world.

My earliest days in Townhead, as part of a family controlled by a monstrous father and a disturbed mother with the strength drained from her, had passed without my knowledge because I was a baby. There was now only the faintest remembrance of being in care – and then secreting food down the back of the sofa in the home of the doctors who wanted to adopt me. My all-too-short stay on North Uist, so remote from the mainland that it created its own natural barrier, was little more now than a bitter-sweet memory. I believe the truly defining period in my life before Quarriers had been living in Drumchapel, where the extent of our poverty and fractured family life had not equipped me – any of us – to deal with the world. As for Quarriers, it was for me a place of terror, and still occupies a deep-seated part of my psyche. In spite of this growing sense of awareness of something positive on the horizon, my life was still a cry suppressed. I was never far from the screams. I don't think I ever truly will be. Today, though, I am protected against them by those who love me. But, back then, I laboured against a dichotomy between fear and burgeoning hope. This split personality allowed me to live with the fear while applying myself to the constructive. I was, believe it or not, a bit of a singer. I had won a leading part in a school production of *The Pirates of Penzance*, although my teacher said that in terms of ability I was a fiver rather than a tenor. Music-teacher joke. They don't get out much. Any aspiration, however, to a glittering theatrical career was destined to be as short-lived as my ambition to make the starting eleven for Scotland: my voice broke during rehearsals. On the night, I croaked my way through the performance. The audience cheered loudly, anyway. I still believe they thought I was bringing some new and comic element to the part. It was a comfort. Any applause was better than none. I swam in the joy of it.

There were other comforts. There was Sandra, my first girlfriend. Dear, dear Sandra, where are you now? I still think fondly of you. From this distance in time, I find it almost incomprehensible that I managed in any way to relate to a girl. I was hardly coming to first love and sexual awakening by the most natural route. The Beast had seen to that. I could not and have never been able to expunge him from my mind. I think of the Beast every day and cannot bring myself to say his given name. Time may have dragged its layers over the memories, but, individually, they are gossamer-thin and even an accumulation of them over my lifetime has not covered them entirely. I still see their shadows. They can never be eradicated. As a growing boy, they were as painfully sharp as a finely honed blade and dogged those first tentative steps towards adulthood. I felt somehow unclean, a dreadful burden to weigh on immature shoulders, which distanced me from my peers. I was sexually mature beyond my years, but not in a wholesome way. Yet I still had the mind of a child.

I had, by now, come to realise that what had happened to me had not been of my making but was the machinations of a manipulative pervert. It was little comfort to me to know that it was not my fault, but the realisation of my innocence of any personal wrongdoing was arguably the biggest single step forward I had ever made. It was no Road to Damascus revelation, though. The clues to the knowledge lay in the children around me at school. Slowly, but surely, I saw, in their behaviour, their conversations, the way they acted, that the life I was leading was far from normal. They spoke of their fathers as men who were safe, protective. Their mothers were homemakers who cherished them, helped them with their homework and threw the blanket of security around them. Their brothers and sisters were with them, in some cases sitting just a few classrooms away, and at the dinner table of an evening. They were as innocent of my world as I was of theirs. Now, though, our worlds were touching and the collision was increasingly liberating to a boy who had to live with such a different set of rules.

The others were unlike me. The boys were brasher, more confident individuals who stood up to the world, while I, metaphorically, stood sheepishly in the corner. The girls were easygoing, possessed of a coquettish innocence, able to flirt with me. It was most forcibly brought home to me when I was invited to dinner at Sandra's home. It was a revelation – could the atmosphere in which she lived really be devoid of anger, stress and a constant watchfulness? It was. There was an air of comfort, welcome and friendship. I did not know the meaning of true friendship. In a children's home, there is no one to trust, no one capable of being trusted. Had the system turned me – all of us – into some kind of animal of prey that could never for a second lower its guard? I realised that it had. But how could I trust? Who could I trust, when the Beast came for me in the bathroom or despoiled the Sabbath by leading me up the stairs of that bell tower? But at least now I was beginning to realise that it was outwith my control. The knowledge somehow offered me a kind of protection, as did my emerging success as a lady's man.

Male generations before mine, ones that lived through the Great Depression and fought World Wars, would probably have dismissed me as a 'pretty boy', but that was no bad thing to be in the early 1970s. With my longish dark hair and fresh face, I had the 'look'. It was a blessing and a curse. I believe if I had been the usual type of boy to emerge from a rough housing estate such as Drumchapel, the Beast would perhaps have left me alone, but now the curse was emerging as a blessing of a kind. I realised as a young teenager that I might actually be good-looking. It may seem strange that any boy can reach the age of nearly 15 and not be aware of how his face is perceived by others, particularly girls. Most boys of that age have worn out at least a couple of bathroom mirrors, preening and posing. I avoided mirrors. If I didn't see myself, perhaps I could stay hidden, and I didn't want to see myself as the Beast saw me. I was small, timid and alone, the perfect victim in many ways, but girls, with their nurturing nature, are quick to identify and be attracted by vulnerability. Right now, it was working in my favour. I had more than a few admirers among the girls in the Village and at school. Vanity battled with confusion. I liked – no, I loved – being the centre of attention, but how was I to respond?

To be honest, it is a state of confusion that has more or less followed me my entire life. When I had my first sexual encounter, not that long after I escaped from Quarriers, it was stilted, awkward, as if picking up an object with a hand composed of five thumbs. My relationship with Sandra was gentle and non-sexual, apart from innocent kisses and cuddles. That was enough for youngsters of our generation. We seemed to be carved from the same stone, although physically I was as dark as she was fair. We dated and flirted. I took her to the school dance. She took me home to meet her family. But there was always an emotional clumsiness in me – what we Scots call a cack-handedness.

Nevertheless, I was flexing emotional muscles that I had not known existed. There was a growing confidence in me. I began looking in the dreaded mirror and did not quite see the boy I had been just a few months before. I was close to something new, but what?

That day, when Mr Cooke sent me running on my way, all of these jumbled thoughts and emotions were bubbling inside me. Sandra. School. *The Pirates of Penzance*. Ambition. Hope. Dreams. I reached the changing rooms and began pulling off my football boots. There was a movement behind me. I could smell the Silvikrin hair lotion. A soft voice said, 'David …'

CHAPTER 16

Escape

The water shone clear and blue, its surface sparkling with pinpoints of diamond light. It looked so inviting. I stood in my swimming trunks at the edge of the pool and watched my shuddering reflection in the water.

'Do you want to go in, David?' This person had not attached the now almost obligatory 'Whelan' to my name. The voice was kind but unctuous. 'You can go in on your own if you like,' the voice added.

I think of him now as the Man. The Beast had arranged a 'special visit'. He was the Beast's friend. I was alone with him. His home was opulent. He was obviously wealthy. The Beast had told me the Man wanted to speak to me, wanted to give me advice. The Man, said the Beast, had influence. He could help me. We had arrived as a group from Quarriers. I can't remember how I got separated from the others, but I was now alone with the Man at the side of his swimming pool. I have to concede that he may have been altruistic and innocent in his intentions, but suddenly I felt like a weak animal that had been separated from the herd by a predator. I could read the signs: he stood too close, the sidelong glances, small smiles, the furtive body language. Something inside me warned me that I should never fall under the influence of this person. A few years, even a few months earlier, I would have been frozen, been too afraid, but my growing sense of confidence – courage? – came to my rescue.

'I don't really feel like a swim today,' I told the Man, sharply. I turned, walked away, heading back to the safety of the herd. I could feel his eyes on my back, willing me to look over my shoulder. A smile was playing on his lips, but there was disappointment and puzzlement on his face.

The Beast seemed surprised to see me back so soon. 'Everything all right, David?' he asked, the tone of puzzlement in his voice reflecting the look on the Man's face. 'Didn't you want to stay for a swim?'

'NO!' I said, and the word had finality. I had never before quite said 'No' with such vehemence. There was strength in it. I had repelled him. A turning point. If I had identified a new-found strength in myself, then so too had he. The Beast would never touch me again. From what I now know about paedophiles and the way they operate, there comes a time when the victim steps beyond their reach. It may be as a result of the victim becoming too strong, physically or mentally. It may be fear of exposure. It may simply be the victim has grown too old for the abuser's sexual predilection. In retrospect, in my case, I recognise that all three reasons may have played their part. In spite of what I said about the Man's motives, I believe I was about to be passed on to him. Perhaps I am wrong, but every instinct I possess screams that was what was happening.

Had I become too mature for the Beast? Like most paedophiles, the Beast obviously had a preference for boys of a particular age. His other known victim, whose evidence helped send him to jail, was even younger than me – aged eight – when the Beast began abusing him. Before my abuse came to an end, the Beast had already chosen my successor. I would only discover this many years later, when the Beast was exposed and brought to justice.

The overriding consideration for any paedophile is fear of exposure. There comes a moment when they can sense their grip loosening on their victims. In my case, the Beast had just witnessed the beginning of the end. Something in the tone of my voice, spitting out that 'No!' had alerted him. He could no longer be certain of my silence. Now there was that possibility of exposure. Today, I believe that was why the Beast tried his best to maintain his control over me, albeit from a distance.

Quarriers had transformed the old Cottage 32 into a half-way hostel for young teenagers. It was designed to equip them for leaving the Village, preparing them for the wider world. At the time, this scheme represented progressive thinking on the part of Quarriers. Many of the children had been cloistered since the day they were born. The world was a big place and largely alien to them. The charity had installed a number of extra kitchens in the cottage and each teenager was provided with their own space, and the responsibility for effectively looking after themselves. It was a good idea, offering the opportunity of a kind of independence. Most Quarriers kids of my age longed for the day when we were considered mature enough to live on 'our own'.

The Beast, however, did not want me out of his sight and blocked my attempts to go there. I was unclear as to his motive. I may have taken huge strides forward, but I was still, in many respects, the confused child under his control. I realise now that he was afraid I would blow the whistle on him. I was on the cusp of 16, but still living in Cottage 7.

From the more solid platform of my growing assurance, I demanded answers. 'Why can't I go?' I asked the Beast.

'You're too young, David. You still need looking after. You'd be too easily influenced by bigger boys. You'd be too easily led.'

I sensed something new in the Beast's voice, a different tone, of solicitousness. His words were not delivered in the usual hectoring, domineering fashion. I knew our relationship had changed. At first, I had thought that it was my fault that I could not move on to the hostel. Paedophiles are expert at transferring blame from themselves to their victims. I felt isolated, and still very different from the other boys. However, the Beast had realised he was no longer able to bludgeon me into submission. There were no more nights sitting in the bath in fear of his arrival. There were no more Sunday trips up those dreaded stairs. He stopped calling me into the staff sitting room when the others were asleep and Helen was out of the house. On my birthday, he presented me with a tennis racket. It is the irony of ironies that, since then, I have been a lover of the game. One of the highlights of my year is Wimbledon fortnight. The constant confusion that had characterised my life began to dissipate.

However, it did not matter to me that the Beast had suddenly decided to become my 'friend' rather than my tormentor. I was going to escape, no matter what. I decided to stop fighting him on the issue of the hostel. I hadn't surrendered; I had merely devised a new line of attack. I knew that within a few weeks the Beast and Helen were planning to go on holiday on their own. By a twist of fate, their plans had coincided with another fortuitous event. Trust House Forte, a big hotel chain, was about to visit our school for a careers presentation. I put my name forward to attend. This could be my way out. I decided I was going to leave that conference with a job.

On the day, I paid particular attention to my appearance. I pressed my school uniform and shirt. My shoes were burnished to a high shine. I was immaculate. I had done my homework on the industry – and Trust House Forte – with the help of my supportive cookery teacher. By the time the hotel people arrived, I was first in line. A smooth, well-dressed man and woman presented their world of opportunities. It was everything I had hoped for. Not only would I get a job and the chance to carve out a career, but it would provide me with somewhere to live. I was not going to be consigned to some dreary flat in an insalubrious area of Glasgow. I was going places. My knowledge of their business, my inquisitiveness and enthusiasm impressed the glorious couple. I left with a job. Now … to end my days at Quarriers.

After I returned to Cottage 7, I told no one of my secret plans. Time dragged. It was only days to go until the Beast and his wife departed abroad for their sunshine holiday. The waiting seemed endless. I watched them pack their bags on the eve of their flight, and I did not sleep that night. My head was swimming with thoughts of liberation, escape and a new life. The following morning, literally seconds after they had left in a taxi for the airport, I ran to my dormitory and began packing. I had precious little to pack, precious little I wanted to take from that place.

I secreted my bag under my bed and headed for Holmlea – the Quarriers office headquarters in the Village. Boys and girls moving on from the Village needed permission to leave. I was worried that, with my house parents being away, it would be difficult to obtain. My fears were unfounded. Joe Mortimer, the superintendent of the Village, seemed happy to be seeing me on my way. I practically floated back to the cottage, recovered my suitcase and left without a backward glance. I did not even say cheerio to any of my 'brothers' and 'sisters'. I hadn't wanted to be placed in the awkward position of having to reveal where I was going. I did not want anyone to follow me.

I walked, almost jogged, towards the gateway of the Village and onto the country road that would take me the two miles to Bridge of Weir and civilisation. I passed the bed of flowers that still spelled out 'Suffer the little children' – the same biblical demand I had seen when Irene and I first set eyes on Quarriers. It seemed so long ago. As I walked away, I looked over my shoulder, back towards the place that held so much fear and so little happiness. The bell tower still reached for the sky, still dominated the landscape and still pointed the way to Heaven and Hell, but with every step I was walking out of its shadow. The sense of relief was immense.

The big orange and cream Graham's bus came towards me along the main street of Bridge of Weir, smoke belching from its exhaust pipe. I was standing alone at the stop. As the bus drew in, I looked up into the cab and the driver smiled at me. I was so grateful. I returned the smile. I stepped onto the platform to begin a journey that would take me much further than the mere five miles from Bridge of Weir to Glasgow Airport and the Trust House Forte Excelsior Hotel.

The sense of relief stayed with me all the way to the hotel foyer, a golden cavern of chandeliers, embossed silken wallpaper and carpets so thick your feet sank into them. I realised I had never before walked in silence.

The female half of the golden couple who had recruited me was waiting to greet me. 'David, welcome,' she said.

I offered a hesitant 'Hello' and held out my hand.

She took it and squeezed it gently before releasing me. I felt the warmth of her hand as she showed me around the hotel, the dining rooms, public areas, the kitchen and the bedrooms. This would be my domain as a management trainee. I had never been so happy. This was a palace from one of the books I had read as a child. It glowed. I glowed. I was introduced to Alastair, the flamboyant head waiter, who smiled at me with warmth. Chef René, who I knew instinctively would run his kitchen with military precision, offered me the cursory greeting of a man who knows his (important) place in the world. The rest of the faces blurred into a single entity as I tried to absorb this magical space.

'You'll be sleeping in the staff quarters,' I was told, and I was taken to an annexe and shown the first room that I could ever call my own. It was spartan, but, to me, it might have been a salon in Buckingham Palace. I stowed away my suitcase and sat on the bed. I looked around me. The journey from Quarriers had been just a few miles, but I had travelled to another world.

The day passed in an instant. I was ordered to get some rest and be ready to start work the following day. As darkness fell, I undressed and lay down on the bed, pulling the fresh-smelling sheets up to my chin. They felt crisp. I felt clean.

As I drifted towards sleep, I was drawn back by the fading echo of a voice speaking my name. 'David,' it said in a soft, sibilant tone. This time, though, there was no smell of Silvikrin. I surrendered to sleep. I was safe.

Chapter 17

Climbing the Ladder

I shaved slivers of peel from the vegetable into the colander until it became the perfect five-star Excelsior Hotel carrot. It rested in my left hand, smooth and pristine. In my right, I clutched the metal peeler. The last time I had held such an implement, it was being used against me in Quarriers as a psychological weapon. The Misses Davidson, in their attempt to break my spirit, had ordered me to peel the mountain of potatoes. As I had tried to complete the Herculean task, they had taunted me until I had erupted and chased one of them from the kitchen. Now there was no frustration, no anger and no resentment.

Chef René's shadow fell over me. 'Nice carrot,' he applauded. 'Now, impress me – transform it into a work of art.'

I set about the task of turning the vegetable into a rose to adorn a salad plate. In the time that had elapsed since I began my new life, I had settled to a happy contentment. I knew that this shiny, self-contained world of seemingly endless possibilities was where I wanted to be. The old world still had me in its grip, but, day by day, I was more determined that I would escape its grasp.

Weeks before, I had awakened on that first morning after a dreamless sleep. For a few seconds I was disoriented and confused suddenly by being alone. There was no one in the next bed. Then I realised there was no 'next bed'; this was *my* room. I was flooded by the same sense of relief that had carried me through the gateway of Quarriers Village. I wore the feeling lightly, though. I was still not wholly confident that this new beginning would not be snatched from me. After all, I had grown up learning not to hope. However, as the days and weeks passed, hope did rise in me as I waged the internal battle to prevent the past from sullying the present – and the future.

One of the most wondrous things that happened to me at that time was the realisation that there was no longer any need to be afraid. I bathed without fear of those dreaded knocks on the bathroom door. I ate with my colleagues in an air of conviviality, no longer sitting at tables of six where we dared only to look at our hands. The banter flew back and forth across the table and my accent became the subject of debate.

'Where are you from originally, David?' they asked.

'Glasgow,' I replied.

'No … you don't sound like a Glaswegian. Your accent's not hard enough.'

'There might be Inverness in it,' suggested one of my dining companions.

'No!' said another. 'It's more Borders.'

I began to revel in my mystique. It was my cover as well as something that made me, in some way, feel special. 'I'm from

Glasgow,' I said, and added, 'but I spent the last few years in Renfrewshire.'

'No, that's not it,' said the original enquirer. 'Where are you from really?' he demanded to know.

I relented. 'I spent a part of my childhood on North Uist,' I revealed.

'That's what it is!' said Alastair, the head waiter, a man who was himself no stranger to a homogenous accent, which he had developed over a number of years of association with well-heeled patrons.

Alastair would become my role model, a template for a polished persona. The apparent softness of my accent was my first clue to the possibility that I could perhaps overcome my roots and rewrite my own history. If people can't pin you down, you can, in effect, become anyone you want to be. I certainly did not want to be that scared little boy from Quarriers any more.

The accent conversation at the dinner table was a gift. I was learning. I was learning, too, that there was a world that I knew nothing of. My distant memory of the doctors' villa in Newton Mearns reflected a grander way of living, but it had long been subsumed by the subsequent experience of poverty in Drumchapel and the soulless regimentation of life at Quarriers. However, now, on a daily basis I saw the evidence of five-star living. Well-groomed men and perfectly coiffed ladies arrived with their matching luggage and loud, confident voices. In the beginning, they were players on a stage and I was still in the audience. It would be some time before the apprentice was allowed to interact with these impressive beings. For the moment, I was content living in the shadows, learning my trade while absorbing their manners and affectations. In those days, the Excelsior was one of the top hotels and a wonderful place, I would discover, to learn how to be a 'gentleman'.

But first, the day-to-day … I was like a sponge, absorbing everything around me, from the menial task of burnishing the cutlery to setting a table for a gala dinner. I polished crystal glasses until they captured the light from the chandeliers high above us. For the first time, nearly five years of regimentation at Quarriers stood me in good stead. The tables had to be laid with such precision that the distance between every fork, knife and spoon was measured with a special stick. Pristine starched white linen crackled as it was spread across the tables. We became origami masters in the art of napkin folding. After the barrenness of my childhood, the sheer opulence of it all delighted me. There were so many times in my early childhood when we didn't have enough forks and knives to go around. Now there were forks and knives for every course. I remember placing a strange new set of cutlery on the table and asking Alastair what they were for. 'The figs, dear boy!' he said. Mercifully, he walked away before I could ask him what a fig was. Before the day was out, I had ensured I knew what a fig was. I was a quick learner, and everything around me was a revelation.

Within a very short time, I was regarded as 'polished' enough for front-of-house duties. I was soon interacting with the golden people. I learned quickly that people at the very top of the tree were the best mannered and the most polite. It is my experience that it is so often the case that it is the aspiring who believe treating 'servants' with disdain is somehow a sign of class. The opposite is true. When I eventually went on to associate with royalty, and some of the most influential people in the world, I found them to be delightful. But I was still a long way from that as I ushered beautifully clad women and their consorts into the Excelsior's dinner dances and gala receptions. These men, and especially these women, were outwith my experience. Morag, with her wellies, and Ma, with her fag and padded dressing gown, had been to couture what a sow's ear is to a silk purse. I discovered that money had a look all of its own.

Alastair, the head waiter, may not have earned a fortune in his career, but it did not prevent him from acquiring the polished presentation of our clients. He was my mentor. There is an old saying that 'Clothes make the man.' I would counsel any young man or woman to take this advice.

'First impressions count,' Alastair would say, as he adjusted his perfectly knotted silver-grey tie. His advice was delivered while he was in the process of instructing me how to 'seat' a lady. 'Don't pull the chair out too far, or too quickly,' he said. 'One doesn't want the client to end up on her arse!' Good advice. I have yet to deposit anyone on their arse while assisting them to sit at a dinner table.

Depositing wine into a glass in the proper manner was also one of Alastair's great skills. 'Cloth over the arm, bottle held from base to centre, tip slowly, and so ...' he said, as the red wine flowed perfectly into the crystal glass. 'Try this,' he said with a conspiratorial air, as he poured an inch of Montrachet into a spare glass. 'It is a *very* good year,' he declared.

I sipped my first taste of fine wine – my first taste of any wine. I never drink wine now without thinking of Alastair.

My days and nights merged one into the other in a circle of shift work. It was tough but fun. We were a young bunch and all driven by the same enthusiasm. The older waitresses fussed over me, becoming surrogate mums. This was a new and welcome variation of the concept of a house parent. My colleagues became like brothers and sisters because, in effect, we all lived as a family. The similarities to Quarriers were inescapable, but this was different; this was a non-threatening atmosphere of calm and freedom. Rivalries were friendly, not mean or vicious.

I began to make real friends for the first time in my life. This was another step forward for the boy who could not trust. The barriers were slowly coming down. Margaret was one of the first people I allowed to chip away at these barriers. To save her blushes, I have called her Margaret. It isn't her real name. She was my first true girlfriend. Sandra had been puppy-love. This was the real thing. Margaret was a wondrous creature who worked as a trainee hairdresser and beautician. I remember being captured first by her smell, a waft of perfume that made me turn and look at her. From the moment I saw her in the hotel foyer, I was smitten. Margaret lived in Glasgow and was the same age as me. My weekly wage of £8 could not stretch to wining and dining her at the Excelsior, but a staff discount and my growing sophistication mightily impressed her. She came from a good background. By now, my background had become the Excelsior Hotel and all that I was learning there.

Margaret didn't know it – how could she? – but she was leading me towards one of the most momentous events of my life: my first sexual encounter with a woman. There comes a time in every blossoming relationship when, by almost tacit approval, sex becomes inevitable. Something different is felt in the kiss, the closeness of your bodies, the hint of going to another level. Margaret and I had reached that juncture and I was terrified. That evening, I drank something a little stronger than Montrachet. Any normal kid reaches such a point in a state of some turmoil. Imagine mine! I was sexually 'experienced', wasn't I? But, God help me, not in any way that Margaret might expect.

On the big night, I had smuggled Margaret into the staff quarters. The normal excitement of such an event, the embarrassed looks and hurried whispers, masked what for me was a battle with the Devil. As we fumbled on the bed, I tried to focus only on her, but the Beast was in the room with us. When she touched me, it became his touch. When she whispered to me, it became his voice. My replies seemed hollow and false. I panicked. I made the excuse of going to the lavatory. I sat in the bathroom, calming my whirling senses. My head was bowed as I sucked in great gulps of air. Drink, I thought, take another drink. I did. I paced the floor, desperate to exorcise the monster from my head. The alcohol kicked in. It was now or never. I returned to the room and made the transition from boy to man.

Afterwards, we held each other. We fell asleep. It was the first time I had fallen asleep in any woman's arms except for my sister. This was different. I awakened the next morning on the proverbial Cloud Nine. Margaret was demure, somewhat embarrassed. This aftermath was all crushingly normal, I was to discover through later experience.

Our relationship was in a new place of heightened intimacy. We were inseparable. When we were not working, we were together. It was on one of our dates, to the cinema in the nearby town of Paisley, that I was brought face to face with my old life at Quarriers. We were coming out of the picture house when I heard the voice calling my name. 'Davie ... Davie ...' The voice was urgent. I recognised it instantly as belonging to one of my old dorm mates, Tommy. The voice dragged me straight back to Quarriers and my heart thudded in my chest.

'Stay here,' I said to Margaret. I turned towards where the voice had come from and saw Tommy on the other side of the road. He hadn't changed. He was just bigger. I strode across the road with a false smile painted on my face. 'Tommy!' I said.

'Where have you been?' he said without ceremony. 'No one would tell us where you'd gone.'

'I've been … about,' I said lamely.

'You should have seen the fuss when you disappeared,' Tommy said. 'Uncle John and Auntie Helen were raging.'

'What were they raging about?' I asked.

'They came back from holiday and you were offski,' he said. 'Not happy!'

'I got a job … in the city,' I said.

'How's it going?' he asked.

'Great, great … Different world,' I said.

Before Tommy could ask any more, I was rescued by Margaret's voice finding me from the other side of the street. 'Bus is coming, Davie. Hurry up!' she shouted.

I had experienced the fight-or-flight response from the moment I had heard Tommy's voice. I fled. 'Nice seeing you, Tommy,' I said, as I bolted for the bus. From the safety of the upper deck I looked down on the bemused Tommy, whose face revealed more questions than I had answers for.

'Who was that?' asked Margaret.

'Nobody,' I replied.

For weeks after the encounter with Tommy, Margaret would return to that evening with enquiries about the 'mystery boy'. Her female intuition had gone into overdrive. She knew I was holding back something. By deflecting her questions, it had created an invisible barrier between us. Our intense relationship was about to come to an end, but even I could not have predicted that one of my new friends at the hotel would be the reason. He stole her from me, the rat. In truth, our relationship was already unravelling by the time of this betrayal.

Margaret and I had arranged to go skating at the ice rink in Paisley, but I pulled an unexpected night duty that I couldn't get out of. She would be waiting for me at the rink, but in the days before mobile phones it was impossible to let her know I was not going to make it.

My pal offered a solution. 'I'm not doing anything tonight. I'll go and tell her,' he said.

'Thanks, mate,' I said with gratitude. 'You're a lifesaver. Tell her I'm sorry and I'll see her tomorrow.'

I never saw Margaret again. Some girlfriend! Some pal! If truth be told, I wasn't too broken-hearted. I had already made a decision to move on. I was told there was 'better money' at the Centre Hotel, in Glasgow. I had learned so much at the Excelsior that I believed I could excel at another, less glamorous hotel.

Alastair agreed when I asked for his advice. 'Go for it, dear boy. You'll be a shining star as a result of my tutelage.'

I went for it. I applied for a job and got it. I had taken another step up the managerial ladder. Margaret and my treacherous mate were quickly forgotten. I stayed at the Centre Hotel for barely a year before I moved on again, this time to a hotel in the country, where news of a tragedy would propel me back into the heart of my estranged family.

Chapter 18
A Family of Strangers

Ma hadn't changed. Older, of course, more drawn certainly and tired-looking, but the eyes were still those of a child bewildered by a world too big to understand. Her pride and joy, the once-lustrous jet-black hair, was now shot with grey. The skin under her eyes was loose. She was still wearing the same padded dressing gown that I had last seen in Drumchapel. I was, in an instant, transported back to 34 Katewell Avenue. I shrugged off the memory. It was a place I didn't want to visit.

'Hello, Ma,' I said. I hadn't seen her for years? How many?

She barely responded. The inevitable Senior Service burned between her fingers. She was looking out of the window without seeing. Ma had the glazed expression of someone who wasn't quite there. It was a look I remembered well. Drink? Pills? Both? Who knows. I may have been different, but Ma wasn't. She was a mess. The house was a mess. Everything was a mess. Some things never change. And now she was carrying the burden of having just lost her first-born and favourite child. Ma never tired of telling us that Johnny was the only one of us that she ever truly wanted. Now he was gone, dead by his own hand at the age of 27, a poor, dear, demented soul, tormented to his grave by a past he could not overcome.

Jeanette said, 'I'll make some tea.' The panacea for all Scottish ills, no matter where we are in the world.

At that moment, we were in a hovel at Lindore Road, in Battersea, London. I've never known why Ma was drawn to the south of England. She had lived there before our ill-fated reunion in Drumchapel and gravitated back there after she deserted us. Only the frequent stays in Woodilee Mental Hospital kept her north of the border. When they ended, she headed south, as did the rest of my brothers and sisters.

Ma lit another cigarette from the butt of the first. She seemed not to care that her house was about to be filled with mourners. Jeanette and I looked at each other. We had to get the place clean, but where to start? Dishes overflowed in the sink. God knows the last time the floor had been washed. The bathroom was filthy. Every surface was covered with grime and dust. No one had cleaned this place in months. My sister and I went into overdrive. Ma might not have cared, but we did.

As Jeanette and I scrubbed and cleaned, my thoughts flew back to the moment when I heard the fateful news. I was in the hotel dining room when the voice dragged me from my work ... 'Someone on the phone for you, David. Family thing. Take it in my office,' the manager said.

It was 21 January 1978. I was puzzled. I hadn't had any 'family things' for such a long time. I picked up the receiver, which was lying on the manager's desk in the Queen's Hotel,

Helensburgh, a coastal town on the Firth of Clyde, in Dunbartonshire, 25 miles from Glasgow.

'Hello?' I said. My initial bewilderment turned to concern when I heard Jeanette's voice. 'Jeanette? What's wrong?'

In the previous five years, my relationship with my eldest sister had been confined to birthday greetings, Christmas cards and the occasional catch-up phone call. She was living in England and I was still in Scotland, working my way up the management ladder.

'Johnny's gone,' she said.

'Gone? Where?' I said.

'He's dead, Davie,' she replied.

Time stopped. Jeanette's voice was breaking. I hadn't seen Johnny since childhood and he was all but a stranger to me. The difference in our ages – nearly seven years – had always acted as the natural barrier that exists between the youngest and oldest in any family, but my memories of him were sharp, going all the way back to those halcyon days in Uist, when Johnny would hoist me into the air or push me around the croft in a makeshift cart. Later, much later, there was that other, deeper connection between us, when I realised that he, too, had probably suffered abuse in the borstal where he was sent for stealing those doormats to cover the cold linoleum at Katewell Avenue. And now he was gone. In spite of not having seen him for years, my sense of loss for that sweet-natured boy was immense.

'How?' I asked Jeanette.

She was reluctant to tell me. At the age of nearly 21, I was suddenly the child again. Jeanette was, as usual, being the mum and I was still the baby of the family who needed to be protected.

'Tell me, Jeanette!' I demanded.

'He took an overdose, as far as we know,' she said, and added, 'He'd been in hospital, a mental hospital, but he'd been out for a bit. He'd been given lots of pills. We think he took too many. Don't know if he meant to do it.'

I said, 'I'm on my way.'

The journey had been a blur, but now I was here. So many memories assailed me. I heard a sound behind me and turned. Irene looked exactly the same. The face of the child was still evident in the face of the woman standing before me. I had last seen her seven years before, on 8 April 1971, the day she disappeared from Quarriers. We didn't speak. We didn't need to. We just held each other. We didn't even cry. The years receded and the sounds in the room faded. It was as if we were alone.

'I'd say you haven't changed a bit, but you have,' she said.

'You're just the same,' I replied. She was slim, athletic and probably still a better footballer – and fighter – than I was.

The air rushed back into the room and I saw the faces of people I hadn't seen for years. Jeanette had done a good job of making Ma presentable, and she was lost in a corner, surrounded by some of those who had come to pay their respects.

'Davie boy!' someone said in pure Glaswegian, an accent that somehow manages to be friendly and menacing simultaneously.

It took two beats before I recognised the face of the old man. 'Uncle Charlie,' I said. 'How you doin'?' I added, hearing the long-forgotten tone creep into my own voice.

'Fine, laddie, fine. How you been?'

'I'm great, Uncle Charlie.' I was rescued by my namesake.

'Uncle Davie,' I said.

'Hello, son,' said a stranger.

The long trip down to London had passed in a blur and suddenly I felt very tired. From seemingly nowhere, my brother Jimmy materialised and embraced me fiercely.

'Davie boy, Davie boy,' he whispered.

Jimmy had been drinking and he was in sentimental mood – a common character flaw of some of the people from my home town. Irene rolled her eyes.

Jeanette was all business. 'It's time we were going,' she said.

She had given me an opportunity to escape. I didn't appreciate it would be as trying as this. It was a blessed relief to be able to leave that house. The atmosphere wasn't right. There was something in the air – aggression? I was almost ashamed. I looked around and asked myself what I had in common with these people now, with the exception of Irene and Jeanette. My two uncles flanked Ma, expressing a solicitude that had been notably absent in Drumchapel all those years before. You should have done more for her, I thought. You could have done more for us. You could have done more for me.

'The cars are outside,' someone said, breaking the spell.

The service at Streatham Crematorium was pleasant enough, an inadequate description, I know, but it was. Afterwards, we negotiated a carpet of flowers as the mourners headed for the pub – I think it was called the Latchmere.

I moved through the throng towards Ma, who was sobbing. 'Ma,' I said.

She looked up at me. 'Davie,' she said softly, 'what am I going to do now?'

I said, 'It'll be fine, Ma. C'mon now, you've still got us.'

'But it's just Johnny I want,' she said.

Somehow, I managed not to cry – not tears for Johnny. For myself. I was bereft. Even at the very worst moments of the abuse, I don't believe I have ever felt so without value. With those six words, my mother had rendered my life meaningless. If she couldn't love me, who could? I was unable to speak. The psyche of the abused child took over. No matter that she had just rejected me in the most thoughtlessly cruel manner, there was something in me still craved her approval, even if it was impossible to have her love. I retrieved a small gold cross and chain from my pocket and placed it round her neck.

She fingered the cross and said, 'Thanks, son. You're a good boy.'

For now, that would have to do. For the moment, it stilled my desire to cry.

Uncle Davie and Uncle Charlie escorted her from the crematorium. I was glad she had been taken away, not just because of how I felt emotionally, but because it gave me the opportunity to explore the circumstances of Johnny's death with Jeanette.

Poor Johnny. Johnny had never defeated his history. He was a lost soul prone to depression as an adult and haunted still by the abusive actions of our father. Johnny suffered from terrible nightmares in which he was being beaten by Da. He would wake from sleep screaming. As a result of his tortured childhood – and the time in the borstal – he continued to wet the bed. He was deeply ashamed of this and it affected every relationship he had. Johnny found it particularly difficult to maintain a relationship with a woman because of it. He was attracted to older women, Jeanette said. What would a psychologist make of that? Searching for a mother's love? Probably.

Jeanette told me, 'I believe he was looking for the emotional security that had been impossible to find with Ma.' Suddenly, I knew all too well what she meant. She went on, 'He never felt safe, Davie. He did find happiness, though – with an older girl – and for a while, thank God, he seemed to be happy.'

All of our lives had been perennially dark. Each of us, in our own way, was trying to get to the light. If Johnny saw a chink of brightness, then I was happy for him. However, small pinpoints of light could not change the fact that Johnny had probably been doomed from the beginning. He had been living in London for the last decade. On a Friday evening, several weeks before his death, he had lost all of his wages at the bookmaker and had nowhere to go. He went to Ma's house for a bed for the night, but she refused to take him in. By now, Johnny's behaviour had alienated even our mother, his biggest supporter.

Jeanette went on, 'One of his friends found him at two in the morning standing crying on Battersea Bridge. No one wanted to know him, he said.'

By now, Jeanette had moved away from Central London to Bromley in Kent. She was usually one of his saviours, allowing him to stay with her when he was down on his luck, but she was too far away now. The friend who found him apparently took Johnny in for several weeks, but his depression deepened and he was on medication. Just before his death, he phoned Jeanette.

She explained to me, 'I'll always feel really terrible about his last days. He phoned right in the middle of a family crisis. "Can't this wait until tomorrow?" I asked him. I told him to call back the following day. Johnny said, "If you don't see me tonight, you won't see me for a long time." I said, "Johnny, I'm having a few personal problems of my own here. I wish I could help you tonight, but I just can't."

'The next day, the police arrived to tell me he had been in an accident and was in a bad way in the intensive-care unit of St Thomas's Hospital. I rushed there and found Ma, wailing and crying for her own ma and da. Jimmy was sitting at

Johnny's bedside and he wasn't much better. Ma was ranting and raving. Jimmy was so upset he was being physically sick. I was the only one able to speak to the doctors. They told me the next twenty-four hours were critical. Davie, I sat with Johnny all night, holding his hand, talking to him about North Uist, the only time in his life I believed he was happy. I promised that when he got better we would go back there together. In the morning, the doctor took me aside and told me his brain was dead. Ma was demanding that Johnny be kept alive, no matter what.'

As the tears poured down Jeanette's face, I put my arms around my sister and asked her what happened next. She told me, 'The doctor and I went into this private room and I told him about our family life and about Ma's psychiatric history. He agreed I should be the one to make the decision about Johnny. The doctor said his life was over, Davie. It was the most difficult and horrible decision of my life – to switch off his life support. It was the kindest thing to do, wasn't it? I decided not to tell Ma. Don't say anything to her. She thinks Johnny just gave up. I had to physically drag her away from his hospital bed, as it was.'

By the time Jeanette had finished recounting this story, I was, like her, drained and in tears. Heaven knows the effect it must have had on my sister, having to make that terrible choice on her own. Perhaps the saddest thing of all is that Jeanette believes that Johnny might have, in his confused state, reasoned that his suicide attempt was probably the only way to bring together his broken family. It did – for his funeral.

By now, we had reached the pub and we composed ourselves before we entered. The place was bedlam. Jimmy was already roaring drunk. My uncles had obviously decided to join him. Inevitably, a fight broke out. Jimmy grabbed a chair and threw it through a window. The police arrived. As I looked around at this mêlée, at this family of strangers connected to me only by genetics, my sense of detachment was complete. I didn't speak like them. I didn't think like them. I didn't act like them. I wasn't one of them.

I turned to Irene and said, 'I'm out of here.'

CHAPTER 19

Return to the Lair of the Beast

'David!' The smell. 'David!' Knocks on the door. 'David!' The door rattles. 'David! Are you clean? David! I'll make you clean. DAVID ...'

I awoke screaming, entangled in crumpled bed sheets and drenched with cold sweat. I had never known such terror. The darkness clawed at me. I whimpered. The light. Get to the light. I scrabbled across the bed, disentangling myself from the sheets, located the switch on the lamp. The shroud of darkness was dispelled.

'Davie!' I thought I was still in the nightmare, but it was Irene's voice. 'What's wrong?' she shouted. She was standing over me. I had not seen her enter the room.

'What ... ?' I said, unable to complete the word.

'You were screaming. What's the matter?'

'Nightmare ... nightmare,' I whispered.

'I thought someone was trying to kill you, for God sake.'

I looked up at Irene, her face etched with concern. There was a movement behind her. Someone else had entered the room. I looked over Irene's shoulder. The Beast was standing there. 'David,' he said.

It had been 24 hours since we laid Johnny to rest and Irene and I had escaped from our family of strangers. When I had said, 'I'm out of here,' she'd grabbed her bag and joined me. We went back to Ma's house, where we had left the overnight bags. It was then Irene told me about the phone call. My back was turned to her when she said, 'I called John and Helen.'

My shoulders stiffened. I turned, slowly, trying to appear unconcerned. 'John and Helen?' I said.

Irene was packing her bag and, mercifully, was not looking in my direction. I was relieved she couldn't see my face. I felt hunted. 'John and Helen?' I repeated.

'Yeah,' said Irene. 'I called them to tell them Johnny had died. They were asking for you, by the way.' Her back was still to me.

'They didn't know Johnny,' I said lamely.

Irene shrugged. 'Just thought I'd tell them,' she said, as she fumbled with the zip of the suitcase. She was looking at me now. 'You look pale. Are you all right?'

'Fine, I'm fine,' I lied. Thank God she could not see the image of the Beast in my head.

'You don't look it,' she said, and added, 'Are you up for a trip?'

'Where?' I asked, knowing instinctively what the dreadful answer would be.

'To John and Helen's. They've invited us,' Irene replied.

I could hardly speak. 'When?'

'Now! No reason to stay here, is there?' she said.

How could I explain? How could I tell her she was taking me back into the dark? As far as she and the world knew, they were just Uncle John and Auntie Helen.

'I don't know, Irene … Work …' I said lamely.

'They won't be expecting you back for a few days,' Irene said, and added, 'Look, you've got to go back to Scotland anyway and I really want you to come with me. I don't want to go on my own.' Irene, too, was conflicted. She had not suffered as I had, but still Quarriers had not been a happy place for her. 'I don't really know why I want to go back,' she said.

I knew. The abused are often drawn to their abusers like moths to a flame.

'It's just something … I don't know,' she went on. 'I want to go back. Come with me? John and Helen will be really pleased to see you.'

It was a *fait accompli*.

'I didn't know you kept in touch,' I said.

'Just the odd letter and phone call,' my sister said. 'I know he gave us a hard time and I got dumped out for standing up to them, but it wasn't all bad, was it, Davie?'

Dear God, she had no idea.

She went on, 'I don't know why, but what with Johnny and everything, I just feel I'd like to go there. Please come. I need you.' It was the first time Irene had ever said anything like that to me. She had always been the strong one. I had always needed her, but now she needed me. How could I deny her this one request, no matter the cost?

'Just for a day,' I said.

Irene had not stopped talking, the cadence of her words merging with the rhythm of the train's wheels. I heard almost nothing of what she said. She was talking more to herself than to me. She didn't need answers, which was just as well. I didn't have any. The steady tempo of the train should have lulled me into a state of meditation, but my inner voice was screaming, *What am I doing? What, in the name of God, am I doing?* My pale reflection in the window revealed frightened eyes. I was going back to a place I believed I had left behind for ever. As every minute of the long journey passed, the abuse I had suffered was replaying itself like in a film in my head. I tried to smother the images, but failed. I felt like a child watching a horror film through laced fingers.

My sister's voice suddenly intruded. 'It'll be kind of nice to see them again, won't it?'

Irene's perception of life at Quarriers was infinitely different from mine. My memories were my nightmares. It had been years since I'd walked through the gateway of the Village. I never believed I would return. My sister was unwittingly leading me back into the lair of the Beast. I don't believe I'm being unnecessarily melodramatic. He was and always will be a monster to me. For three years I had been his prisoner, broken to his will and a hostage to his depravity. My state of mind, as an abused child, has been likened by psychologists to that of a concentration-camp survivor. The rational part of my being shies away from such a comparison. I feel it somehow insults those poor people who suffered so dreadfully, but as a therapist once said to me, 'David, asking you to go back to Quarriers is like asking a victim of the Holocaust to return to Auschwitz.'

This sense of foreboding followed me every mile of that seemingly interminable train journey to Glasgow. It ended finally with our arrival at Central Station. Within a few minutes of leaving the station, we had boarded a bus that would carry us to the Village.

The city fell away behind us as we rolled into the green Renfrewshire countryside. By now I was in emotional lockdown. There was no comfort in seeing the familiar hedgerows teeming with birds. There was no joy in their song. The bus deposited us in Bridge of Weir. We walked the last few miles. I saw the bell tower. It still loomed over the Village, as it did over my life. The floral message at the gate still offered the same hollow words. As we walked into the heart of the Village, I was bombarded by familiar sights and sounds that had been dormant for so long. I realised I had been suppressing all my thoughts of this place for years.

I took an involuntary sharp intake of breath when I saw Cottage 7. The ordinariness of the building belied the horrors I had suffered behind that closed door. All around me was peace, tended lawns and manicured flower beds. If I had not suffered as I did, it would have been inconceivable that anything bad could happen in this place. Anyone seeing the Village with fresh eyes – as I did for a few seconds that day – would have been lulled into believing it was a place of harmony and goodness. For many children like me, however, it was the perfect hiding place for evil.

Irene's voice once again broke my reverie. 'John and Helen don't live in Cottage 7 any more,' she said, pulling me away. 'They aren't house parents any more. I think Helen's a carer at the epilepsy centre and John's just the fire officer now. They're living at Carsemeadow.'

Carsemeadow was the name of a collection of staff cottages on the edge of the Village, across from where Quarriers' old fire station used to be. The Beast's wife had told Irene to look for the red-brick cottage, with a Pets' Corner in the garden. This turned out to be a collection of hutches for rabbits and guinea pigs.

As we approached the cottage, a ghostly face appeared at the window and disappeared quickly as we approached the door. Before we could knock, it was opened by Helen.

'Irene, David ... welcome back,' she said. Helen hadn't changed, but it had only been a few years. Her facial features were still strong and her voice – even mouthing platitudes – remained strident.

Helen prattled about how we had changed, how grown-up we looked. I was not listening. My eyes were searching beyond her into the darkness of the hallway. Where was he? He had to be there. He would not have missed this opportunity. I could smell him before I could see him. Silvikrin. He was still using it on his hair. I was robbed of speech; my heart thumped against my ribs. He emerged from the darkness. Steady, steady, steady, I told myself. He no longer has power over you. He can't hurt you. I wasn't convinced. He offered me his hand. For a few seconds, I did not respond. I felt Irene and Helen's eyes on me. I took the hand.

'David,' he said.

Tomorrow, I thought. I just have to make it through until tomorrow.

We were sitting at the dinner table. Helen and the Beast were silent. Irene was prattling. I don't know what had got into Irene that day, for she had not stopped talking since we left London. It was almost as if silence would allow the past to crowd in on her. She seemed to be trying to exorcise ... something. I knew she had many unhappy memories, but perhaps the passage of time had made Quarriers seem more tolerable than it really had been. Perhaps it had been Johnny's death, or meeting Ma again, that had stirred up in her a need for some sense of permanence and familiarity. I don't know. The Beast's children were playing in another room, leaving the grown-ups to themselves. We could hear their laughter filtering through the house.

In one of the rare breaks in Irene's chatter, Helen spoke proudly of how many of 'her' children had come back to Quarriers to see her and Uncle John. 'It's good that you two have come back,' she said.

I felt like a traitor to myself. I know abused children are drawn back to their abuser. I was following a pattern, but I had been dragged rather than drawn. Every cell in my body told me I didn't want to be here. I sat at the table, virtually silent. I had nothing to say to these people. The Beast had not taken his eyes off me. As Irene prattled and Helen preened, he was not listening to them, not looking at them. He was looking at me. Throughout the conversation, I had been feigning interest, in order that I did not have to look at him. I could feel his eyes burning into me.

'How have you been, David?' he said at length.

They were innocent words, but I read their secret meaning. He wanted a sign. I turned in his direction, focusing my eyes on the bridge of his nose. A smile played on his lips, the secret smile I had seen so often. I was suddenly afraid, a child once more.

'I've been fine, thank you,' I said, and the child was in my voice.

'What have you been up to? Are you working?'

'I'm working in hotel management,' I told him.

'Where?' he asked.

'In the city,' I lied. I didn't want this man to know where I was. I had decided that this would be the last time I was ever going to be in his world. I would, of course, see him again, when he sat in the dock accused of abusing me and another child, but that would be a lifetime away. For the moment, the conversation was desultory and banal. He had lost interest. He had not received the sign.

Darkness had fallen outside when Helen said, 'Well, you two will want to get to your bed. You must be tired.'

We rose from the table and Helen directed us to our rooms. I shut the bedroom door behind me and searched for a lock. There was none. I sat down heavily on the bed. Just tonight, I said to myself, just tonight. If I can get through tonight, I'll be safe. I didn't undress. Not in this house, not with that man in another room. It was perhaps irrational, but it was as if my clothes represented some form of protection, a flimsy suit of armour. I took off only my shoes, laid my head on the pillow and pulled the coverlet up to my chin, holding it with both hands like the small and frightened child I had become. Another psychological layer of protection? I was enveloped in darkness. I heard a noise at the door. It opened. He had been waiting, too.

'David,' said the soft voice.

I knew it! He could not resist!

'David?' he said again. 'Are you awake?'

I was in an instant back in the bathroom, the sitting room, the bell tower.

'Are you OK?' he asked.

'YES!' I said, my voice stern, strong, adult. I knew suddenly, definitively, that the Beast no longer had any power over me. My hands dropped from the coverlet and I raised myself up in the bed. 'It's been a long day. I've just lost my brother. I want to sleep – leave me alone!'

The door slid shut. He went as quietly as he had come. There was such a release of tension that the need for sleep began to overwhelm me. Not even the knowledge that the

Beast was in the same house could keep me awake. He would visit me again that night, in the nightmare that drove me into the arms of Irene. The Beast came too, alerted by the sound of my screams. I stared into his eyes and held them. Neither of us spoke, but we both knew his spell had been broken for ever. As Irene lay down beside me and held me in her arms, I was finally, physically, beyond his reach.

Nevertheless, his shadow would keep me in a dark place for many years, driving our secret far below the surface of my life. One day, I would step out of the shadow, but the price of making what would become the most momentous decision of my life would be so very high.

CHAPTER 20
The First Cracks

In the security of the darkness, illuminated intermittently by flashing neon, it was usually the fifth or sixth drink that made the memories easier to live with. Over the years I had become adept at masking my emotions, presenting a face to the world that revealed nothing but a smile. The hard-earned facility was failing me now. The secrets were eating me alive from the inside. I looked up into the heart of the glittering orb, circling on the ceiling of Victoria's Nightclub, in Scarborough, and I was lost for a while in its hypnotic dance.

'Are you a Bay City Roller?' the English girl's voice shrieked through the rainfall of light.

She was tipsy. I was drunk. Drink had become a troublesome friend to me in recent times. It loved me one moment and disapproved of me the next. I was unravelling. I had been ever since that night spent in the home of the Beast, when I had awakened screaming from the nightmare. I had left the following morning, offering stilted, peremptory goodbyes, believing that his hold over me had at last been loosened. But I had believed that before and found it to be untrue. I was wrong, again. Since I had left his lair, I had been sliding ever faster down an emotional slope.

I raised my arms wide and declaimed, 'What makes you think I'm a Bay City Roller?' The smooth Caribbean groove of Typically Tropical had been replaced by the more soulful voice of George McCrae singing 'Rock Your Baby'. I felt mellow, inordinately pleased by the attention of this pretty young woman. It was the 1970s, and my platform boots and trousers, with a tartan flash down the outside leg, had persuaded my new friend that I was a member of the hottest boy band of the era.

'Your accent,' she said, and added, 'You sound just like Les McKeown.'

'I'm David Whelan,' I said, trying to disabuse the girl of the notion that I might be the lead singer of the group.

'Are you the one who plays guitar, then?' she demanded, somehow convinced still that I was indeed extremely famous but attempting to remain incognito.

'I'm David Whelan,' I repeated, suddenly feeling self-conscious, as if being David Whelan wasn't good enough.

At that moment, it wasn't. The meeting with the Beast had unhinged me, slowly, to a degree that I was falling into the trap that so often lies in wait for the abused child – the belief that they are in some way to blame for the abuse they suffer. The feeling had been sweeping over me for weeks. A Christian upbringing can leave most of us carrying a heavy burden of guilt. Think of the expression 'I must have done something terrible to deserve this' and you will appreciate my state of mind. I was still a long way from the realisation that paedophiles are so very skilled at promoting such feelings by shifting the blame from them to their victims. We all only have to remember our mothers saying to us, 'Look, see what you've done,' to recognise the milder aspects of that syndrome.

My new best friend had lost interest in whether or not I was a Bay City Roller and she had wandered off through the thin shafts of brilliant white. It was time for me to go, too. I thought that maybe I would feel better in the morning. Over the years, I had also developed more than one way of deluding myself.

After Johnny's funeral – and my brief visit to the Beast – I had gone back to my work at the Queen's Hotel, Helensburgh, but my life had changed. It was arid, as if something vital was missing. At first I thought it was just because Irene had left me to return to Brighton, where she was working in a hotel. I didn't realise how much I would miss her. I knew she had her own life to lead, but the events of Johnny's funeral and the impromptu trip to Quarriers had reaffirmed the once close relationship we enjoyed. Her departure left me unsettled. I felt absolutely alone. My coping mechanisms, which had helped me deal with the horrors that crowded my mind, were crashing. For no apparent reason, I would plunge into moods which swung from lofty highs to crushing lows. I started drinking.

At first, it was a little, a few drinks to take off the edge, but I eventually started drinking to excess. It did numb my growing sense of uncertainty, but like all self-medication it can become a bigger problem than the one it is seeking to cure. I was also having trouble holding down my job. I was suffering increasingly from flashbacks to the abuse. My nights were spent sweating, awakening from nightmares in which I was being hunted by the Beast. I would throw on the lights to illuminate the dark corners of the room and lie there in my bed until morning. I was in despair, convinced there could be no escape from someone who can follow you into your dreams. I also continued to be plagued by self-doubt and low self-esteem. I had to get away. It was time to move on. I was running.

The obvious destination was England, where my family lived now. I had been to Scarborough on holiday and it seemed as good a place as any to make a fresh start. During that holiday I had met two girls, Val and Jill, who were from Hull originally. They were working in a local hotel. I had kept their number. It took one phone call for them to arrange an interview with the manager. I packed a bag and headed south.

When I met the manager, he was impressed. I had a track record of working at good hotels with a strong reputation. He hired me. The job came with accommodation. I loved Scarborough and looked forward to be being there for the summer season. It would be hard work, but there were nights at Victoria's Nightclub to offer light relief and the blessed forgetfulness induced by alcohol. In many ways it was a happy innocent summer, but by season's end I was ready to move on again.

London seemed now to be the logical place to go. By now Jeanette had three children and was living in Kent with Colin, the wonderful man who was to become her second husband. She could put me up until I got on my feet. When I arrived, Jeanette was happy to see me, and it was great to see her again. I soon had a job in a local hotel, but I realised that, in spite of putting miles between me and Scotland, I had not travelled very far emotionally. I might have run, but I could not hide. I was helped by the fact that Jeanette and I had become ever closer since the death of our brother. In retrospect, I should have been able to share my innermost thoughts with her, but that is the realisation of a man in middle age and not the boy I was then. Heaven knows, she would have been the last person to judge me and the first person to offer me support, but at the time the secret was buried too deep. All Jeanette could see was the increasingly erratic behaviour of someone she loved spinning out of control.

I'd like to put a glamorous complexion on what was happening, tell of a romantic drunk who was pouring out his pain in poetry, but this was classic stuff – tired and wearisome. I just drank too much, mostly on my own. The periods between sobriety were getting shorter. I leaped from one casual relationship to another. I wasn't doing my job properly. I wasn't living; I existed. Worst of all, in my heart and head I existed as the abused child I had once been and not the determined young man I aspired to be. I would awake in my bed after a night out drinking, curled in the foetal position, a little boy rather than an adult. When I looked in the mirror at my pale face, with its tired eyes, I saw more than my own reflection. I saw a shadow from the past, shallow and indistinct, but well defined enough to frighten me. The Beast's face was never far from me. I only had to close my eyes. I reached the point where it was becoming increasingly difficult to push back the tide. I struggled. This was a fight I couldn't win but which I knew I couldn't afford to lose. I dreaded surrendering to the past. For years I had suppressed my secrets, held them at bay in my determination to become a normal person like everyone around me. But like Atlas, with the world on his shoulders, the burden had become too great. I collapsed under the weight.

With one word, Jeanette began the process of guiding me through the emotional maze. 'Enough!' she said. I was lying on her living-room couch, gripped by a hangover, debilitated by lethargy. 'You have to do something about this, Davie. It can't go on,' she said. 'See a doctor!'

My first instinct was to protest, take the route of the belligerent drunk and claim that everything was just fine, but before

I blurted out the usual litany of excuses I paused, realising that Jeanette was right. As usual, my sister knew what I needed better than I did myself. Jeanette may not have known my secrets, but she saw deep enough into me to know that I was in pain. And there was something else … something bad. I had been beginning to think like Johnny.

'What would happen to his children?' I asked. 'If he went to jail, what would happen to them? They'll end up in care … like I did.'

Dr Keith Stoll, the clinical psychologist I had been referred to for counselling by Jeanette's GP, considered my questions. He had leaned back in his chair, resting his chin on steepled fingers. This was the first person in the world who knew any part of the secret, but it would never leave this room. I had, moments before, revealed a little of what had happened to me at the hands of the Beast. Dr Keith's immediate reaction was to suggest that I tell the police. My first thought was not for myself or the pursuit of justice. I thought only of the effect that exposing the predator would have on his young children. My reaction may seem bizarre – and only another abused or abandoned child would understand. In my heart, I didn't want another child to suffer as I was suffering, and I did not want them to end up in the care system, as I had done. Irrational, perhaps. But the thought of being responsible for breaking up a home and plunging those children into a life of uncertainty seemed to me unutterably cruel. What had they done? They were innocent.

The session had started as these things do, with me painting my life in broad brushstrokes – the drinking, the issues affecting my work, the sense of emptiness. Dr Keith sat opposite, hearing more than the words, seeing more than I was revealing. He probed quietly, firmly, and suddenly my belief that I could end up like Johnny was out there. I told him of my sense of worthlessness, my fear that I, too, would die by my own hand. It was not the only revelation. Suddenly, I was talking about my childhood, the time in the children's homes, the deprivation of Drumchapel, the sense of being without value, an ever-present accompaniment to my life. And then I told him. Words I thought I would never utter flowed from me. I spoke about the Beast. I didn't tell him everything, just enough to deepen the look of concern in his eyes. Psychologists rarely react to revelations, but he sat forward. It was as if this was what he had been waiting for. I thought, What have I said? But the words were out there now.

When I sat back, I was drained. I had thought once that if I revealed what had happened to me, there would be a sense of relief, a lightening of the burden. There wasn't. In fact, his suggestion that I go to the police, however well intentioned, had added another brick to the burden. He was right. The correct thing to do would be to go to the police. The fear of what I might be doing to the Beast's children was the major concern. But there was another. At that time, in my confusion, I did not yet associate the police with justice. I saw them as the people who took away my brothers. My mother had drummed it into me as a child that they were the enemy, as were all figures of authority as far as she was concerned. People from my world did not trust the police. They were regarded as invaders, not guardians. As soon as Dr Keith mentioned them, I froze. When he gauged my reaction, he pulled back, not probing any deeper. He said that we should continue with the counselling sessions and suggested that my doctor prescribe a mild antidepressant. The psychologist also advised that I concentrate on seasonal work in the hotel trade, so that I was not subject to the responsibilities of a long-term job.

Although I could not tell him everything, or follow all of his advice, I am eternally grateful to the man. He had proved to me that I could reveal my secrets. Or at least some of them. I just wasn't strong enough yet to handle the consequences of revealing all of them. That would come later, when the police did become my guardians. For now, Dr Keith had given me the confidence to get back on the path. I realised what a burden I had been on Jeanette and I decided it was time to give her a break by taking charge of my life. I wanted to put as much space as I could between me and the past. I didn't realise how far that journey would take me. Around the world, in fact. My first foreign port of call would be the Normandy coast of France, where I got a job. In the years following I would move on, circumnavigating the globe on the most glamorous cruise ships, visiting the most exotic locations – Barbados, Jamaica, Hawaii, St Lucia, Acapulco, Caracas, Cartagena.

It was a glorious time in my life. I had buried the past, or so I thought, under the weight of fresh experiences. I threw myself wholeheartedly into this world, which took me to new horizons, where people accepted me at face value. The skills I had learned and, bizarrely, my accent were a passport. I read somewhere recently that the Scottish accent is the most trusted in the world. My accent certainly made me popular with wealthy Americans. They asked for me specifically to be their guide on shore excursions. The little boy from nowhere was soon taking them to see the greatest sights in the world. And it all stemmed from getting the post at the prestigious Hôtel du Golf, in Deauville.

If I thought that working in British hotels was glamorous, it was nothing compared to the French experience. France – and the palatial mock-Tudor du Golf – changed my life. I learned the language as well as the secrets of French cuisine and wine. My Moroccan colleagues in the kitchen even taught me how to swear in Arabic, a skill I have not utilised to any great degree, I'm happy to say. The du Golf was a sporting hotel and I developed a reputation as a bit of a tennis star among the staff. I realised that the only good thing the Beast had ever done for me was to give me a tennis racket for my birthday. I pushed the thought away. I was having the time of my life – and I was changing. The bouts of depression that had afflicted me were receding, and I was learning how to hold back the black mood swings. I was determined not to go backwards, and I was growing in confidence. The hotels I had worked in before had knocked off my rough edges. The Hôtel du Golf buffed me to a high-gloss polish. I was ready to take on the world – and eventually I would.

At the end of the summer season, I applied for a position on board the Norwegian *Royal Viking Sea*, the flagship liner of the Royal Viking Line. I was living the dream. I was the first member of my family to go abroad. Now I would be heading for America. I had applied for this job through the same trade magazine that enabled me to work in France, and my employer had helped me with a glowing reference. While I waited for a reply, I returned to England. By now, Ma was living with Jeanette, whose children had in my absence grown up at an alarming rate. Ma hadn't changed, as if she ever would. I had been home for a few days when it dawned on me that she wasn't wearing the gold cross I had given to her on that terrible day when she laid Johnny to rest and effectively told me she had never wanted me.

'Where's your cross, Ma?'

She fingered her neck as if she couldn't remember what I was talking about.

'The cross, Ma. I gave it to you before I went away,' I said.

Jeanette appeared, to tell us the tea was ready.

Ma thought for a moment and said, 'It's with the rest of my jewellery.'

In the excitement of the following days, while I waited for a reply from the cruise-ship people, I forgot about the cross. A letter arrived eventually from Royal Viking. I had got the job. I had to leave almost immediately, for Fort Lauderdale in Florida, where all the biggest cruise ships gathered. I packed my bag in a state of high excitement. Jeanette laughed as she sat on my bulging case as I struggled to close the zip. Even Ma seemed excited – almost.

'Take care, son,' she said, as she hugged me.

The cross was still not there. 'Where's the cross, Ma?' I asked again.

'It's with the rest of my jewellery,' she said.

I was about to say more when Jeanette ushered me away. At the front door, she whispered, 'Don't ask her again. It is with the rest of her jewellery – in the pawnshop!'

Why is it that it's always the simplest of things that pull the rug out from under your feet?

As the taxi drew away, my mother waved to me. It would be the last time I would see her alive.

Chapter 21

A Single Tear for Ma

I leaned over and looked down at the face of a woman made old before her time. A single teardrop fell in slow motion from my eye. Just the one. She was 49 but she looked so wearied. Death had smoothed some of the lines around her mouth and eyes, but not all of them. The face was careworn, but it showed, at last, a trace of peace. My mother was dead. I can't know if she ever fulfilled her ambition to be reunited with her Johnny in that place she conceived as Heaven, but she had begun the journey.

I was 23 years old, but how long had I actually been my 'mother's child'? How long had we lived under the same roof, shared the same day-to-day life? How long had she looked after me? Had she ever really looked after me? I calculated that, if I subtracted all the years I had been in care, she had been a mother to me in any normal sense of the word for less than three of them, during that dreadful time in Drumchapel. But even when she was not physically there, she had been omnipresent. Her decisions shaped the course of my life. I wish I could say those decisions had always been for the good, but there had been precious little good in anything my mother had a hand in. Her actions consigned me to the children's homes. They prevented the doctors in Glasgow from calling me their own. They sent me to North Uist, to rejoin a family I had not known. They prevented us remaining with Morag and Willie and growing up in a rural idyll, surrounded by love. They dragged me back to deprivation. They sent me to Quarriers. My mother delivered me to the Beast.

She had a lot to answer for, but as I brushed away that single teardrop I realised she would always be my mother and I would always be her son. However, too many precious childhood years had passed without being loved for her to deserve more than that single tear. It had fallen involuntarily. Believe me, I tried, as I had learned to do, to block even that small display of emotion. But the tear fell anyway. After all, you only have one mother, don't you?

I was in Paris when Ma died. I had been looking forward to a few days' break, visiting old friends in a hotel on the Champs-Elysées, near the Arc de Triomphe. I had kept my ties in France even after I left to work on the cruise ships. Irene and Jeanette knew how to reach me. It was Irene who called.

'Ma's dead,' she said without ceremony. There was no hurt in her voice. 'You'd better come home,' she added, and the line went dead.

I have no memory of the journey from France to Kent. My first recollection of being back in England is Jeanette opening her front door to me. She was upset, unlike Irene. Ma had spent the last months of her life living with my oldest sister. Jeanette was taking it hard. Jimmy was in the house, half drunk as usual, maudlin as usual. Uncle Davie and Uncle

Charlie, and my mother's sister, Jenny, would be arriving soon. The usual suspects.

Once I was settled, Jeanette explained that since Johnny's death Ma had lost the will to live. She had drifted into a no man's land, so depressed she was continually abusing her medication and alcohol.

'She was comatose most of the time,' said Jeanette. 'Nothing could reach her. All she wanted was to be with Johnny. She talked about him morning, noon and night. Ma couldn't get over losing him. None of the rest of us seemed to matter.'

Jeanette had, as usual, borne the burden of Ma's erratic behaviour, the reverse-charge midnight phone calls when she was drunk and raving about losing 'her Johnny'. It became easier eventually to have her in Jeanette's home. 'She was causing chaos,' said Jeanette.

Irene sat opposite Jeanette, saying little. Suddenly she interjected, 'You know she wasn't a good mother!' It was a statement, not a question. 'She abandoned us,' added Irene.

Jeanette said, 'She didn't know any better, did she?'

Irene's pain was palpable. 'What mother would do that?' she asked. It was a question she would now never find the answer to.

The crisis had been precipitated after Jeanette had taken Ma for lunch. Jeanette only ever allowed Ma to have a single drink when she took her out. Ma called her a 'snob' because she spoke properly and didn't drink like Ma or Jimmy. On that day, Jeanette had taken Ma back to her own home. Two hours later, Jimmy was on the phone, ranting and raving, telling Jeanette she ought to be ashamed. He had gone to Ma's house to borrow money as usual and had found her apparently roaring drunk. Jimmy blamed Jeanette. Jeanette told Jimmy Ma only had one drink. My sister had the foresight to realise something was terribly wrong and urged him to call an ambulance. Ma was taken to St James's Hospital, in Balham, where she was given a series of tests and admitted. She had cried wolf so many times that her 'attack' was presumed initially to be the result of taking alcohol on top of her medication, but the following day doctors called Jeanette and asked to see her immediately. Ma had meanwhile been transferred to a specialist unit at the Atkinson Morley Hospital in Wimbledon. Jeanette went to the hospital.

'When I saw her, I was shocked by her appearance,' said Jeanette. Ma was deranged and rambling in a strange voice. She told Jeanette she was being 'taken down to the firing line' and that rats were running around at her feet. Jeanette was at her bedside, trying to calm Ma, when a nurse arrived and said the doctor wanted to speak to her in private. Jeanette had a dreadful sense of foreboding, just as she had with Johnny.

My sister said, 'As soon as I saw the woman's face I knew it was bad news. When I reached the doctor's office, there were three people in the room. The consultant said there was no easy way to tell me that Ma was riddled with cancer. The disease had travelled from her lungs to her brain. She had a brain tumour and little hope of survival. He could, he said, operate, but there was little point. Even if the operation was successful, she would have very little quality of life. The alternative was to take her home to live out what little time she had left in relative peace. The decision was mine, he said. I was going to take her home with me.'

When Jeanette went back to Ma's bedside, Jimmy was showing his usual impatience, demanding to know what had been said.

'I took him aside and told him Ma was dying,' Jeanette told me.

Jimmy refused to believe it, but Jeanette swore him to secrecy. She told him, 'Don't dare tell her, Jimmy. Why make her last few months any more miserable than they need to be?'

Jimmy took his normal course of action in a crisis. He headed for the nearest pub.

The last seven months of Ma's life were difficult for Jeanette, not least when an idiotic carer in the hospice, where Ma went while my sister was working, let the cat out of the bag. She told Ma she was dying. Ma was furious, raging at Jeanette for being a 'lying bastard'.

Jeanette told me, 'I came home from work and she was lying down on the sofa. As soon as she saw me, she started cursing and swearing at me. She said I knew that she was dying and what sort of daughter was I, to be hiding such a thing from her? Ma said, "You're a whore. You've been taking me to the park and for walks in the garden, pretending everything is rosy when you knew I was dying."'

Jeanette tried to convince her that the carer had got her case mixed up with someone else. Ma was having none of it. She turned her face to the wall. All the fight went out of her.

Jeanette said, 'I tried everything I could to make her comfortable, but those last few weeks were very hard. I did ask Irene to help me out once, but she said, "No. Ma never looked after me, so now I don't want to know about her." I didn't hold it against Irene. I knew how she felt.'

Jeanette nursed Ma right until the very end. She spent only the last few days of her life in hospital. Ma took the decision to die in hospital. It was an uncharacteristic act of kindness. She had decided she didn't want her grandchildren to see her dying. Ma passed away on 21 October 1980.

When I got back from France, we put a notice in the local newspaper announcing her death. Five people from outside the family came to the funeral at Streatham Crematorium. The family arrived in two cars. The first vehicle held her surviving children. The second brought her brothers and sister. The cortège took the same route as it did on the day we laid Johnny to rest. Ma would have been pleased. There were a few floral tributes for Ma in the garden of remembrance. When the service was over, we gathered her ashes and scattered them near those of 'her Johnny'. It is what she would have wanted. I brought flowers and laid them on the ground. Irene sat, resolutely silent, still refusing to shed a tear for her mother. As far as I know, she never did. Jimmy and his two uncles went to the pub and got drunk. This time, thankfully, the police were not called.

Ma was gone, but however inept she may have been, however selfish, weak and inadequate, a physical – and emotional – bond existed between us. She had done nothing in her life to strengthen that bond, the opposite in fact. None-theless, it existed as the slimmest of threads. I realised that when I reached into the casket and brushed the single tear I'd shed from her cheek. It dried quickly under my warm hand. One teardrop. So little to show for a lifetime. Irene was unable to offer Ma even that smallest of tokens. She remained dry-eyed, outwardly calm, and it was a calm edged with anger. Even in the presence of death, which often settles old debts, Irene still couldn't forgive. The scars inflicted by Ma's desertion ran deep and remained raw. Even then, Irene still regarded Morag as her real mother, but Ma was our real mother, no matter how feeble she was.

As I stood alone with her in the small chapel of rest, I sensed rather than heard her voice: 'Davie, give your ma a kiss.' They were the first words I remember her saying to me. The scene was vivid in my mind. I looked down at the tired old woman, with her steel-grey hair, who bore little resemblance to that dark, exotic creature who had greeted my arrival in Drumchapel. I cried then. Not just a single teardrop this time. My tears were not for Ma. They were for the lost years, the opportunities missed, the love she could not give me, for the pain, for all that was and all that might have been. I cried. I cried for my sense of loss. I cried in anger for all that she had not done. I cried with sadness for what I had been unable to do for her. I cried for my stolen childhood.

CHAPTER 22

Finding Morag

The death of Ma, following hard on the heels of losing Johnny, had affected us more than we realised. I shed only one tear for Ma on the day we laid her to rest, but over the few weeks and months that followed I cried many more. For her? For me? For all of us? Life had to go on, but there was still … emptiness? I tried the best I could to continue to write new chapters in my life, but it was difficult. Something was missing. There had to be an answer somewhere. And, as usual, it would fall to Jeanette to find it. She went in search of Morag …

The wheels of Jeanette's car passed over the dimpled metal platform that connected the ferry to the concrete pier at Lochmaddy with a satisfying metallic *thunk*. My sister had returned to North Uist after an absence of two decades and she was overwhelmed. She had come in search of those answers, some kind of closure, trying somehow to find one mother to replace another. Would she succeed? Time would tell. She heard her husband, Colin, say, 'Well, here we are!'

'Go left,' she told him, and their hire car left the tiny but bustling port and headed towards the interior of the island. Jeanette began laughing, she told me later, a schoolgirl giggling at the memory that had assailed her.

'What you laughing at?' said Colin.

'Charlie,' she replied.

'Who's Charlie?' he asked.

'Charlie was a horse,' said Jeanette, and added, 'There, just there, that's where Charlie ran away with Johnny on his back, hanging on for dear life.' Laughter consumed Jeanette. She was recalling the day when Johnny and Charlie, a workhorse owned by Morag and Willie, went on an unscheduled tour of the island. Charlie was a big beast conditioned to pull things – he was not trained to handle a rider. Anyway, such a term could only have been loosely applied to our late brother. There was a standing order on the croft not to attempt to mount Charlie. That was more than enough of a challenge for cowboy Johnny, a child of the *Bonanza* generation. Johnny had been eyeing up Charlie for ages.

'Now, now, Johnny, ye'll ken a' aboot it if ye hoist yersel' onto that old Trojan,' Willie would warn.

What did Johnny do? You've guessed it. First chance he got, he grabbed Charlie's mane and vaulted onto the beast's back. The animal, terrified by this mad thing in a bright-yellow oilskin jacket, took off like the proverbial bat out of hell. With bulging eyes, and foaming at the mouth, Charlie and Johnny galloped off with Willie, Morag and the entire Whelan clan in hot pursuit.

'Johnny was hysterical,' Jeanette told Colin, and added, 'He didn't know whether to laugh or cry, so he howled with a mixture of both. We were shouting, "Hold on, Johnny!" and Johnny was shouting, "I'm trying!"'

When Jeanette told me later about her memory, it brought it all back to me. Willie had leaped onto the tractor and we piled into the bogey at the back of it. We took off after Johnny and the bucking bronco of North Uist.

'Get back here … ye bugger!' Willie shouted. It was the nearest thing to swearing for Willie and I wasn't certain whether he was talking to Charlie or Johnny.

We kept horse and rider in sight – just – until we could see only Charlie galloping towards the sands. At some point the horse had deposited Johnny somewhere on the shoreline. Where was he? Our question was answered when we reached the *machair*. Johnny's legs were poking out of a clump of rough tussock grass. He was still laughing, in spite of his bare limbs being shredded by the grass, which is as tough as barbed wire. We extricated Johnny from the tussock and threw him onto the cart.

'Ye wee bugger!' said Willie, and I knew then that he had been talking to Johnny earlier and not the horse.

Willie blew a shrill whistle and Charlie, now relieved of his unwanted passenger, trotted happily behind the tractor back to the croft. The memory was a moment of light relief for Jeanette, diverting her thoughts from why she had returned to North Uist. It was for all of us, but primarily for me. I was still in the bad place. She didn't know yet about my abuse, but she knew me well enough to know I was unsettled and deeply unhappy. Jeanette reasoned that if she could revisit the only truly happy period in our lives, she might heal some of the wounds of our past. She wasn't just doing it for me. It was for all of us. Jeanette's natural nurturing instinct persuaded her that our fragmented family needed to be made whole again.

This was the first step, a focus for us to come together with a common purpose. Her plan would culminate on a special Christmas Day, when we were reunited with Morag. The idea had come to Jeanette soon after her marriage to Colin. She witnessed the workings of his loving family, which supported each of its members. Jeanette had spoken to Colin's relatives about our dysfunctional childhood and how North Uist had been the one beacon of light in an otherwise bleak emotional landscape. Colin's family encouraged Jeanette to reignite that light, and her new husband's honeymoon gift was the trip to North Uist.

In reality, Jeanette's heart had been drawing her back to Uist for years, but she was scared of what, if anything, she would find there. Was her memory erroneous? Had it truly been idyllic, or had our experiences on the mainland been so bad that they had imbued Uist with an undeserved romanticism? Those thoughts haunted her on the train journeys from Kent to Glasgow Central. When she arrived, it was a Glasgow she didn't know and felt little affection for. She and Colin picked up the hire car and prepared to head north.

'Can we make a detour?' she asked him.

'Where to?' he said.

'Drumchapel. I want to see the old house,' Jeanette told him.

My sister told me later that if I had thought Drumchapel was bad in our day, it had got far worse, more run down, even more devoid of hope. Our old school was gone, she said, as was 34 Katewell Avenue, which had also been demolished. She didn't linger. There was nothing for her there except emptiness and more bad memories.

Colin pointed the car north and headed for Fort William. They drove through the long, eerie stretch of Glencoe, the road crowded on both sides by towering peaks shrouded in impenetrable mist. Jeanette told Colin about one of the darkest periods in Highland history, the massacre of Glencoe, when Willie and Morag's clan, the MacDonalds, were slaughtered by Campbell soldiers. Life was cheap in the Highlands of the 17th century. The killers had lived for days with their future victims. The Campbells' greatest sin was to accept their hospitality, with murder in their hearts. It was the ultimate betrayal, but one expected of the untrustworthy Campbells, who were the factors for a repressive regime. Strange as it may seem to modern English eyes, the incident is still very much part of the Scottish psyche. More than 300 years later the Campbells are still tainted by the repugnant behaviour of their ancestors. And anyone who has ever passed through the 'Glen of the Weeping', even in bright summer sunshine, will suppress a shiver in a place still haunted by its history. Jeanette passed through it *en route* to laying to rest a few ghosts of our own.

Colin and Jeanette arrived in Fort William at bedtime. The following morning they set off for the Isle of Skye, where they would take the ferry to Lochmaddy. From the moment Jeanette set foot on North Uist, she was bombarded by memories. The Hebrides are an unchanging landscape of the mind as well as geography. Familiar places and faces surrounded her. She and Colin went to a local tourist office to find a bed-and-breakfast place. They were directed to the home of yet another MacDonald, who lived nearby. When they reached the B&B, they were ushered into the house by Mrs MacDonald.

'Is this your first time on the island?' she asked, the standard question to all visitors.

'No,' said Jeanette. 'I used to live here as a child, with Mr and Mrs MacDonald at Knockintorran.'

'You'll be the oldest Whelan sister, Jeanette?' said the woman without hesitation.

Jeanette was taken aback. She told me later that somehow she felt as if she had just come home. 'How did you know?' she asked Mrs MacDonald, who had gathered her up in a warm hug.

'I watched you grow up,' said Mrs MacDonald. 'And your brothers. And wee Irene, too. How is she?'

Jeanette felt as if the years had melted away and that Colin was finally beginning to realise the huge part this place had played in her life.

With typical Highland hospitality to one of their own, Mrs MacDonald refused to take any money for their overnight stay. But she had bad news. Morag was no longer on the island, and Willie had passed away. Jeanette felt as if she had been punched in the stomach. She had come all this way. She was so close and yet so far.

'Where is she?' Jeanette asked.

'Morag is in Caol at Fort William now,' she was told. The irony of having passed through Fort William only the day before was not lost on Jeanette. Mrs MacDonald went on, 'Morag's been there for many years – from soon after you and your brothers and sister left, in fact. They just couldn't settle after you were taken. It wasn't the same for them any more. They lost heart.'

Jeanette learned that before Morag and Willie had left for the mainland they had given the croft to their nephew and his family. Colin and Jeanette headed for Knockintorran, where they were met by a couple who looked like a younger version of Morag and Willie. They had known of course that Jeanette and Colin had been on their way. There are no secrets on the islands. The tea was already on the table.

The afternoon whiled away as Jeanette spoke to the couple about her life on the croft. Jeanette was handed a clutch of old black-and-white photographs of us all together during those halcyon days. She was numb, on the verge of tears, buried under the weight of her memories.

'Would you like to see round?' they asked.

'Yes, please,' said Jeanette, grateful for the opportunity to move away from the table.

She went up the stairs to the upper floor, torn between sadness and joy. The old sideboard, where she had once packed the ironing, was still at the head of the stairs. The bedroom she had shared with Irene was the same but for the décor.

'There's electricity now!' she exclaimed. 'When I was here we had to go around with candles and Tilley lamps. All mod cons now!' she laughed.

Jeanette experienced the years dropping away. It was as if she had left months rather than years ago. The couple told Jeanette that Willie and Morag had never got over the loss of their 'family'.

'It was too much for them,' said the nephew. 'It broke their hearts, not being allowed to stay in touch. In the end, they just decided there were too many memories and they had to leave.'

Jeanette's earlier excitement had been replaced by a sad and sober frame of mind by the time she left the croft.

'We have to go to Caol,' she told Colin. 'I can't go back without seeing Morag.'

The door opened. 'You look thin,' said the old woman.

'You look the same,' said Jeanette. My sister was in Morag's arms, murmuring words that made no sense.

'Come in, come away in,' Morag soothed.

Jeanette and Colin were directed into the bungalow's homely living room. My sister gave herself up to the tears that had been suppressed for nearly 20 years. There were childhood photographs of us on the wall. Morag had not forgotten us. We were still in her heart.

'Where have you been?' said the older woman. 'Where have you been? Willie's gone. Did you know?'

Jeanette nodded, still unable to speak.

'I'm sorry,' said Morag. 'It was my fault.'

'No!' said Jeanette, finding her voice. 'You didn't let us down. Everyone else did. You and Willie never did.'

The old woman heaved a sigh of relief. It was as if a burden she had been carrying for years had been finally lifted. 'Willie never stopped talking about you all, wondering about you all. We never knew what happened to you. We weren't allowed to.'

Jeanette said, 'Johnny's gone.'

It was as if Morag had been slapped in the face.

There was no sleep for the two women that night. They sat up talking into the wee small hours, laughing and crying in equal measure at the memories of life on the croft and the pain of separation.

Morag told Jeanette, 'They day you were all taken away was the worst day of our lives. We were heartbroken, but we couldn't let our feelings show. It would have made it harder for you, but when the car took you away we were both crying. Part of us had gone. Life was never the same. There was never another child on that croft. You were like our own. We couldn't replace you. We didn't even want to live on the island any more. There's been a hole in my life for 20 years. Having you here now is the best thing that has happened for years. I'm only sorry that Willie isn't here to see this day.'

Jeanette and Colin stayed with Morag for a week, promising it would be the first of many reunions, and it was. My sister demanded that Morag come for Christmas and meet the rest of us. Jeanette left Morag's home with a new sense of belonging, a new sense of connection to her childhood and the proper family life that had been snatched away from all of us. She returned home a different and determined woman. Her husband and children saw the change, realising now how big a part North Uist had played in her life. 'Now they could understand,' she told me later.

There was great excitement about the planned visit of Morag for Christmas. Irene was delighted. I had never seen her so happy or animated. It brought it home to me just how cruel it had been to take her from Morag. My sense of loss for Morag was great, but Irene had been her 'baby' for almost nine years. It was the only truly happy period of her life and her loss had been devastating. I realised that now as I watched Irene revert to the joyful little girl I had not seen since our time on Uist. It was a revelation. It also occurred to me that I had no memory of ever having spent a normal family Christmas with my natural mother. There was a reason for that. We hadn't.

I was as excited as Irene and Jeanette at the prospect of recreating the times we shared on the croft. Jimmy, Irene, Jeanette and I decided to put on a slap-up Christmas dinner for Morag. The week before she was due to arrive, we all clubbed together to buy a table and enough chairs to accommodate us. We were determined to sit together like any family. It may seem like a small thing to those who are used to such certainties, but to us it would be a profoundly special occasion. We laid on the best of food. The Christmas tree was dressed with precision. Everything had to be perfect.

Christmas Eve arrived and we were as excited as pre-school children. Colin and Jeanette picked up Morag from Victoria Bus Station in London, where she arrived after the long journey from the Highlands. I wasn't there when Morag arrived at

Jeanette's house, but my sister told me later that the reunion
with Irene was heartbreaking and joyful in equal measure. I
had been working, but I left for Jeanette's home as soon as I
could.

'Quiet,' she said, holding her finger to her lips, and guiding
me towards the living-room door, which was ajar. She pointed
to the space and I looked in. Morag was on the sofa. Irene's
head was on her breast and the old woman was stroking her
hair. I didn't want to break the spell, but some change in the
atmosphere alerted Morag to my presence. I pushed open the
door and she rose to meet me. I was enveloped in a fierce
embrace. She would not release me.

'My bairn,' she said.

'Mum,' I whispered. I had not realised just how much she
had meant to me, this buxom, grey-haired woman with music
in her voice and the glow of wild and remote places in her
eyes. Suddenly I was a child again, the innocent child, the one
whose play parks were fields and the *machair*, where the land
meets the sea in a multicoloured riot of wild flowers. In that
moment I was no longer the fearful child, subjugated and
degraded by a sexual predator. In the almost surreal surroundings of a typically suburban living room in Bromley, in Kent, I
was again the boy running free, with the wind from the Atlantic blowing me towards a world of promise. Morag … dear
Morag. I'd never thought I would see her again.

In years past, the thought of her, and Willie, and the croft,
had sustained me through many of my darkest moments. I had
last seen her through the tears I would shed for days, the grief
of parting, which began on North Uist and lasted until well
after my arrival in a warren of utility housing in a Glasgow
estate. I had last seen her as Irene was being dragged screaming from her arms. Morag was now looking back and forth

between the two of us as if Irene and I had stepped out of a dream. The three of us cried, but there was no sadness in it. Morag was wearing the same quiet smile I remembered so well, a smile that knew everything but gave away little.

My natural mother was gone, a woman who, in truth, was incapable mentally, morally and emotionally of nurturing any of us. I realised that buried deep within me was the knowledge that Morag was probably the only real mother I had known. She, and Willie, had given us everything and asked for nothing. I didn't know what to say to her. The lights blinked on the Christmas tree, reminding me that this was the season of reunions – and beginnings. Irene offered us a beatific smile as Morag held me in her arms as she had when I was a child. I had no need of words. I cried.

Bless Jeanette. Her plan had succeeded. I would soon go on to work with the world's most famous people, be surrounded by celebrity and opulence, but being reunited with this simple island woman had, for the moment, freed me from the past.

CHAPTER 23

Dining With Diana

When Her Royal Highness the Princess of Wales enquired after my family, I could hardly speak. I had heard that one may be struck dumb in the presence of beauty. Until that moment I hadn't realised just what that meant. She and I were 'old acquaintances' who had 'met' on many occasions at glittering balls, lavish weddings and intimate royal lunches and dinner parties. She was the fairytale princess, and I was attending to her every need. Diana came from a world of absolute privilege; I came from a world beyond poverty; but we had much in common. We both had secrets; we both knew pain. Neither of us showed our true face to the world. I had always thought her beautiful, but in that dress …

I found my voice eventually. 'They are well, Your Royal Highness.'

'And you, David? Haven't seen you for some time,' she continued. Diana was almost unique in royal circles in that she could be positively chatty and had a wicked sense of humour.

'Very well, thank you, Your Royal Highness,' I replied, instilling my voice with the degree of formality demanded by the occasion. She may have been the most egalitarian member of the Royal Family, but there was a professional line you did not cross.

I was not aware then of the momentous machinations that were taking place that evening in the life and faltering marriage of the princess and Prince Charles. I would have to read the papers the following morning to understand fully all that was going on. But I had attended the princess often enough to realise that she was unusually unsettled. She was ordinarily the most relaxed of women, always with a ready smile or a shy laugh.

Her napkin slid from her lap and I bent quickly to whisk it from the floor, replacing it with a clean one.

'Thank you,' she said quietly.

'Ma'am,' I said.

We were in the Serpentine Gallery, in London, for a charity reception and dinner hosted by *Vanity Fair*. I was working for Mustard, the elite catering company, which provided a corps of butlers trained to the most exacting royal standard. There was hardly a magnificent event in or around the city that was not handled by Mustard's boss, Glynn Woodin, and his prestigious team. His people were not directly employed by the royal household, but we were expected to provide the same calibre of service. Which was why, at this moment, I was Princess Diana's butler for the evening.

The atmosphere was electric. She had arrived earlier on her own, stepping gracefully from a black limo into a lightning storm of camera flashes. The paparazzi almost outnumbered the glitterati. It was 29 June 1994. There had been much speculation about what Prince Charles would reveal that evening in a planned television interview with Jonathan Dimbleby. Would there be a 'confession' of adultery with Camilla Parker-Bowles? the media was asking.

No matter what revelations might emerge, Diana was never going to be upstaged. She knew full well that the eyes of the world would be on her when she arrived at the Serpentine. And, boy, did she put on a show. Even from inside the gallery we could hear the gasps as she arrived. She was beyond stunning in what the media would describe later as the 'Revenge Dress' – a fabulous and daring creation by Christina Stambolian. The black dress was complemented by a choker of flawless pearls with a large blue-black sapphire, surrounded by diamonds. If Prince Charles had believed he was going to make the front pages the following morning, he was sadly mistaken. He had been well and truly outmanoeuvred by his media-savvy wife.

The princess readjusted the napkin on her lap as I filled her glass with water. Throughout the course of the evening she did her job, smiling and laughing at poor jokes and tedious stories, but sadness and loss were things I could recognise from a mile away. No matter what the cameras captured that evening, I could see – up close – the tears in her eyes.

Strange as it may seem, it was the death of Ma and the reunion with Morag that had set me on the path to the world of Diana, Princess of Wales. The two events were catalysts. Life was short, I realised. I had been drifting, troubled, uncertain, without a focus for too long. Would I end up like Johnny? A sad wreck. Like Ma? A woman who lived and died without knowing real love. Or like Morag? For ever living with a sense of loss. It was time, as we Glaswegians are wont to say, that I got a grip.

I tallied up the credit side of the balance sheet. I was person-
able, skilled at what I did and well trained. There was work
out there for people like me, good work, jobs that had already
propelled me into a world that, as a child, I couldn't even have
dreamed of. I began looking for something more. Life on the
cruise ships had begun to pall. It was outwardly glamorous,
but, in truth, I saw more ports than I did historical landmarks.
There were highs, of course, but even lobster thermidor loses
its appeal. I felt I still wanted to go abroad, but I wanted to
be settled in one place.

I made a shopping list – job, security, good wages and sun.
Within a month I was working in Hamilton, Bermuda, in the
Fisherman's Wharf restaurant, the finest in the Caribbean. I
squinted against the harsh light of the sun and checked the
shopping list. Perfect. The scenery and the chowder were
equally spectacular. I really had landed on my feet. My life was
back on track and I took up residence with an elderly ex-pat
lady who treated me like a son.

For the next nine months, life could not have been any
better. I worked insanely hard in the restaurant, but I could top
up my wages with $800–$1,000 a week in tips. In what spare
time I had I learned how to barbecue and scuba dive, in that
order. I haunted the harbour, coveting the yachts of the fabu-
lously wealthy. It was an earthly paradise, but, perversely, I still
missed the British seasons, especially after I spent 10 days in bed
with sunstroke, an affliction that did not amuse my superiors. I
had rather stupidly been showing off my tennis skills and did
not legislate for the ferocity of the sun. I ended up very much
like the aforementioned lobster. I lived in an idyll, but I missed
Jeanette and Irene. I even missed the rain. I came home.

Jeanette was still living in Kent, but Irene had moved on
to Forest Hill in south-east London. Before taking up a job in

a five-star hotel, in Torquay, in Devon, I spent time with both of my sisters. Jeanette was, as always, my Jeanette, and Irene seemed content and happy for the first time since living in North Uist. She doted on her young son, Paul, and kept me up all night, asking me to regale her with stories of my foreign adventures.

One night she dropped the bombshell. 'John and Helen were asking for you,' she said.

'Who?' I asked.

'John and Helen … Porteous,' she told me.

I felt a cold chill in my stomach. The Beast had never been far from my thoughts, but in the last year I had suffocated his influence over me.

Irene sensed something was wrong. 'What's up?' she asked.

'Nothing,' I lied. 'When did you hear from them?'

'They send cards at Christmas and birthdays and always ask for you,' she said.

I teetered on the edge of telling Irene, but instead I said cryptically, 'John Porteous should not have been looking after children.' However, yet again, I suppressed the urge to tell her what had happened. 'Time for bed,' I said, delighted to escape.

It was not long before I left for Devon and the summer season. Irene's mention of the Beast haunted me throughout the summer, causing me to drink a little more than I should. However, this time I nipped it in the bud, fearful that it might become too much of a crutch. I took up cycling and swimming, sweating away my demons with physical activity. Although I could hardly have been described as a problem drinker, I attended Alcoholics Anonymous meetings, learning new coping skills to keep the blues under control. Even so, there were times when I was like a taut string.

When I returned to London I got a job with the Ritz group of hotels. I was doing very well by any standard, but the words I had heard so often from the Beast in my childhood crowded my mind – that I came 'from nothing', that I would 'come to nothing', that no one could love me. I fought the negativity tooth and nail. I worked every hour that God sent. I had soon left the hotels and was helping to run a restaurant in Chancery Lane, near Fleet Street. My life was truly on track now.

The owner of the restaurant treated me like a member of his own family and helped me raise a deposit to buy my first property, a two-bedroom terraced house in Luton. I took on additional jobs and shifts to help me pay for it. It was a sacrifice worth making. I felt that I was at last leading my own life. Within a few years I was managing the directors' dining rooms and the catering department for one of London's top investment banks. I beat off stiff competition from the Bank of England to win the coveted Company Restaurant of the Year Award in 1989. The food, service and ambience of my restaurant were judged by the top writers and critics of the day to be the best. I was presented with the award at a glittering ceremony. For the first time in my life I was the centre of attention for something good and positive. I still have the trophy and I am inordinately proud of it. Winning the award raised my profile in the industry and I featured in a number of publications.

My success won me an even better job, this time running the catering department of a blue-chip firm of accountants in the City. I now had a reputation, and I was approached by a member of Mustard's staff to come and work for them. I did my first job for Glynn Woodin and he was impressed enough to put me on the team. He was a genius and all-round good man. This was the breakthrough. Mustard Catering was and still is an astonishingly influential organisation, regarded as the best in the business. The nature of my job with the company meant I could continue working in other areas, which gave me a greater earning capacity.

I had big plans. I had started to dream. I wanted my own business. In the meantime, I was more than happy to rub shoulders with the very rich and famous. And how many jobs are there where you are able to elicit a wink from the Iron Lady? Baroness Thatcher had just relinquished the position of prime minister when I attended her at a banquet.

As I, and another colleague, fussed over her, he said, 'Excuse me, Prime Minister.'

I took a sharp intake of breath, waiting for us to be chastised – she did not suffer fools or slips of the tongue. She turned to us very deliberately and winked. I was somewhat taken aback. My colleague's face was a picture. I was surrounded by wealth and privilege, but I also learned that such attributes mean very little if you can't get into your own 'do'.

Lord and Lady Sainsbury, of the supermarket empire, were hosting a dinner at the National Gallery for Princess Margaret. Unfortunately, Lady Sainsbury had forgotten her security pass and the upmarket bouncers wouldn't allow the hostess through the door! Glynn Woodin had to come to the rescue and he was none too pleased.

His troubles weren't over. Princess Margaret spilled red wine on a brand-new carpet. She turned to my colleague and said, 'You'd better clean that up. Her Majesty is coming tomorrow!'

My friend was soon down on his hands and knees with salt and soda water scrubbing away – under the personal instruction of the Queen's sister, who was, unlike her illustrious great-grandmother, highly amused.

The royals and Margaret Thatcher were not Mustard's only clients and we catered many celebrity bashes. I know it has become fashionable to sneer at the *nouveau riche* and dismiss celebrities as upstarts, but I met a horde of them who were uniformly courteous – Mick Jagger, Jerry Hall, Dame Shirley Bassey, Sir Elton John, Bryan Ferry, Naomi Campbell, Kate Moss, Sir David Tang, Joan Collins and Joan Rivers.

I seem to remember the perennially pleasant Ms Collins had a penchant for leaving diamond bracelets all over the place. Fortunately, Mustard's staff were as honest as she was forgetful. Although on one occasion her sense of humour had the bosses of Tiffany, the diamond people, in a quandary. The jeweller had laid on a celebrity breakfast and photo shoot. Ms Collins was there with her great buddy, the flamboyant actor Christopher Biggins.

The actress was draped in exquisite and very expensive gems when she turned to her friend and said, 'I do get to keep these, don't I, Biggins?'

Biggins took his cue and in a pantomime voice said, 'Indeed you do, Joanie. That's the deal, isn't it?' He had turned to a seriously discomfited Tiffany executive, who began spluttering and fidgeting in a most alarming manner. The poor man was almost apoplectic by the time Ms Collins and her chum dissolved into gales of laughter. The look of relief on his face was as priceless as some of his jewels.

I also discovered that Joan Rivers, the American comedienne, is also a lover of fine things – particularly sumptuous mink coats. At one event she turned up in a fabulous black mink, which was checked in to the cloakroom on her behalf. The coat girls, who had never seen such a wonderful garment, took a real shine to it. They took turns trying it on and parading up and down behind the racks.

'I do so love this coat,' said one.

Mercifully, Miss Rivers is as loud in person as she is professionally and she could be heard approaching from some distance. The cloakroom attendant whipped off the mink just in time to present it to the star.

'How did you know it was mine?' drawled the star.

'Only you could wear such a fabulous coat, Miss Rivers,' said the quick-thinking girl, who was rewarded with an arch smile and a handsome tip.

I don't know what happened to that young lady, but I expect that, by now, she is making her third or fourth million.

Working for Mustard was heady stuff. I doubt whether I passed a day without being surrounded by the clients of Yves Saint Laurent, de La Renta, Balenciaga, Galliano and Valentino. The ladies competed with each other to see who could be the most glamorous. In such an atmosphere, it was not uncommon for those who served their needs to get a bit carried away by an overinflated sense of their own importance. One of my erstwhile colleagues watched one butler having a hissy fit and declared, 'In here, there are more prima donnas and queens than in all of the royal houses of Europe.'

It was the members of those royal families and the social elite who were our biggest and most prestigious clients. In the course of only a few years, we catered celebrity parties for Sir David and Lady Carina Frost, Lord and Lady Heseltine, Lord and Lady Lloyd-Webber, as well as Lord and Lady Rothschild. There were royal occasions too, for Prince Charles, the Kents, Princess Margaret's son, Lord Linley, as well as Lord Frederick and Lady Gabriella Windsor. One of the most glittering occasions was when virtually all the kings and queens of Europe attended the wedding of Crown Prince Pavlos, the eldest son of the King and Queen of Greece. These functions were held in some of the most beautiful and historic places – Windsor Castle, Kensington Palace, Blenheim Palace, St James's Palace, Hampton Court Palace and Spencer House, which had been built by an ancestor of Princess Diana.

In my opinion, Diana was unique, and certainly the most accessible, human and down-to-earth member of the Royal Family. However, my first encounter with her was less than auspicious. She was attending a glittering event and wanted to go to the loo. Rather than use the royal conveniences, she popped along to the ordinary ladies'. What she didn't know was that some of our staff were getting changed into their uniforms. Princess Di's lady-in-waiting knocked on the locked loo door and a waitress shouted, 'Sorry, you can't come in. We're changing. Come back later!' The lady knocked again and the door was unlocked. Three rather sheepish girls were confronted by an uncomfortable-looking Princess of Wales. With a hurried curtsey and whispered 'Your Royal Highness' they fled for their lives. Thankfully, the Princess saw the funny side and laughed out loud.

It was a wonderful period, and my Scottish accent seemed to endear me to the Queen and her mother. The minute they heard it, they warmed to me. Her Majesty and the late Queen Mother adored Scotland. I had by this time developed a great respect and affection for the Royal Family, but, if I'm honest, Diana was the One, radiating charm and elegance. She was as beautiful as we were discreet and professional. We heard many things behind the scenes. Reveal them? Certainly not! Duty prevails.

CHAPTER 24

Success on a Plate

The boy from nowhere, who once drank tea from a jam jar, was now sitting by the window admiring the view and sipping a particularly fine French red wine from the Médoc region. Dear God in Heaven ... these days I lived on a different planet. I suppressed a self-conscious smile. It occurred to me that the wine had come from the Gironde estuary. The fine details of the wine's provenance were imprinted on my mind. These fripperies were second nature to me now, part of who I was and what people expected me to be. I smiled again. If they only knew.

It had been an incredible journey. Most of those who thought they knew me were aware only of the last few staging posts. Every word that came from my lips was still carefully guarded, lest I give too much away. I turned my attention from the window, and its magnificent view of London and the Canary Wharf skyline, and looked up at the high, ornately corniced ceiling of my Victorian villa in London's Blackheath.

I raised the crystal balloon with its slender stem to my lips and toasted the reconstructed David Whelan. I now ran my own very successful and high-profile recruitment company, providing staff for the sort of events I used to work at myself. Since my breakthrough with the big City firms and Mustard, I had launched Premier Crew Recruitment Consultants, which could call on around 200 temporary and permanent staff. We had plush offices in Fleet Street, in the heart of the City, which appealed to the calibre of clients we wanted to attract. I had worked really hard in the last few years, saving enough money to start the business. I had gone to college to learn business skills and had passed with distinction. I had been determined to make it, and now business was good.

On a personal level, I'd just come back from the south of France, where I was considering buying a property. I had already acquired a seafront flat in Brighton, which waited for the weekends. Papers relating to a portfolio of other properties resided in my desk drawer. I had recently returned from Australia and Asia, and I was planning a trip to Russia. Life was good, too. Could it get any better than this? Probably not. But this halcyon day, when I toasted the new and improved David Whelan, would be the last day in my life that I could truly call my own. I didn't know it, but I was enjoying the lull before the storm. The phone hadn't rung yet, but it would … soon.

The last few years had passed almost in a blur as I strived for bigger and better things, while continuing to push my secrets to the dark side. The year before, the sudden and unexpected loss of my brother Jimmy had put into perspective the vagaries of life and so-called achievement. For a time, my success seemed rather hollow. Poor Jimmy. He had been a fleeting presence in my life; initially, he was the big brother who loved playing the fool, a lovable rogue who laughed his way out of trouble. The adult Jimmy was another matter – an angry, mentally unwell victim of our past. He was a sad soul who did more harm to himself than he ever did to anyone else. His last years were troubled. He had been estranged from me, Irene and Jeanette for long periods. We were reunited with Jimmy shortly before his passing. It's something I'm grateful for, even though he had by then become a shell of his former self. At the end, it seemed that the biggest thing in his life was his drinking buddies, but even they would steal from him as he lay dead in his flat.

Jimmy was living in Dorset when we tracked him down. He was due to go into hospital, in London, for heart bypass surgery. He survived the operation, but when he awoke from the procedure he was blind. His health deteriorated dramatically. Jimmy was found dead behind the door of his flat. He had lain there for three days. He was 46 years old and the sum total of his material possessions was a mouth organ, a watch, a tobacco tin, a dental plate and an empty wallet. His pals had taken the cash and his bank card, which they used to steal the few pounds in his account. They would even steal the floral tributes from his funeral. It broke my heart to think his life could be summed up by so little. We took his ashes to Streatham, where he joined Ma and Johnny. Now there was only Jeanette, Irene and me. We didn't count our father. Why would we?

As I sipped the wine on this best of days, I thought about Jimmy and Johnny and Ma and what they would say if they could see me. History had taught me that they would probably not have been too impressed. I was, after all, according to them, the 'snob' of the family. If I had been a believer in such things, I might have thought that my focus turning from the good life to the bad times was an omen. In a sense it was. The phone rang ...

CHAPTER 25

Three Phone Calls Change My Life

The telephone on the desk in my office mocks me, daring me to lift it and tear down the meticulously constructed façade I have hidden behind for so many years. I want more than anything to let this moment pass and get on with my life, but suddenly my life does not seem to be worth very much. I know it will never be the same again if I stay silent. I know it will never be the same again if I speak out. There is so much to lose.

It is a dreary workaday Monday morning and it has taken a weekend of soul-searching to arrive at this moment. For that is what I am contemplating – baring my soul – and I don't know if I have the courage. I am comforted and strengthened by the words spoken to me by Jeanette on the previous Friday evening: 'You have to do this, David! You *have* to do this.'

It is such a massive step. Taking me forward? Backwards? Who knows? I am bombarded by two distinct voices in my head to the exclusion of all else. Both of the voices are my own. One of them urges me not to break cover, to stay hidden and enjoy the life I have built. The other, which is growing stronger, demands I divest myself of the burden. I have grown so used to living a lie in this house of cards without foundations. The stronger voice tells me my life is an existence, no more than that, no matter my success, the money and the enviable lifestyle.

With a monumental effort of will, I reach out and place my hand on the receiver. Still I hesitate. I face exposure, perhaps ridicule. It is impossible for anyone who has not been at this crossroads to appreciate or understand the conflict. It may sound verbose, but the torment of it has seeped into the depths of my soul. Someone once famously said that a lie bloats itself on silence. My lie, my secrets were engorged.

Bizarre as it may sound, there was a part of me that was concerned for the man who had abused me. It's a psychological syndrome, I have since learned. The abused cling to their abusers, for ever connected by silence and secrets until it becomes, quite incomprehensibly, almost the duty of the abused to protect the abuser. It is common, for example, for an abused child to enter a room full of adults and go straight to their abuser, almost as if the child believes that by making him- or herself appealing, the pain will stop. As I said, incomprehensible!

My fears for the Beast's children are more easily understood. I am worried about the effect on their lives. It is not the first time I have worried about what would happen to them if their father was exposed. He is a monster, but they have done nothing.

Decision time. Three decades of silence. Now or never. A few feet away, one of my employees, Daniel, is getting on with his job, unaware of my inner turmoil, that I am debating the biggest decision of my life. I would be a great poker player. My face would never betray the bluff. If I have learned one thing over the years, it is how to mask true feelings.

I find my voice eventually and make it as calm as I can. 'Would you mind stepping out of the office for a minute?' I ask Daniel.

He smiles. 'Sure,' he says.

I have not made an uncommon request. I can read his thoughts. David wants to make a sensitive phone call, he thinks. If he only knew just how sensitive. He departs, and I am alone with my thoughts, one step closer to a decision.

I am still afraid. It is impossible to find the words to describe my emotions. Imagine for a moment that you are a person in early middle age. For as long as you can remember, you have walked around with a time bomb strapped to your body. You have no idea when it is due to explode. Time and familiarity have inevitably bred contempt for the device, but there has never been a period when you did not long to be free of it, a nagging, perennial longing to lay down the burden. My fingers close around the receiver, and as I lift it from its cradle I refer to the scrap of paper in front of me. There is a number scrawled on it that was given to me 48 hours earlier by directory enquiries.

I take a deep breath. Shakespeare was correct. If it is to be done, it is better to be done quickly. I dial. My nerves scream. A click at the other end. The call is picked up. An anonymous, if soothing, female voice with a Scottish accent says, 'Strathclyde Police.' Soon, there will be no more secrets.

Three days before … The insistent ring of the phone in my living room in Blackheath had dragged me from my bedroom, where I had been unpacking after returning from a holiday in the south of France. I felt good; the break had refreshed me. Sun, rest, fine food, even finer French wine. Perfect. I was tired, but I felt fresh enough to be contemplating a big Friday night out. I was alone and in the best of moods. It wasn't to last long.

I cast aside clothes selected for the laundry basket, glad of the chance to put off the mundane task, and made my way through the detritus of house renovation work to the living room. The remodelling had been part of the reason for escaping to France. I caught the call on the third ring, oblivious that it was about to change my life for ever.

Before I had the chance to speak, a voice – female, strident and abrasive – said, 'Hi, David. It's Helen.'

I was momentarily nonplussed. Helen who? I asked myself silently. The voice was, however, strangely familiar and the tone in her voice dictated that she knew me. Recognition was hiding on the edge of memory. We've all been in that position; our first instinct is a wish not to appear rude. Telephone conversations are intimate, two voices in the dark. This woman knew me and assumed I knew her. I didn't want to embarrass her by asking bluntly who she was.

Instead, I said, 'Hello, Helen,' in a cordial tone, hoping that she would offer me a clue that would drag her voice back into my conscious mind and give her a name. Then I realised! I did know who it was. I felt cold suddenly, numb. My head was spinning – how the hell did *she* get my number?

'How are you?' she asked.

I was utterly mystified. Not long before, Helen Porteous had written to me out of the blue, an innocuous letter filled with family news. In the letter, she wrote of how she and the Beast thought of me often. 'Drop us a line, or phone, or better still pay us a visit,' she wrote. As if! And now this?

I heard her say, 'Some children have made disgusting allegations against Uncle John. They are so ungrateful. We can't understand it. You will speak up for him, David, won't you?

We always treated you as one of our own. We need your help. We need your support. I know we can rely on you.'

God help me, I thought. This woman was asking *me* to be a character witness for *the Beast*. Helen was such a pious woman that everything in the tone of her voice screamed that these 'disgusting allegations' were sexual. I was in no doubt of that and it was obvious to me that there were legal proceedings in the wind. I could tell by the urgency in her voice.

'What they are saying is, of course, all nonsense,' she went on. 'Uncle John would never hurt anyone.'

Her words stabbed at me, every syllable activating a memory ... the bathroom door ... the bell tower ... the staff sitting room ... his hands touching me ... his weight on me ... his filthy words ... the smell. My hand was crushing the receiver. I eased my fingers from the phone and sensed they were indented with the shape of the instrument. She went on ... lies ... mistakes ... ingratitude. Suddenly, I was very angry, uncontrollably angrier than I have ever been before, angrier than I ever thought I could be. I cut into her monologue, demanding to know why she was phoning me, telling her she had no business to call me. There was silence. It spoke volumes. She was obviously shocked.

'David?' she said, a question mark in her voice.

I shouted, 'Terrible, unspeakable things were done to children in Quarriers – they were done to ME! I don't want to speak about this.'

I needed to get away, fast, but I was frozen, deluged by the flashbacks, which I now realised had never been buried as deep as I believed them to be. Nausea overwhelmed me. It was as if I was alone in a darkened cinema with the screen playing images of the younger me, the child who could not escape from the terrible things that were happening. I had not viewed those images with such clarity for so long. They had always been there, but I had buried them under success, money, possessions, status. The sharpness of the colours had dimmed. Now, they were revealed again. Why now? Why me? The phantom smell of the Beast's hair lotion assailed me, plunging me into a black hole. I felt his soft hands, saw his hard eyes and the look that came into them when he brought his face close to mine. I heard the inevitable catch in his breath, which was deepened by his perverse lust. I struggled to climb out of the black hole. I supported myself against the wall of a room that had become a Dalí painting.

Helen seemed unaware of this; she was speaking rapidly.

I exploded. 'I can't talk about this!' I shouted again. She was stunned into silence. 'I can't talk about this,' I said for a third time. She remained silent. 'I can't talk about this.' A mantra. And then I screamed, 'You've no business phoning me – he abused me!'

I slammed down the receiver, which had suddenly become red hot in my hand, and leaned against the wall. I had always dismissed the concept of the spinning room as a myth. It wasn't. I was in a spinning room. Slowly, inexorably, the room stopped moving and came back into focus. Call Jeanette. Call Jeanette, I thought. She'll know what to do.

I composed myself and dialled my sister's number with trembling fingers. As I listened to the phone ringing, I realised that I was about to reach yet another landmark. And I was about to change her life, too. After all these years, Jeanette still did not know that I had been abused. The call connected and Jeanette's voice, as calm and self-assured as ever, answered with a cheery 'Hello!'

I sucked in a deep breath. The sound of her voice comforted me. A safe haven. She always knew what to do. I dispensed with formality. 'There's something I need to tell you,' I said without preamble.

There was a momentary silence. 'What?' she said, an edge of uncertainty competing with the smile in her voice.

'I've just had a call from Helen Porteous,' I told her.

'Yes?' she said. Some of the uncertainty gone. We were back in familiar territory.

'There's something I need to tell you,' I repeated.

'What?' she said. The edge crept back into her voice.

'Helen said he's been accused of abusing children,' I told her.

'John?' she said, and added, 'That's awful. Why did Helen phone you?'

I said, 'It's obvious this is going to court and she wants me to be a character witness on his behalf. Why else would she phone me?'

'Oh, I see,' said Jeanette. 'So, what's the problem?'

I took another deep breath and said it quickly. 'He abused me.'

There was a pregnant pause and Jeanette said very quietly, 'When?' Her voice was catching with emotion and I heard the beginnings of anger.

'After Irene left Quarriers,' I replied.

There was a long, dark silence on the line. Eventually, the silence was broken by a voice that had gone very small and quiet.

'Why didn't you tell me?' She was hurt and angry in equal measure.

'I couldn't. I haven't been able to tell anyone,' I said to her, the tears welling in my eyes. Suddenly, I could not see.

'Oh, Davie,' she said in a voice that was so tired. It had been the first time in her life, or mine, that she had heard this. It was the proverbial bombshell.

Then the words flowed out of me, too many words, too much emotion, an avalanche, as I described the abuse. How can one, in a few words, capture a pain suffered for years, or explain the passage of time spent suppressing that pain? I'm certain she didn't hear or understand half of what I said as the words tumbled out of me. When I finally stopped talking, the silence seemed to last for ever and I felt the anger coming in waves towards me. I knew my sister well enough to realise instinctively that the anger wasn't directed at me.

After what seemed like an eternity, Jeanette said, 'Davie, you have to do something about this.'

'What?' I pleaded.

'You must do what you need to do to make this right,' she said, and added, 'You must go to the police. You have to. You have to do this, Davie.' Her anger was palpable, the mothering instinct she had shown me all my life reached out to me, trying to comfort me, to ease the pain, to guide me away from it.

'I don't know, I don't know,' I said in a little voice that had more child than adult in it. It was all I could think of to say.

'Listen, listen, Davie,' she said. 'We have to make this right.'

'I'm so sorry,' I told her.

'No, Davie, I'm so sorry.' All of her adult life, Jeanette had lived with the belief that Irene and I had been so lucky to have been placed in Quarriers.

It would take me three days to make the phone call …

So, here I am, sitting at my desk, my fingers clamped tightly around the phone.

'Strathclyde Police,' said the woman.

'Hello,' I said. 'My name is David Whelan.'

Silence was no longer an option.

CHAPTER 26
Pandora's Box

'We've been looking for you, David.' It was the man who spoke.

My heart was a drumbeat on my ribs. He had a soft voice and an open, kindly face, but there was a look in his eyes that suggested he would be capable of toughness if the situation demanded it. As every respectable, law-abiding citizen knows, innocence of wrongdoing is no defence against that feeling of guilt that somehow overwhelms you when you are in the presence of a police officer. Unlike my father, I had always strived to stay on the right side of the law. Within the walls of this police station, though, I felt somehow that I was about to be put on trial. Silly, I know, but you cannot help yourself.

'We knew you were out there, but we just didn't know where,' he continued.

'We were quite taken aback when you phoned,' added his colleague. The woman went on, 'I take it you hadn't realised we were looking for you?'

I told them I had no idea; it had only been the call from Helen Porteous that had prompted me to contact the police.

'That's an unusual set of circumstances, David,' she added. 'But we are glad you called.' She looked to her side and offered a quiet smile to her colleague. Something unspoken passed between them. I sensed they believed they had made a break-through – a breakthrough in what I had yet to learn was the biggest ever police investigation into the systematic abuse of children in care. The inquiry had been going on quietly for years and would eventually explode in a rash of arrests and convictions. I was unaware that my story was the one they were waiting for. It would place the final pieces into a massive jigsaw that had spanned three continents, two generations and thousands of police man-hours collecting witness statements. In the end, eight abusers would be convicted, including the Beast – all of them monsters hiding in our midst, who had believed their camouflage of respectability and the passing of time had concealed their wickedness.

For the moment, though, I knew nothing of the bigger picture. I was in this quiet room, with my sister Jeanette by my side, and I was scared. Half an hour before, after I arrived at the police station in Rue End Street, Greenock, in Renfrew-shire, the two officers had introduced themselves as Detective Constables Alan Harvie and Mairi Milne. Greenock was the hub of Operation Orbona – named after the Roman goddess of orphans and unwanted children – because it was the nearest main station to Quarriers. These two officers would be the first to hear the full story. I had only touched on certain aspects of it with Dr Keith, the psychologist. I wasn't ready for it at that time, but, now, in the course of the next several hours, all would be revealed …

* * *

The pilot's voice crackled over the intercom: 'Good morning, ladies and gentlemen. We will soon be arriving in Glasgow. On behalf of the crew, we hope you have a pleasant onward journey.' I wasn't sure if my onward journey could be described as pleasant or even where it would take me. Laying bare your soul doesn't appear on too many maps. Jeanette was silent, gathering up her bits and pieces and stuffing them into her bag. Mercifully, she had asked me no more questions since the weekend, when I had blurted out the story of Helen Porteous's phone call and my revelation that I had been abused. She had of course agreed immediately to accompany me to Scotland. My sister had once more assumed the role of mother.

We had departed from Gatwick Airport little more than an hour before and the trip had passed in relative silence. I was terrified of what lay ahead. Over the weekend, after Helen's fateful phone call, I had allowed Jeanette to catch a glimpse of what had been a secret for 30 years. I had travelled so far from Drumchapel and Quarriers. I had created my own business. I had a lovely home in a very desirable part of London. I had a millionaire lifestyle and a portfolio of properties. In the course of my working day, I rubbed shoulders with royalty and the most famous people in the world. None of them saw the filthy urchin who drank tea from a jam jar, the child whose head was once crawling with lice or the frightened little boy who wore cast-off clothes from a stinking Welfare warehouse. There was no sign of the terrified child who cowered behind the bathroom door or the abused boy afraid to climb the stairs to the bell tower. In the eyes of those who thought they knew me, I sipped Krug from cut-crystal flutes. I was a successful man by any yardstick. Before long I would be stepping back in time to again become nobody's child.

The skidding wheels of the aircraft touching down arrested my thoughts. It taxied to the terminal building. We processed up the narrow aisle of the aircraft and exited into a typical Glasgow day. As we descended the uncertain metal stairs to the tarmac, the sky was 10 feet above my head. Welcome home … for the first time in years. I wanted to experience some sense of belonging, but I didn't. We Scots are often sentimental about homecomings. In my life thus far, there had been little room for sentimentality.

Jeanette and I had arranged a hire car and booked a hotel in Glasgow. I would be interviewed by the police the following day. As we drove towards the city, I realised it had changed dramatically since I had seen it last. The new high-rise flats, so reminiscent of London, were a far cry from the drab multi-storey buildings of the 1960s. I couldn't believe how elegant and sophisticated the city had become. It wasn't hard to understand why it had been accorded the honour of European Capital of Culture. But the revised skyline was not uppermost in my mind. We reached the city centre and suffered a moment of confusion in the one-way system before we arrived at the hotel.

An early dinner, at which I picked at the food, was followed by an early night. As Jeanette and I separated, to go to our rooms, my sister put her arm around my shoulder and said quietly, 'This isn't just about you any more, Davie. There are no choices left. Just tell them what happened.'

I headed for bed in a sober frame of mind. Naturally, I didn't sleep. I lay in bed, dozing fitfully until the first rays of morning light fell on my face. It was time to go. I rose and dressed carefully, as I always did. Old habits die hard. And then, of course, there were those all-important first impressions.

I don't remember much of breakfast, but I do remember the car journey to Greenock, which took me past so many familiar places. We arrived at the police station early for the meeting and parked in front of an architecturally anonymous building that screamed the 1960s at me. There was a moment of deep anxiety. Wrapped up against the sharp coastal wind, I paced back and forth outside the station and for a while I didn't believe I was going to make it inside. The silence had gone on for so long. Could I really break its evil spell after all these years?

I felt Jeanette's hand on my arm. 'It's time, Davie,' she said.

We walked into the police station. There was no going back …

'You'll feel more comfortable in here, David,' said Detective Constable Milne. She, too, had a soft voice and a kind face. Her face didn't have the same capacity for toughness as her male colleague, but it was strong and resolute. I was immediately calm and at ease. It's the strangest thing, but I have always been more comfortable in the company of women when intimate matters need to be discussed.

She led me into an airy room with pastel walls. A settee sat to one side, opposite two chairs.

'Take a seat, David,' said Detective Constable Harvie, indicating the settee.

The detectives took the chairs. We were separated by a coffee table. My eyes were drawn to the tape machine, which sat in isolation on the table. It seemed incongruous there, in what effectively looked like someone's living room. I had seen enough cop shows on television to realise that I was in what they call the 'rape suite'.

Jeanette joined me on the settee. I was grateful for her silent support. She had begun to cry silently, even before a word was spoken. My initial sense of calm was beginning to desert me. The detectives must have sensed it, identified something in my eyes and body language.

'Nice trip down, David?' said the man.

I nodded.

'Changed a bit since you were last here?' added the woman.

'It has,' I said.

They were consummate professionals. They knew how difficult this was for me and they were trying to divert my attention from what was coming.

DC Milne said, 'Don't worry about this, David. We just want you to tell us what you remember.'

'All we are doing now is asking a few questions, tying up a few things,' said DC Harvie. He added, 'If at any time you want a break, or a glass of water, just tell us.'

I told them I was fine and I wanted to get it over with as quickly as possible.

'That's fine,' said the woman.

She maintained the conversational tone as she asked me if I consented to being interviewed. I said I did. They asked me if I was happy for Jeanette to be present. I said I was.

'If you're ready, then,' said DC Harvie, as his hand reached down to the coffee table.

I felt nauseous. Could I do this? His finger depressed the button on the tape machine, which beeped once and settled into an insistent but almost inaudible hiss. DC Harvie's voice assumed a more authoritative tone: 'It is eleven a.m., 28 March 2002. Present are Detective Constables Alan Harvie and Mairi Milne.'

'What is your name?' DC Milne asked me.

'David Whelan,' I reply.

'What is your date of birth and current address?' she went on.

I answer both questions.

'What is your occupation?' she asked.

'I run my own recruitment consultancy, based in London.'

'Who is with you, Mr Whelan, and are you happy to have her present during this interview?' said DC Harvie.

I confirm who Jeanette is and inform the detectives that I want her to be with me. My hands are shaking. I glance at Jeanette and she, too, is obviously distressed. She is still crying. This is going to be as tough for her as it is for me. She is about to take on a burden of guilt that will never leave her, although what happened to me is no fault of hers. In spite of all the promises I had made to myself to be strong, I, too, begin crying. The tears won't stop.

'Would you like a drink of water?' asked DC Milne.

My mouth is suddenly too dry to respond. I nod.

She poured water from a carafe into a glass and handed it to me. The tape would not record her reassuring smile and the warm touch of her hand.

DC Harvie took a deep breath and said, 'In your own words, Mr Whelan, tell us about your time in Quarriers.'

Pandora's box opened. I told them what the Beast did to me. It took five hours.

CHAPTER 27

Telling Irene

The woman who sat opposite me was all business. It had been 24 hours since I was interviewed by Detective Constables Harvie and Milne. I was back in Greenock, but this time the soothing pastel shades of the rape suite, with its comfortable settee, had been replaced by a grey and inhospitable room trapped within a grim Victorian building. An atmosphere of informality had been replaced by a sense of urgency. The woman was Cath White. She was the procurator-fiscal and she was building a case. There was no time now for chit-chat.

Under Scots law, the Procurator Fiscal Service acts on behalf of the Crown to decide which cases should go to trial. It is the Scottish equivalent of the Crown Prosecution Service in England. However, the two services differ in that a Scottish victim of an alleged offence has no influence over whether or not charges will be brought. The English system still offers the victim in some situations the opportunity not to press charges. In Scotland, the procurator fiscal is the one who decides. I would learn of this signal difference between the laws of the two countries before the interview is over. The PF is also technically in charge of the police inquiry and has the authority to direct officers. When the fiscal has built the case, an advocate depute, who is usually a QC, presents the case for the prosecution at trial on behalf of the Lord Advocate of Scotland. It is a system that dates back to Roman times, hence the use of the word 'procurator'.

'I just want to go over a few things in your statement, Mr Whelan,' said Miss White, as she opened a manila folder.

I was with Miss White and a police officer from Operation Orbona. I had decided that two such interviews would be too much for Jeanette. She had been physically and emotionally drained by the experience of the previous day. We had driven back up the M8 to Glasgow in the evening and immediately gone for a much-needed drink. The weather had turned unseasonably warm and we went for a walk in Sauchiehall Street and ate fish and chips. There was too much information out there now for Jeanette to take it all in. However, she was quick to reassure me I had done the right thing in exposing a pervert. Jeanette finished her fish supper and wanted to go back to the hotel. I needed some time to myself, so I stayed out, absorbing the night-time sounds of the city. I thought about the following day. I had agreed to return to Greenock to meet with the Procurator Fiscal. Eventually, I walked back to the hotel on weary legs. This time, I had no problem getting to sleep.

We were up early. Jeanette wanted to come with me, so when we arrived I found a café where she could wait for me. I was more confident that I could deal with this on my own, but my confidence took a knock when the police officer ushered me into Miss White's drab office. It wasn't her job to mollycoddle me. She wanted – needed – to put bad people in jail. I was the means of achieving it. There was a tower block of files on her desk. Given my institutional upbringing, I had longed since mastered the ancient art of upside-down reading. I realised that my Social Work file was on top of the pile of documents. I asked if I could see the file.

My request unnerved her. 'It's confidential,' she informed me in a sharp voice.

She, too, had a tape machine running. Miss White asked me to recall some of the things I had told the police. She began dissecting my statement, clarifying where this particular person was at a specific time, which cottage this or that child was in. She was obviously piecing together other cases they were working on.

'What was your experience like at Quarriers?' she asked.

With massive understatement I replied, 'Overall it wasn't a good experience.' I wasn't trying to be facetious. It was just the way it came out. I almost laughed at my ludicrously inadequate assessment. It was a bit like saying that a train crash causes a bit of a mess.

Miss White asked me more questions and I was suddenly overwhelmed by the enormity of what was happening. I had spent so long keeping everything to myself, I was suddenly anxious that the secret was no longer under my control. What would it do to the successful life I had so carefully built? Desperately trying to wrest back control, I blurted out, 'If Porteous is prepared to acknowledge what he did to me and apologise to me personally, I will drop the charges.'

Miss White's reaction confirmed what I already knew in my sinking heart – the matter was outwith my control. Anxiety and nausea washed over me. I was like a child again, the terrified child I had once been.

'But I don't want Mr Porteous to go to jail,' I told the Procurator Fiscal. I was once more in Dr Keith's office, when I had become so worried about the effect any revelation of mine might have on the Beast's children.

'It's not just about you, Mr Whelan,' Miss White said in a quiet but firm voice.

She was correct. The police had told me nothing of their investigation, but I had an inkling that this was much bigger than just me. I took a deep, calming breath. The genie was out of the bottle. Nothing I could do about it now. I listened as Miss White detailed key points about my time in Quarriers, asking me to clarify certain details. Had I been in touch with any of the other Quarriers children, or had I spoken to anyone about what had happened to me or to others? I told her I hadn't, apart from the briefest mention to Dr Keith. She seemed pleased. This would be of vital importance at the coming trial, I would learn. Our evidence would be untainted by any suggestion that we had swapped stories.

The interview was short compared to the previous day. Miss White's manner softened as we came to the end of it and she shook my hand and smiled warmly as I left. Once out of her office, I fled down the stairs of the old building and into the comfort of daylight and fresh air.

Jeanette was waiting for me where I had left her. 'How did it go?' she asked.

'OK,' I said, not certain if I was telling the truth.

'You do know you'll have to tell Irene,' she added.

'I know,' I said.

Three hours later we touched down at Gatwick. I gave myself a day of grace before I phoned Irene.

'Can I come and see you?' I asked.

'Sure,' said my sister. 'I'll see you in my lunch break.'

Her lunch break ate into the afternoon and early evening and it was dark by the time I had finished my story. Irene looked at me for a long time without blinking. She had not interjected once during my monologue.

Eventually, she said, 'That dirty bastard!'

I looked down at my feet, unable to meet her eye. I knew she felt guilty. In spite of her bad memories of Quarriers, she had remained in touch with the Beast and Helen. I knew she was thinking about the time she had cajoled me into returning to Quarriers after Johnny's funeral. I knew she was remembering the occasions years ago when she had inveigled me into sending Christmas cards. It was easier to keep the peace by doing what she asked rather than telling her my secret. It was the path of least resistance. I knew also that she felt betrayed that I had not been confident enough in her to tell her what happened.

Irene said, 'Why in heaven's name did you wait so long to tell anyone?'

How many times had I asked that question of myself?

She put her arms around me and said, 'It's OK. We'll get through this.'

Now everyone who mattered knew … the police, Jeanette, Irene. And soon the Beast and the rest of the world would know.

I was bone tired as I trudged home through the rain. I was rescued from my thoughts by the deep-throated growl of a London bus. I turned in time to be washed by warm yellow light from its welcoming interior. Pale white faces looked at me through the windows of the bottom deck and then they were gone. How many of them had their secrets? How many of them should have spoken out long before now? How many of them were monsters yet to be exposed? I pulled up the collar of my coat and dug my hands deep into my pockets. I was soon at home and in bed. It wasn't long before the nightmares came.

CHAPTER 28

The Others

'You had a more sinister side to your character'

LORD HARDIE TO JOHN PORTEOUS

I found the white envelope lying on the mat at my front door. No other post came that day. I knew instinctively what it was. I tore open the envelope with fingers that would not work and unfolded the single sheet of paper it contained. Her Majesty's Lord Advocate of Scotland summoned me to appear at the High Court of Justiciary, in Glasgow, as a witness in the trial of John Porteous and his wife. I wanted to run and hide, but it was too late. Cath White, the procurator fiscal, had already made it clear that I was no longer in control of the silence. Come what may, I would have to walk into that court and break the dark spell that had been cast so many years earlier.

I called Jeanette. 'It's arrived,' I told her.

'At last,' she said.

'Will you come with me?' I pleaded.

'I can't, Davie. My back. I couldn't face the journey. I wouldn't make it,' she said. Jeanette had been suffering from debilitating back pain for a while. I was going to have to do this on my own. So be it.

The following morning, I went to work and rescheduled my diary for the next fortnight. I booked a train ticket. Normally, the journey to Scotland relaxed me. Not this time, I thought.

The cadence of the train's rattling wheels failed to work their usual magic, as I had expected. In fact, I could not spend more than a few minutes at a time in my seat. I prowled the aisles, hiding in the gap between the carriages and pressing my face against the cool glass of the door window. The countryside, blurred by the speed of the train, hurtled past. I was in no mood to take in the scenery. The journey seemed interminable. Throughout, I was drawn back to the summons. I kept opening the letter. The words hadn't changed. It was really happening.

By the time I reached Glasgow Central, I was soaked with sweat. Get to the hotel, I thought. Relax.

I checked in, showered and took the sleeping pills my doctor had prescribed. Tomorrow, I thought, it all starts tomorrow.

I awoke in the silent darkness of a Scottish winter morning. The soundtrack of the city had yet to begin. My sleep had been dreamless. I showered and dressed and went to the breakfast room. A buffet table groaned under that most magnificent of all things, the Scottish breakfast, but I couldn't face it. I felt nauseous. I needed fresh air and walked through the rear entrance of the Central Hotel, which led into the concourse of the station. I vomited. No one noticed. Mercifully, people in transit are too busy with their own affairs.

I walked back into the hotel on shaky legs, in time to see a man at the front desk telling the receptionist that the coach for the High Court had arrived. A coach? For me? The Procurator Fiscal had said she was laying on transport, but I hardly needed a coach. Then I saw them. A group of people, filing onto the bus. A middle-aged woman turned towards me and there was a moment of awful clarity. God Almighty, I'm not the only one.

'Hi, David,' said the woman.

I answered, 'Hello.' Wholly inadequate. There were others, I realised. Throughout the years of silence, it had not occurred to me there might be others.

I took my place on the bus and, suddenly, I recognised some of them. I saw the children they once were in the faces of the adults. I was stunned. No one spoke. A voice from outside the bus, accompanied by the blast of a car horn, shattered the silence.

'Move that effin' bus,' shouted a taxi driver, trapped behind the coach.

'I'm a police officer,' Detective Constable Mairi Milne told him.

'You should effin' well know better, then,' said the cabbie.

I almost laughed, in spite of myself. Welcome to Glasgow.

In what seemed like the blink of an eye, we were outside the High Court. The bus came to a halt and the doors opened with a pneumatic hiss. People were milling in front of the Alexander 'Greek' Thomson façade, with its Doric pillars. We were taken through the airport-style security into a cavernous atrium. The tension was palpable. Our group of familiar strangers was guided into a witness room. We had the look of the condemned. It was as if we were on trial. In a sense, we were.

An older woman was comforting some of the younger women and I recognised her as Marion Fraser, the wife of the Reverend Arthur Fraser, minister of Mount Zion Church, in Quarriers Village. She smiled. I smiled. Her presence comforted me. I had always had affection for the Frasers. They were good people.

A court officer appeared and asked if we would mind if the public gallery was opened. There was uproar. The women were crying. Bad enough we should face the ordeal. We did not need gawpers. Reporting restrictions would guarantee our anonymity. We were regarded still as 'children' because of when the offences allegedly occurred. The downside of this was that it would be difficult for the media to report. Much of the evidence revealed in court would never reach the public domain. As a result, media interest waned until the end of the trial. While we would have liked all that had been done to us to be revealed, it would not.

Our priority, however, was justice. So for now we sat in this airless, claustrophobic room, afraid to speak for fear of being accused of contaminating each other's evidence. We waited …

CHAPTER 29

Accused

'You presented a face of respectability'

HIGH COURT JUDGE LORD HARDIE TO JOHN PORTEOUS

The Procurator Fiscal had laid 14 charges against John Porteous before he went on trial at the High Court in Glasgow in October 2002. Ten of the charges were alleged offences of a sexual nature against me and four others – two girls and two boys – which were said to have taken place between 1969 and 1982. The offences, it was alleged, occurred when some of us were as young as 7 years old and continued allegedly until some of us were 15. The charges included alleged crimes that ranged from shameful indecency to oral sex, masturbation and unnatural carnal connection. Three of the charges were not of a sexual nature. They related variously to the alleged physical abuse and intimidation of three children in his care – me and two girls – in the late 1960s and early 1970s. Helen Porteous was charged with six offences that alleged that she had physically abused or ill treated three girls in her care between 1968 and 1976. The charges variously alleged she had punched, kicked, force-fed and deprived children of food. She was also accused of rubbing a child's face in soiled bedclothes and repeatedly failing to obtain medical attention for a child. John Porteous and his wife, Helen, were jointly charged with wilfully ill treating and neglecting me in a manner likely to cause me unnecessary suffering or injury to my health, depriving me of food, repeatedly re-serving parts of uneaten meals and locking me in a room.

You will have noticed that the only 'child' identified is me. The law of Scotland protects the identity of children under the age of 16 who are involved in court cases, as well as the identity of all alleged victims of a sexual crime. I have relinquished anonymity. The others have not. When I refer to them, I use aliases.

Chapter 30
The Yellow Bird Café

'These were children who came to regard you as a father figure'
LORD HARDIE TO JOHN PORTEOUS

We were in the witness room. It was claustrophobic, tense, a powder keg.

Miranda prattled incessantly. '… And he's so big now – he'll soon be as big as his dad. And clever, he's very clever. I can't even do his homework any more …'

The voice tailed off into a droning sound that went to the centre of my brain. Stop! For God's sake, stop! I screamed internally. I know the poor woman was only trying to alleviate the tension she was obviously feeling, but the incessant chatter about her perfect son was driving me crazy. Wrapped in our cocoon, we were unaware that the morning of the first day of the trial was being consumed by legal arguments. It was, we learned from a court officer, par for the course, but every minute, sitting on this edge of near hysteria, seemed like an hour.

'… And he's just as untidy as his dad, always leaving his stuff lying about the place. But at least he doesn't spend all of his time on the computer. He's out and about and …'

I stood up, unable to sit for one second longer. I began to pace, but there was nowhere to go. Please God, let her be called first.

'… And what an appetite! Eats as much as his dad. You should see our grocery bills. And he's skin and bone, too. Not a pick on him!'

The door of the witness room opened. She stopped speaking. Saved! A court officer entered and pointed with his right hand to a watch on his left wrist. 'No one will be called until after lunch. Why don't you take a break in the cafeteria?'

Thank you, Jesus.

There was a near stampede for the door. In the corridor, the life of a supreme court was being played out. Bewigged advocates processed at a stately pace, dragging behind them the wheeled carry-on luggage that held their court papers. Three police officers wearing 'stab vests' huddled, speaking in whispers, their tired expressions revealing they would rather be on the streets. Court ushers in blue uniforms moved at speed, performing a slalom manoeuvre through the lawyers, cops and citizens whose participation in the panoply of the law was transitory. I don't quite know why, but the entire scene was incredibly intimidating. I was, however, just glad to be out of that overheated room where the tension had cranked up to breaking point. I began to cry. If the others noticed, they said nothing. There would be no judgements from them, that was for sure. I hurried on, embarrassed. I also needed to eat.

The cafeteria was bustling. I slid the brown plastic tray along the serving rail, the others following me in a line to the cash desk. I hoisted the tray from the rail and found a seat. I passed a group of people who were sitting at an adjacent table. As I was joined by the others, the group began to mutter and point.

'What?' I asked one of the group, Thomas.

'Supporters,' he said. 'They're here to support the Porteouses.'

I looked at the people at the other table, who were glaring. 'Finish up quickly,' I said, 'and let's get out of here.'

Thomas wanted a cigarette, so we walked outside, some way from the main door, towards Glasgow Green. He lit his cigarette and expelled smoke in a long, nervous breath. 'Christ!' he said suddenly.

Something in his face made me look at his line of vision. The Beast ... and Helen.

'I'm going to say something,' Thomas said.

'NO!' I said, shocked by the tone in my voice. 'No,' I said, more quietly. 'Leave it. This isn't the time. They'll use it against you. There's so much at stake. Don't do anything that could derail the trial.'

Thomas was placated.

The Beast and Helen were looking straight at us. I held their gaze. I could still feel the heat of Thomas's anger, but I was calm, coldly calm. Porteous and Helen disappeared from view, round the corner of the building.

Thomas was called to the witness box after lunch. He had alleged that he had been sexually abused by the Beast in the early 1980s, long after I left Quarriers. I later discovered he was the child who accused Porteous of abuse in 1982. The allegation could not be substantiated at the time and he was moved out of Quarriers. The vestiges of his earlier anger had translated into cockiness. He leaped to his feet and walked to the door of the witness room with a look on his face that said, 'I'll show them!'

He was a different man when he returned, deflated and defeated. And he was staring at me. He beckoned me into a corner of the room and hissed, 'If you had reported it when it happened to you, it wouldn't have happened to me!' He had been torn apart in the witness box and, poor man, was now hovering between tears and rage. Thomas was so close that his spit peppered my face, his accusation burning like a branding iron. The cockiness he displayed earlier was gone. I was devastated by his words. I knew exactly how he was feeling; that sense of impotence so common to children like us. I would have felt the same in his position. His anger was not directed at me, but after what he had gone through I was the only target. My heart broke for him. I wanted so much to put my arm around him after the outburst, but I couldn't. The constraints of the law prevented me from any conversation with him about the case. It was just as well. I had no answers. The words were locked inside me – that I, too, was in pain, that I wished I'd had the strength to tell someone, anyone, when it had happened to me, that I'd gladly rewrite history if I could. I'm sorry, I'm so sorry, I shouted after him, but as he snatched his jacket and fled from the room the words were only in my head.

The door was still lying open when a court usher came into the room. 'That's it for today, ladies and gentlemen,' he said. 'See you tomorrow.'

I was drained by the time I got back to the hotel. I didn't want to speak to anyone – even if I could have. I went to my room and collapsed on the bed, glad to be alone and grateful for the silence. I don't remember falling asleep, but I remember the dream ...

Two knickerbocker glories sat in the middle of the Formica table. I had never seen anything so beautiful. I was nine years old. Irene was next to me in the dark leatherette booth, her eyes dancing with delight. We were in the Yellow Bird Café in the centre of Glasgow. Mirrored walls reflected countless Davids and Irenes. The place smelled of sweets and coffee. I ran my finger down the side of the sundae glass. It was cold. Ice cream – vanilla, strawberry and chocolate – spilled over the top, running onto my finger. Irene giggled.

'You like that?' said Mr Black. The kindly social worker had taken us for a treat. We had been to the Welfare warehouse for clothes. I can't remember why he had taken us, but I think Ma was having one of her episodes.

'Yes,' I replied. 'I've never had this before. Ma doesn't buy ice cream.'

Irene leaned forward and licked raspberry sauce from the top of the wonderful creation. She giggled again. The hiss of the espresso machine dragged our attention away from the sundaes.

'Can I have another white coffee?' Mr Black shouted to the man in the white coat, behind the stainless-steel counter.

'Coming up,' said the man over his shoulder.

I dug into the sundae with a long-stemmed spoon as a shadow fell over me. I looked up. It was the man in the white coat. 'Hello, David,' said the Beast.

I awoke with a start, bile rising in my throat. I sat for two hours on the edge of the bed, rocking myself as I had done so long ago when the Beast left me to return to his own bed.

CHAPTER 31
Witness for the Prosecution

'It is impossible to determine what psychological damage you have caused them'　　　LORD HARDIE TO JOHN PORTEOUS

'Calling David Whelan.' I heard but did not hear my name. 'Calling David Whelan.' Louder this time.

I rose from the chair like a man bound for the execution chamber. All eyes were on me. I followed the broad shoulders of the usher who had called me. He led me through a heavy door and offered a reassuring smile.

'Thank you,' I whispered, as I entered the witness box.

This moment had been coming for 28 years. The Beast sat in the dock, stripped of his power. He was 69 years old. His wife, Helen, sat beside him, wearing a look of disdain … and something else. What was it? Pious indignation, I realised.

He was standing trial, accused of sexual offences against me and four other children. She was accused of the assault, ill treatment and neglect of three girls in her care. I had watched a succession of witnesses leave the claustrophobic room and return with the haunted look of the walking wounded. Would I be one of them? I was gripped by nerves.

Porteous and his wife look at me. I cannot take my eyes from them. I am drawn like a moth to a flame. Behind my nervous tension, though, there is resolve. Cath White had been correct. The time was long overdue to get this out in the open. Even separated by the width of the courtroom, I sense tension in the couple in the dock. But Porteous projects defiance. Not for long.

The court is deathly quiet. If I thought the corridors of this august building were intimidating, the court itself is terrifying. Like most people, my only experience of the courts is what I see on television crime series. The royal crest hangs above the judge's 'throne'. Lord Hardie looks stern, in his red robes and white wig. Two teams of advocates sit at separate tables, legal gladiators facing the clerk of the court, who sits below the judge. I feel like a Christian among lions. Fifteen jurors face me. All I can do is tell my story. The rest is up to them.

'Would you like a glass of water, Mr Whelan?' asks Lord Hardie.

I nod. My mouth is too dry to reply. I feel faint. The water appears before me and I lift the glass. It offers me a few moments to compose myself. And so it begins …

Lord Hardie raises his right arm. Did I swear to tell the truth, the whole truth and nothing but the truth? I concur. One of the bewigged men at the advocates' table rises. Norman Ritchie QC, prosecuting on behalf of the Crown. In answer to his prompting, I tell him my name, my age, my occupation and my address.

Could I, he then asked, identify and point out the accused in this courtroom today? My finger pointed like an invisible laser beam aimed straight at the heart of the old man with white hair and defiance smouldering in his eyes. I promised myself that, by God, before this day was out I would replace that look with fear. Porteous shook his head disdainfully.

It had been suggested to me that some juries find it difficult to equate bad acts with older people. The Beast had been so adept at hiding in plain sight for so long. Would the jury now see beyond the apparent venerability and fragility of his age? Would they see the younger man? The man who crept into my bed and committed those unspeakable acts? Would they see the truth, or would the mask continue to hide the face of a monster? Was I strong enough to overcome my embarrassment and, yes, the sense of shame that had held me captive and ensured my silence for so long? I had for as long as I could remember trained myself to disassociate my emotions from the abuse. However, one cannot merely shut down a single part of the psyche – every emotion is affected. People that didn't know me might assume I was cold. Would my air of detachment, my defence mechanism, go against me now? How could they see the maelstrom of emotion, the fear, anger and distrust that were hidden by *my* mask? Would this jury of my so-called peers, with their normal lives and happy childhoods, understand how pervasive are the effects of childhood abuse, how it eats into every corner of your very being? All of these thoughts rattled through my mind at lightning speed. I was pulled back by the voice of Norman Ritchie.

His first questions were innocuous. Did I own my own firm? How many employees did I have? I told him. Mr Ritchie asked me to confirm when I was at Quarriers. I told him. Which cottages was I in? I told him. Who were the house parents? I told him.

There was a pregnant pause. 'What happened to you in Cottage 7?' he asked in a quiet voice.

The courtroom seemed to hold its breath.

'I was physically and sexually abused,' I said in a loud, clear voice.

'Who did this to you?'

'John Porteous.'

'Where did the sexual abuse take place?'

I told him.

For the following hour, it was only the adult David who answered the questions. The child within was somewhere else, trapped in the bedroom, the bathroom, the bell tower and the staff sitting room.

In the end, I heard a disembodied voice say, 'Thank you, Mr Whelan. M'lord, I have no further questions at this juncture.' Mr Ritchie sat down.

Blood was rushing into my head, pumped by a pounding heart. The next stage of this inquisition would be a lot harder. Derek Ogg QC, defending, stood up. Suddenly I felt very alone. He flicked over pages in a bundle of paperwork, heightening the tension. I waited, sick to my stomach. I can't even recall his first few questions. I was so nervous. But I did hear him say, 'We put it to you, Mr Whelan, that you were never abused physically or sexually in Quarriers.'

This was it. I knew I was fighting for my credibility, my future and my life. I looked toward the jury, silently pleading with them to understand.

'Yes, I was,' I said defiantly.

'You were a very disruptive boy while in Quarriers and did not like being disciplined when you were disruptive,' he said. He continued to flick through what was obviously the record of my childhood in Quarriers – empty words that bore no relation to what had truly happened.

I gripped the rail on the witness box to steady myself. 'No!'

Was I disruptive? Perhaps I was at times, but it wasn't my nature to snap without extreme provocation. I just hoped the court could appreciate the behaviour of a vulnerable abused child who had been pushed over the edge. I prayed that those sitting in judgment of the Beast would not judge me.

'No,' I said again.

Ogg continued in a quiet, mellifluous voice. 'You were upset because your mother never came to see you – it was not because Mr Porteous abused you.'

'No,' I repeated.

'It is not true,' said Ogg, 'that you were sexually or physically abused.'

Only the rail on the box held me up. 'Yes, I was,' I said quietly. 'Yes, I was.' In my mind, I felt the weight of Porteous on me, his fingers groping under my kilt, touching me under the bedclothes.

Ogg was saying, 'You have said you ran away five or six times because of the abuse. That's not true, is it? Wasn't it because your mother never came to visit you?'

Poor Ma, blamed again. She was guilty of many things, but to suggest she was at the root of me bringing an accusation of sexual abuse against an 'innocent' man – I had never heard anything so repugnant. I had accused The Beast because he *was* guilty. My accusation had nothing to do with how my mother failed to visit.

'Mr Whelan, you are confused,' said Ogg.

Confused, I thought. I had been many things, but I was not confused. I have been damaged, I have been for ever marked, I have been afraid to trust, to love … but confused? Never!

'No,' I told Ogg.

He did not seem to hear. 'That was the reason you absconded. Your family did not come to see you and you were upset.'

'No,' I repeated.

He was relentless, claiming I had not been abused but that my accusation was the result of repressed anger, a memory of my family life before Quarriers. And so was his female junior. Ogg sat down and she rose. She continued the attack. I was transferring my anger from a chaotic early life with a father who was a drunk, a wife-beater and a convicted rapist, on to 'Mr Porteous'. It was a statement, not a question.

'I have not,' I said. I explained that my father had done nothing to me. I had only seen him once – on that day I allowed him into the house in Drumchapel when I was 10 years old. There is no doubt that he, too, was a monster, but of a different kind. He had done nothing. He hadn't touched me. The female advocate sat down, and Ogg rose again. I was weary, drained. I knew at that moment that this might never stop, that this trial would not be an end to it. I had to answer these questions, revisit the past, dredge up the nightmare. But I realised that I had believed erroneously that justice would be done and the truth would set me free. It wouldn't. Ogg told me again that the abuse had not happened.

'No!' I said again. 'It did!' All my steely control and my artfully contrived coolness deserted me. My defensive mask was torn from me as I lost control of my emotions. 'I have answered your question *three* times now,' I declared. 'My answer is still the same! It *did* happen.' I turned to Lord Hardie and pleaded, 'M'lord?'

Lord Hardie looked down into the well of the court and said, 'Counsel, I believe the witness has answered your question.'

Mr Ogg took off on another tack. 'Mr Whelan, I put it to you were never in the bell tower,' he said.

'I was.'

'No, you were not.'

'I was!' I closed my eyes and I returned there. The images were so vivid I seemed to be in the bell tower. It was a flashback I hadn't expected. I stunned Ogg into silence as I described in minute detail the stairs, the layout of the tower, the stool, the pulleys, levers and mechanism of the bell in Mount Zion Church. Every single detail poured out, how he had locked the door behind us, how, in that secret place, he had abused me, violated me, in the house of God. The words I was forced to use made me flush red to the roots of my hair. I looked at the jury. I could see their discomfiture. No, it wasn't that. They were horrified by the language of sexual abuse, but how else could they know what I had gone through? I could not be stopped. I was there!

'Grey flannel trousers,' I said suddenly.

Ogg was puzzled.

I went on quickly, 'And a wine-coloured pullover.' I then described in detail what Porteous was wearing when he abused me, this time in the staff bedroom.

When I stopped speaking, there was a ghastly silence. I was stripped bare. My coolness, the aloofness, the carefully constructed barriers were all gone. The defensive mask I had worn for three decades was, in a sense, lying on the floor before the jury. *Now they could see.* And so could Ogg.

He turned to the bench and said, 'No more questions.'

I looked at the jury and every eye was on me. They believed. I knew that they believed me. No matter what was to come, no matter what I would lose, no matter the pain that was awaiting me, they believed me. The sense of relief was immense. I stole a glimpse at my watch. Three hours. It had seemed like three days. A disembodied voice told me I was free to go.

When I looked to the dock, Porteous did not seem quite so defiant and Helen was crying. I walked from the court on leaden feet. The floodgates had been opened and I would be deluged. In the months ahead I would drown; my life would disintegrate. In the darkest moments I clung to that look in the eyes of the jury. In other moments it would be the eyes of the Beast.

A voice spoke to me. 'How do you think it went?' Cath White.

'I told my story … and the truth.'

'How are you feeling?'

'Like having been in the lions' den.'

Cath White raised her shoulders and offered a non-committal smile. 'The jury may come to its decision on the evidence you have given today,' she added. 'Are you OK?'

Was I? The fortress had been demolished. The world knew me now. The silence was shattered. Was I OK? No, I wasn't. I feared I would never be the same again.

CHAPTER 32
Roll of Shame

'A children's home worker nicknamed the "Beast of the Bell Tower" was jailed for eight years yesterday for the sexual abuse of two boys'   *Daily Record*, 8 NOVEMBER 2002

'Did you hear?' said the voice on the phone. It was a former Quarriers girl. 'He got eight years!' she said.

I sat down. I was back in London. After I had given my evidence, I had needed the safety of my home. In recent times so many momentous events had translated into simple phone calls. Helen's original call, asking me to be a character witness, had started it. My phone call to the police had ended years of silence. This was the latest, bringing news of justice. I felt deflated. The cliché response would have been to punch the air and shout, 'Yessss!' but it didn't feel like a victory. There can be no happy endings in a situation like this. I tuned in to the Scottish news. Porteous was convicted on four of the original charges, in relation to me and the other boy. He was found guilty of two counts of shameless indecency and two counts of lewd, indecent and libidinous practices and behaviour. He was found not guilty of the alleged abuse of Thomas.

Sentencing Porteous on 7 November 2002 to eight years' imprisonment, Lord Hardie pointed out that it was ironic that his wife's support and faith in him had resulted in me coming forward to condemn him. He told him, 'There could be no doubt that you presented a face of respectability. It is clear from the discerning verdict of the jury that between 1969 and 1977 you had a more sinister side to your character. You abused two boys entrusted to your care over a period of eight years on numerous occasions. Those boys were entrusted to your care because they had personal difficulties and the last thing that was expected or needed was for you to add to their difficulties by sexually abusing them. These were children who came to regard you as a father figure and it is impossible to determine what psychological damage you have caused them in later life.'

The charges against Helen Porteous had been dropped by the Crown and she was formally acquitted. She was not guilty. When the Beast was led from the dock, he shouted to his family: 'Fight them for me. They are liars, absolute liars!' It was not long before the abusive and threatening phone calls began from men and women with Scottish accents. I was appalled. My number is ex-directory. I called Detective Constable Mairi Milne to report it and asked BT to monitor my line. The phone calls stopped. I later learned that I had not been the only person to receive them.

I took comfort in the knowledge that the Beast was now Prisoner No. 77107 in A-Hall of HMP Invernethie – better known as Peterhead Prison – where Scotland's child sex abusers are sent. The phone calls may have stopped, but the campaign to paint the Beast as an innocent man was about to

begin. While he was in Peterhead Prison, the Beast refused to
address his offending behaviour by taking part in a programme
designed to prevent sex offenders from continuing to abuse
children. He wrote to a newsletter published by a pressure
group called FACT – Falsely Accused Carers and Teachers.
He blamed everyone but himself. The legal system had not
informed him of his 'rights'. The police had been 'underhand',
'trawling' for witnesses and putting words 'in their mouths'.
The lawyers had made a 'farce' of justice. In the same newsletter, his wife published a letter in which she, too, accused the
police of 'trawling'. She suggested only a minority of children
in care *may* (her italics) have been abused. She added, 'My
husband is serving a prison sentence for something he *did not
do'* (her italics). Talk about denial. This is the truth.

The Beast was only one of a group of abusers who blackened the good name of Quarriers. They used good works to
mask their evil. Here is the roll of shame. Porteous's brother-
in-law, Alexander 'Sandy' Wilson, would be convicted in 2004
of sexually abusing girls for two decades. Uncle Sandy was
found guilty of 15 charges. Some victims had learning difficulties. He was brought up in Quarriers, where he and the Beast
ran the Boys' Brigade.

In 2001, Joseph Nicholson – Uncle Joe – was 72 when he
was jailed for two years for sexually abusing a 13-year-old girl.
He was described in court as 'a good Christian who did the
Lord's work'.

The same year, Samuel McBrearty, then 70, who had left
Quarriers to become a senior social worker in Aberdeen, was
jailed for 12 years for repeatedly raping two girls and indecently
assaulting another when they were aged 8, 10 and 11 years old.

In 2005, William Gilmore, then 48, the son of Quarriers
house parents, was convicted of using lewd, indecent and

libidinous practices against two girls and a boy when he was a teenager. He was placed on the sex offenders register and sentenced to 300 hours' community service. One of his victims criticised the sentence and said, 'He ruined our lives.'

Ruth Wallace was 72, in March 2006, when she was found guilty of assaulting and ill treating children between 1971 and 1981. Sheriff John Herald said her conduct was 'inexcusable'. The former Quarriers nurse and house parent in Cottage 17 was placed on probation for three years.

Mary Drummond was 74, in 2002, when she admitted five charges of cruelty. She terrified children with a bogeyman she nicknamed the 'Baw Baw'. She locked up children as young as five and forced a child to swallow food and vomit by holding her mouth and nose. Drummond was placed on probation for three years. For her own safety, she had to be escorted from court.

Euphemia Ramsay, or Climie, was 59 when she was convicted, in July 2006, of three charges of assaulting children while she worked at Quarriers in the late 1960s and early 1970s. Ramsay, who worked as a residential care worker for the Department of Health and Social Security on the Isle of Man, was sentenced to 150 hours' community service. She was cleared of committing a series of sexual assaults against Quarriers children.

Who, I wonder, 'trawled' for their victims? Who put 'words in their mouths'? The truth is that Strathclyde Police and Operation Orbona, the biggest ever investigation into the systematic abuse of children in care, did their job, a superb job. Justice was served no matter how the perverts, paedophiles and abusers seek to justify their appalling behaviour. In fact, Strathclyde Police did such a good job that the model of the inquiry is now used at police training colleges, to instruct officers in how to conduct historic sexual-abuse investigations. Members of the original team work with new recruits, passing on their highly specialised skills.

One of the leading experts is Detective Inspector Ross Mackay, the senior investigating officer on the Quarriers inquiry, who told me, 'We learned a lot from the inquiry and gained valuable insight into the terrible crime of historic abuse. Now we use the techniques we learned to train other officers from all over the country in how to run an investigation and how to interview victims in order that they feel comfortable telling what happened to them.

'We did a great job on the Quarriers investigation. I'm very proud of what we achieved. We had a team of dedicated officers, focused and determined to help those victims get justice and find some closure for what happened to them. At times, the inquiry was like putting together a huge jigsaw. We were covering many decades and people who had moved on in their lives to every part of the UK as well as to Canada, America and Australia. It was a time-consuming operation, much of it taken up tracing people. One thing that struck us was that a number of victims had reported what had happened to them, but no one had believed them at the time. We believed them. And we were determined to do something about it.

'One witness complained about Porteous in the 1980s. That complaint was not handled the way we handle complaints of this nature today. We've learned so much more now about these kinds of crimes. A lot of the Quarriers victims were very badly damaged by what happened to them. Some victims wanted to speak out; others didn't. My officers respected the courage of all of them in facing what they did. They were there to support those who went through the justice system. Some of the victims have gone on to do something positive, supporting others by working with survivors. That's a good thing.'

Detective Inspector Mackay is correct, but it is no better than what his officers did to bring evil to justice. They were highly professional, and without their skills most of us would never have seen our abusers brought to court.

CHAPTER 33
Falling Apart

I was numb. It was as if Novocaine had been injected into my system. I couldn't feel. I couldn't think. My life had flat-lined. The Beast was in jail and I should have been elated. I should have been liberated, but I was as imprisoned by my emotions as he was by his prison cell. Alcohol didn't help me, but it wasn't for lack of trying. Funny thing about booze: three drinks make you garrulous; six condemn you to silence; ten take you to the dark place. I was in a very dark place. I had always been wary about drinking and kept a lid on it, but I began drinking more than I should have.

I had prided myself on my work. I was precise in my business dealings to the point of obsession, but even that was slipping away. I made mistakes. I couldn't go into the office. The telephone was my enemy. Every time it rang, I feared it would be another abusive call. I hid at home, spending my days in tears.

Inevitably, my business suffered. I appointed a manager, but my reputation had been established by the trust built up by dealing personally with clients. I lost prestigious contracts. My five-star business was haemorrhaging stars. I was on the road to nowhere. A lifetime of hurt had caught up with me.

It couldn't get worse, could it? Then it did, ironically on April Fool's Day 2003, with the broadcast of a BBC *Frontline* documentary entitled 'Secrets or Lies?' A few weeks before, I had taken a call from a producer, who told me they were making a programme about the Porteous case. Would I take part? I gave her a full statement, and said that yes, I would take part. I told her everything that had happened to me in Quarriers. I was preparing to leave for a holiday and told her that if she needed more information in the meantime to contact my lawyer, Cameron Fyfe. I received another call from the BBC while I was abroad. I reiterated they should speak to Cameron to make arrangements for my interview. When the programme aired, however, the BBC stated I had declined to comment. I returned to a bombshell – in a phone call from a friend in Scotland. Yet another phone call, yet another disaster. How ironic.

'Have you seen it?' said my friend.

'What?' I said.

Silence. My caller was composing herself. 'Have you heard what they're saying?' she continued.

'What?' I repeated.

'They let Porteous go on television and say he is innocent! That you're a liar, so was the other boy, and they're questioning the safety of Porteous's conviction.'

'WHAT?' I said.

'I'll send the tape,' said my friend.

* * *

I sat in the dark, alone, and watched the machine swallow the tape. The picture flickered and I was confronted by the Beast, obviously in jail. A reporter's voice said, 'This man is a convicted paedophile, accused of horrific sexual abuse. Yet instead of being a figure of hatred, his case has attracted the most incredible support.'

I was aghast. I heard other voices, but not the words.

The reporter continued, 'Exactly how safe is the conviction of John Porteous?'

I felt nauseous. Here was the BBC, the national broadcaster and arbiter of impartiality, apparently siding with a monster who had been convicted of abusing me and another boy and destroying our lives, in the words of the judge.

I watched horrified as the reporter asked him, 'Have you ever sexually abused anybody?'

The Beast looked straight into the camera and replied, 'No, I have not. I'm not that way inclined.'

Had he ever sexually abused any of the children in his care?

'Hand on my heart, I did not,' he said.

I was transfixed. In the programme, I was referred to as 'James' and the Beast's other victim was called 'Robert'. The reporter told viewers that I and my sister had been sent to Quarriers because our mother 'abused' us. Wrong! My mother abandoned us. She had not abused us. The reporter recounted how John and Helen Porteous were to find themselves accused of 'horrific offences'.

Helen said, on camera, 'We just couldn't believe that this was happening to us. We had heard about it happening to other people that had worked in the Village.'

One of the 'other people' would be her own brother, Alexander 'Sandy' Wilson, who would be convicted for a reign of sickening abuse lasting 19 years. Helen was asked if she ever 'beat' children. She replied, 'As I said, I smacked children, but I did not beat them.'

Did she starve them? she was asked.

'Never,' she said.

The BBC reporter, with the cooperation of John and Helen Porteous, went on to tell viewers, 'Police checked Quarriers' records and found that John Porteous had been accused of abusing a boy earlier, in the late 1970s.' Wrong! The accusation was levelled in the 1980s. According to the BBC, that 'accusation', coupled with the testimony of 'Robert' and 'James', 'strengthened' the prosecution's case.

The rest of the documentary passed in a blur and I watched the credits roll with a sense of horror. The BBC was effectively claiming the Beast was innocent and we were liars. The programme-makers had also filmed a so-called dramatic reconstruction within Quarriers, with children from a theatre group, run by a daughter of Porteous, supposedly enacting scenes from *my* life. I couldn't believe it. If my life had been derailed, the wreckage was now on fire. Once more I would have to find the strength to pursue the truth.

Two people came to my aid: my MP, Nick Raynsford, and Mike Jempson of MediaWise, a group that helps people who have grievances against the media. Both helped steer me through the complaints process. It was years before the BBC's Editorial Standards Committee decreed the *Frontline* documentary breached the corporation's code of conduct and I received an apology from its chairman, Richard Tait. The committee concluded the programme had not met the required standards in a 'number of areas', including 'due accuracy and impartiality' and the 'right of reply'. It went on to express concern over the possibility of 'systemic failures'.

I believe the BBC, like many others, had been manipulated by a clever liar who has yet to accept his guilt. I am happy to say that I have since enjoyed a good working relationship with the corporation, in my roles with the government and survivor groups, as well as appearing on television and radio, representing Quarriers abuse victims. Porteous was adept at hiding behind his mask of respectability, which I believe had duped people within the BBC.

In the end I was vindicated, but the burden was intolerable. I became suicidal and was more than once on the brink of taking my own life as I failed to come to terms with this 'justice'. The final straw came in January 2004, when the Beast became the first paedophile in Scotland to use a change in the law to reduce his sentence. The charge of 'shameless indecency' – of which the Beast had been convicted on two separate counts, involving me and the other victim – was removed from the statute. The Beast's lawyer petitioned the court and his eight-year sentence was reduced by three years. Lord Gill, the Lord Justice Clerk, said the remaining charges were 'grave offences'. He added, 'They were committed by him at a time when he had a serious responsibility of care in relation to children who were already disadvantaged.' The Appeal Court judge said that while the sentence on Porteous had to be cut to reflect the change in the law, he should still serve a 'significant' sentence for the remaining charges.

It's important to note that the Beast did not – and has never – appealed his actual conviction. His first application for parole would be denied. I had seen to that by petitioning the Parole Board. I told the board that I feared for public safety because he refused to acknowledge his crimes. I pointed out that even after he had been accused of abuse he had sat on the board of a primary school and had been appointed chairman of his local Children's Panel Advisory Council.

However, the Beast would eventually be released on 3 March 2006 – without ever having addressed his offending behaviour. He and his wife live in a village not far from Quarriers, as does Helen's paedophile brother.

The double blow of the documentary and the Beast taking advantage of the legal loophole was intolerable after everything I had been through. I had even been forced to threaten Helen Porteous with legal action. On 9 January 2004, my legal advisors had written to her: 'Our client has advised us that you have stated publicly at several meetings that no abuse took place and that our client is a liar. If you persist with these allegations, we are to raise an action of interdict and defamation.' It was my final small act of defiance before I went under.

At times, I had worked three jobs to fund my business, my properties and my investments for the future. I lost everything. But I paid off outstanding loans and mortgages, and ensured my staff was looked after financially. The millionaire lifestyle was gone, but at least I had done the honourable thing and went down without owing anyone a penny. I entered a period of utter despair, spending long spells in therapy, dependent on antidepressants and sleeping pills. Nothing brought me peace.

At my lowest ebb, I was helped immeasurably by Ian Stephen, one of the UK's top forensic psychologists, and the real-life inspiration for the television series *Cracker*, starring Robbie Coltrane. Ian, who was the consultant on the series, is the insightful, soft-spoken Aberdonian who saved my life. I was able to express my emotions to him, as I had never been able to do before, and with his therapy I was able to bring all those childhood abuse memories into sharp focus. His advice was invaluable. In his report, he concluded, 'The trial of

Porteous and Mr Whelan being contacted to become involved opened the floodgates. He has been re-traumatised and has suffered emotionally and psychologically. There is no doubt that the abuse perpetrated on him while he was in Quarriers has led to post-traumatic stress disorder and mental-health problems. He will need support to help him cope with the aftermath of the abuse and the recent reopening of his memories.'

My lawyer, Cameron Fyfe, also helped me greatly. He has enormous expertise in child-abuse cases and recognised that I was on the edge, but he encouraged me to fight my way out of the darkness by helping others. He said to me, 'David, you have been through so much, and there are so many others like you. Maybe it's time you helped them.' Cameron is dealing with hundreds of cases of historic child-abuse victims and is at the forefront of attempts to remove the iniquitous three-year 'time-bar' law that exists in Scotland. It prevents so many abuse victims from seeking justice through the civil courts. There is no time bar on criminal cases of historic abuse. That was why the Crown was able to pursue the Beast – in a criminal case. Unfortunately, many historic abuse victims do not get the chance to have their day in a criminal court because it is difficult for prosecutors to pursue the offenders so many years after the crimes were committed. Often, the only recourse victims have is to go to the civil courts to sue their abuser, seeking reparation for their broken lives, or to sue the organisation where the abuse occurred for a lack of care or negligence. The law allows for full reparation for victims, but time bar in Scotland prevents it. Under the current time-bar law, they have only three years from the time of the abuse or from when they reach the age of 18 to lodge that claim. Many other countries across the world have rejected the time bar. They recognise that the crime of child abuse is unique in that it may take the victims – as it did in my case – many decades to come forward. That is what Cameron and I are fighting to change.

Cameron went on, 'You've been through the system. Your abuser has been brought to justice. Why not use that experience to help others?'

His words sowed the seeds of new beginnings, but I still had questions that needed answers. Those answers could only lie in the past. I went in search of my father.

CHAPTER 34
Finding Da

'Ger away tae fuck! Bastards! Fuckin' bangin' ma door! Shower o' bastards!' It was like the sound of an animal at bay, growling its threats, but there was a tinge of fear behind the menace.

It had taken me several moments to identify the sound from behind the door as actual words spoken by a human being. I don't know who had been the last person at this door, but whoever it was must have frightened this creature. The Salvation Army officer who had knocked took a step back. The poor woman's sensibilities were crushed. I'm certain this reunion wasn't going quite as she had planned.

'Mr Whelan,' she said in a small, hesitant voice. Another tirade of expletives erupted. 'Mr Whelan, it's the Salvation Army.'

The Salvation Army had found my father. He had apparently been sleeping rough on the streets of London for many years, but he had been given this council house in a block of maisonette flats in Stepney. I still wasn't sure why I believed I needed to meet with my father again. He was nothing and everything. I had seen him last when I was 10 years old, and only then for a few minutes after I had inadvertently let him into the house in Drumchapel. Somewhere under the confusion, though, there was a need. Something had driven me here. In a lull in the growling from within the flat, I looked across at Jeanette, who had come with me.

The Salvation Army woman went on, 'Remember ... remember I told you I was bringing your children to see you?' she said, in a voice that tried and failed to sound firm.

Silence.

'Oh,' said a strange new voice from behind the door. 'How nice. Just a moment.' The change in tone was so dramatic I almost laughed. The accent was now what we Scots describe euphemistically as 'pan loaf' – an affected posh voice. I knew it was anything but a funny scenario, but, all the same, I had to suppress a giggle at this bloody black comedy that was unfolding.

There was a shuffling movement from behind the door and the lock was turned with a sharp click. It opened to reveal a frail and wizened old man, much shorter than I remembered, with the bruised features of a second-rate pugilist. My father. Dear old dad. He looked benign, but his initial reaction had proved that some things never change. It is said we take comfort from the constants in our lives – the safety offered by unchanging circumstances. I felt somehow this meeting was not going to throw a security blanket around me, after all. But I was in a dark place in my life and I needed to know why. I also wanted to know ... how. I suppose I hoped that an explanation for the present could be found in the past.

My head hurt. I had been drinking the night before. Like father, like son? God, I hoped not. The thought chilled me.

'Hello, Mr Whelan,' said the woman, whose memory of my father's outburst was as fresh as mine. She could not hide the alarm in her voice.

'Do come in,' said the old man, still speaking in the pretend accent.

'This is Jeanette … and David,' she told him.

'Davie, Jeanette,' he said, and added, 'Come in, come in and see your old da.'

Suffering Christ, I thought.

Jeanette's face was a picture.

My urge to laugh had gone. So this was what the Little Bull had come to? Somewhere in this pathetic old man, a shell of his former self, was the monster who struck fear into his family with his quick temper and quicker fists. This was the man who brought trollops into our home and had sex with them as my mother and brothers and sisters cowered under blankets. I was just a baby then, but Jeanette had told me the stories of his brutality. This was the man who raped a woman in a dark alley. This was the man who battered every vestige of strength, hope, compassion and care out of the poor demented creature who was our mother. This was the man who beat his sons and daughters to prove he had power. Now look at him. Living in a drab single room, so like the one in Kennedy Street, in Glasgow, where he had held us hostage to his madness.

He smiled at me. I couldn't smile back. He would live for a year beyond this reunion, but he had been dead to me for as long as I could remember. The smile on his lips never reached his eyes, which were as cold and unforgiving as I had remembered. He scared me still. Not physically, not any more. It was just what he was. That's what scared me. It was the knowledge that I was his son, that I carried his genes. Was I like him? In any way?

The spell was broken by the lady from the Salvation Army. 'Well, I'm sure you have such a lot to talk about, a lot of years to catch up. I'll leave you to it.'

'Davie?' said the old man, uncertain, I think, of which of his sons I was. The Salvation Army woman had introduced me, but the old man probably didn't remember. God help us. 'You look … smart,' he said. 'Doing well for yourself? Chip off the old block?'

I was in no mood for small talk.

'Jimmy's dead,' he said suddenly.

'I know,' I replied. 'Did you know Johnny was dead, too?'

With the Salvation Army woman out of the way, the monster was free to return. The smile faded and his eyes glittered. The voice reverted to pure Glasgow. 'Johnny, eh? Another one oot the way!' he replied. 'One less bastard tae worry aboot.' As if he had ever worried about any of us, but he was like a scorpion, incapable of not stinging.

I bit my tongue to stay silent. I've never had a violent bone in my body, but, God forgive me, at that moment I wanted to drag him outside and throw him from the walkway at his front door.

'Ma's gone, too,' I went on, a cold hand closing around my heart.

'Fuckin' whore,' he spat. 'Good for fuck all, she was.'

The hand tightened. Would there be no end to this unutterable callousness and inhumanity? My soul ached.

'Dad,' said Jeanette quietly but firmly, 'that's enough. We –'

He broke in, 'Fuckin' bitch. Who'll miss that? Nae use tae anybody, yer ma.'

This had been a mistake, a monumental mistake. I tried to collect my thoughts by looking around the room. There was nothing of us, his family, anywhere. No mementoes, no photographs. What had I expected? A family group in a gilt frame? There were, however, several pictures of the Queen, a deeply ironic choice, given that he had spent most of his life as a guest of Her Majesty in her various jails. A few cheap seaside souvenir ornaments sat on the mantelpiece. This tawdry attempt to make the place homely was not of his doing, obviously. They had probably been left behind by a previous tenant. The Little Bull was not a man to surround himself with memories. If he had, the room would have been painted pitch black.

I could not stand it for another second. I was suffocating. I turned on my heel and walked out of the flat, leaving Jeanette alone with him. I stepped onto the walkway and gripped the metal railing. I looked out over the East End of London, towards the Mile End Road, which had grown up around the ancient church of St Dunstan. I could see the bell tower of the medieval church hemmed in by the modern city. The bell tower evoked more bad memories.

'Are you all right?' a voice said.

I had not seen the old woman approach. She was not wearing a coat, so she must have come out of a neighbouring flat.

'Hello,' I said.

She looked from me towards the open door. 'Here to see Mr Whelan?' she asked.

I nodded.

'Such a lovely old man. So kind, isn't he?' she said.

She didn't wait for an answer and retreated at a slow shuffle back into her home. It was just as well. I don't think I could have prevented myself from telling her exactly what kind of man her Mr Whelan was. I stood alone with my thoughts until

I heard Jeanette behind me. I looked at my watch. Less than three minutes had passed since I left the flat. Jeanette's tolerance level was not much greater than mine. My father had followed her. He was about to say something to me, but I walked away. I never looked back. I knew now this old man had no answers for me. Jeanette followed on my heels.

When we reached our car, I turned to her and said, 'I never want to hear his name mentioned for as long as I live.' I realised that it had been a fruitless, ill-conceived plan to believe that our father could offer anything other than cruel indifference.

And there I thought it would end, but a few weeks later Jeanette handed me a letter written on cheap notepaper. It was from him. In a scrawling ill-educated hand, he wrote of how he had 'missed' us. More black lies. The letter ended with the words, 'Hope to hear from you soon. Your old dad, Johnny.' There were six kisses on the bottom – one for each of us and Ma? I crumpled the letter and tossed it in the bin.

It would not be the last letter we would receive about our father. Less than a year later, in February 2004, Jeanette handed me another missive. This time it was from Hackney Council. They wanted £2,000 – the cost of Da's funeral. My father was dead and I could not even shed the single tear I had offered up to Ma. And I certainly wasn't going to pay to lay him to rest. He had given me no rest. He could go to his pauper's grave. I threw away the letter. Good riddance.

CHAPTER 35
Fighting Back

I was wrong. My father did have answers for me. I had just not realised it as I fled from his little flat. There was nothing wrong with his house, where he lived, or those who lived around him. It was he who was marooned on a bleak, uninhabited island of his own making. He had not cared. He had shown no compassion. He had been cruel and insensitive. And now he was alone, unloved, unwanted, without value. His entire existence screamed how *not* to live a life. That was the lesson for me. Cameron Fyfe had been correct. I could, if I wanted, sit in front of abuse victims and tell them, 'I know what you are going through.' I could, if I wanted, persuade them that it was possible to take up the reins of their life and go forward. I could assure them, if I wanted, that they could survive, as I had learned to.

First, though, I had to address the psychological problems that beset me. If I allowed myself to remain with my face in the dirt, could I expect anything but to end up like my father?

He didn't know it, but Da had, for the one and only time in his life, been a father to me and shown me the right path. It was a defining moment in my life. The road lay ahead, clear but uphill. It was time to start climbing.

I was sitting at home – I was living in Brighton at the time – when I experienced the revelation. Cameron had told me during one of our meetings that there was an organisation for people like me, led by an inspirational man named Frank Docherty. Like me, he had been to hell and back, after a childhood of abuse in a home. I had his phone number. I called him. Frank was gruff, down-to-earth, pure Lanarkshire working class, a man whose life had been in tatters until he found redemption in fighting for others. He invited me to a 'big meeting' in Glasgow.

When I arrived for the meeting, in a conference room at the city's university, I was astonished. There were more than 300 people in the room, of all ages and social groups. Every one of them had a story to break your heart – of lives shattered by abuse, drink, drugs and prison. I had never been so happy in my life. A strange thing to say, I know, surrounded by so much apparent sorrow, but there was no misery here. There was kinship, and there was hope. I wasn't alone any more.

Frank gripped me by the hand and said, 'There are some people you should meet.' He led me to a group that comprised middle-aged men and women, even aged grandmothers. I looked at them mystified. 'These are the folk from Quarriers,' said Frank.

The sea of faces misted in my rising tears. Truly, I wasn't alone any more. We took our places in the hall and the meeting began. A campaign was being launched on two fronts: the first was to demand a judicial review into how widespread historic abuse was in Scotland's institutions; and, second, we wanted to end the intrinsic injustice of historic abuse reparation cases being time-barred from the civil courts. Now, I had a cause. This was something worth fighting for.

One of Scotland's top law lords had already claimed that a 'generation of abused children' had been failed and expressed his hope that the law would be reformed. Lord McEwan said, 'I have an uneasy feeling that the legislation, and the strict way the courts have interpreted it, has failed a generation of children who've been abused and whose attempts to seek a fair remedy have become mired in the legal system.'

The only way to change the law is through Parliament, and by now Scotland had its own government. The abuse had held us in invisible chains all of our lives, so it was apt to make our feelings known by forming a 'human chain of misery' round the Scottish Parliament building in Edinburgh. That got the attention of the politicians.

One of Frank's members approached the petitions committee of the Parliament, and its chairman, Michael McMahon MSP, took up the fight. With his help, Scotland's first minister, Jack McConnell, was forced to say sorry on behalf of the people of Scotland. Mr McConnell said the abuse of vulnerable young Scots was 'deplorable, unacceptable and inexcusable'. Hundreds of us sat in the public gallery to hear him tell Parliament, 'I offer a sincere and full apology to those who were subject to abuse and neglect, who did not receive the level of love, care and support that they deserved and who have coped with that burden all of their lives.'

We applauded as he went on, 'It is clear that some children were abused in Scottish residential care homes. Children suffered physical, emotional and sexual abuse in the very places in which they hoped to find love, care and protection. Those children, adults today, deserve our full recognition of what happened to them. They should not have been abused. They were badly wronged. Such abuse of vulnerable young people – whenever or wherever it took place – is deplorable, unacceptable and inexcusable.'

It was, in a sense, a breakthrough, but in many ways the words were hollow. It hadn't been the people of Scotland who abused us. I wanted changes, and so far the hoped-for judicial review and the removal of the time bar have eluded us. Until we achieve those ends, none of us will have received proper justice.

To date, eight people associated with Quarriers have been convicted of abusing children in the charity's care, far more than any other organisation. These perverts and abusers have besmirched the good name of the organisation and what it has always stood for. Throughout the years of its existence, many good and decent Quarriers people have helped give thousands of vulnerable children the best start in life, but what happened to me and those like me, at the hands of a cadre of evil people, remains a national disgrace.

I believed there were enough former Quarriers children alleging abuse to set up our own pressure group. I formed FBGA – Former Boys and Girls Abused of Quarriers Homes, with Christine, Isaac, Jeremy and Stephen. I use only their first names to protect their identity. The name of our organisation was a play on words on the Former Boys and Girls Association of Quarriers Homes, which at one time was chaired by the Beast himself. Our ethos remained the same – a judicial review and the end to the time bar. We have several hundred members around the world, all of whom allege they suffered physical or sexual abuse – or both – at Quarriers.

By now, on the back of all this apparent misery, I had been saved, my life transformed, having found new meaning through my suffering and that of others. I had also learned that to make significant changes you have to fight from within.

I was invited to become an advisor to the Scottish government, to help create a strategy to support historic abuse survivors and ensure the protection of future generations of children in care. It's not perfect. It's a work – an often frustrating work – in progress, but we are making inroads. A survivor service has been set up, funded by the government, and a programme is in place to allow survivors to present their testimony to a specially appointed commission. The Scottish Human Rights Commission (SHRC) has already demanded that this forum should lead to securing 'effective access to justice, remedies and reparation for all survivors of childhood abuse'.

Quarriers have agreed to take part in the 'Time to be Heard' pilot scheme, which FBGA hope will be rolled out to involve other organisations wherever there has been alleged abuse. Professor Alan Miller, chair of the SHRC, commented, 'As well as a time to be heard, it is a time to learn lessons, so we call on the Scottish government to ensure accountability as well as acknowledgement to identify not only what happened but why it happened and how it can be avoided in the future.' I agree, but what I don't want is for this to become a 'talking shop'. We need action. It is, however, a start, and what has begun in Scotland has to be translated all over the UK. That's why I've been lobbying the British government as well, and meeting with MPs to discuss similar strategies across the entire country.

Child-abuse scandals, notably in Ireland, Australia and Canada, have been addressed by the governments of those ntries. Good for them. I wish our government would show same compassion to our abused. The former prime minister Gordon Brown spoke of national 'shame' over the thousands of migrant children sent from Britain to Australia until the 1960s. He set up a £6 million fund to help these 'forgotten Australians' re-establish links with their lost families. I'm happy about that, but the government has turned its back on the victims on its own doorstep. That must change.

The fight to achieve change will continue for many years, but what the battle has taught me is that at the heart of any struggle there can be no room for silence. I have made mistakes in my life – and no doubt I will make many more – but the greatest mistake I ever made was to remain silent for so long. Living a lie is no way to live a life. That is an object lesson for us all. The day I stopped living a lie was the day I reclaimed who I was. Now I am David Whelan, and that means something.

As well as helping survivors across the world, I hold a responsible position in the NHS, working at a leading London hospital, which has been hugely supportive of my survivor work. The energy I once applied to running my business has been channelled into helping those in need. How ironic it was that the final meeting with my father should have had such far-reaching consequences.

Today, I admit that at times I am still afraid, but the scared little boy behind the bathroom door is gone. There is nothing more to hide. I surrendered my anonymity. I have been stripped bare. Most importantly, there are no more stairs to climb. There is no more abuse to suffer. I am no longer nobody's child.

It has been a long journey from the time I held Irene's hand as we passed through the gates of Quarriers and saw those empty words – 'Suffer the little children' – spelled out in flowers. She and I did suffer individually and together for most of our lives, but only one of us survived. If my final meeting with Da changed my life, one of my last conversations with my sister Irene would free me for ever from the spell of the Beast. Her words were spoken to me from her deathbed.

CHAPTER 36
No More Silence

Something good happened to me on the night I lost Irene, something true and noble and liberating. I had only been out of the room for a few minutes. When I returned, she was gone. She was on the bed, still, her face in repose, her body relaxed by the deepest of all sleeps. She had been 49 years old for just six weeks. The last words I had said to her were 'I love you.' How do I explain the loss of my sister … and the realisation that the end of her life offered me a new beginning?

Ma had gone, so too had Johnny and Jimmy, and the man who called himself our father. But when I examined the circumstances of my life, with all of its pain, all of its trouble and, yes, modesty apart, all of its achievements, I knew somehow that my story, in a sense, ends – and begins – with Irene. Jeanette has always been like a mother to me as well as a loving sister. Johnny and Jimmy were loved but often remote figures in my life. Ma and Da? Well, you know enough by now to realise the roles they played. Irene was my sister in the truest sense. She was closest to me in age. My sister ran with me in the bright sunshine along the white sands of North Uist. We roamed together on the streets of Drumchapel, like orphans in a storm. She was with me when we drove through the gates of Quarriers. In the beginning, it was this strong, feisty woman who, when she was little more than a child herself, stood in front of me as my shield. The really bad things did not truly begin to happen to me until she was driven away. Another stain on the soul of the Beast. In the course of our lives, when we were brought together, more often than not by the experience of loss, we re-established a connection that had always existed. Now she was gone.

The others in the room sensed that I wanted to be alone with her. I drew the curtain around the bed. I took her hand, kissed her on the forehead and told her again that I loved her I was grateful that when I had last spoken those words to her she had heard them. I don't know how long I sat with her. I thanked her for the letter. She had written to me from her deathbed, a short but intensely private and personal note. Irene told me she loved me and that she valued our special relationship. She spoke of what had happened to me, to us, as children, but there was no rancour or bitterness in the words. They were imbued with the philosophy of someone nearing death, someone who had learned that to fight the universe is to wage a losing battle.

It was 21 December 2004. Irene had been taken by metastatic carcinoma – the formal expression for a body and brain riddled with cancer. It had happened so quickly. Who can see cancer coming? One day, she was feeling unwell. The next, she was dying. A few weeks before her death, we had spent a lovely weekend together, going to the theatre and dining out. I don't think she had been to the theatre in her life and it was a magical experience for her. I was grateful I had given her that.

Jeanette, as always, was the rock throughout the relatively short period when Irene's health deteriorated rapidly. We had taken her out of hospital for a few hours to a Chinese restaurant to celebrate her 49th birthday. Banners proclaimed her age, the champagne flowed, and she was happy to have her family around her. She wore a paper crown and we treated her like a queen. Now the end had come in a side room, off Ward 6, in Lewisham Hospital, South London.

I had felt anger when I first learned of her condition, but my fury had evaporated. Irene's serenity had calmed me. But deep within me, in spite of this, there remained a simmering resentment against those who had once diminished her place in the world. Those who had told her she would 'come to nothing'. Her life would be without value, they said. She would be as worthless as her mother and father. If she had children of her own, they would be as unwanted as she had been, she was goaded. She and her children would spend their lives dependent on state handouts.

I know that those cruel jibes spoken so many years before stung her to the core of her being, to the extent that she would not take help even from those who loved her. Yes, there were times when she struggled, but if you were going to offer financial help to Irene, you had damn well better find a way to disguise it. Irene was reluctant to take a penny she had not earned. My sister had worked every day of her life in a caring profession, looking after the sick in a series of residential care homes. She had raised Paul, a fine son. So, in the end, those cold-hearted and spiritually bereft tyrants were so terribly wrong. Hers was a life of immense value, unlike theirs. And so was mine, I realised. We had both lived with disdain, with cruelty, with the burden of the past. Not only had we survived, we had triumphed.

Nowhere was this more evident than when, later, we cleared out Irene's home. I found a packet of uncashed cheques.

'What the hell is this?' I asked Jeanette.

We flicked through the cheques, all made out to Irene. They added up to thousands of pounds. Then we found the thank-you letters. The letters – and the cheques – were from the grateful relatives of people she had cared for. She hadn't banked any of them. It wasn't that she couldn't have used the money; she simply regarded her work as a duty for which she had already been paid. So, is this a life without value? Or was mine? I don't think so.

A few weeks before, when we were sitting in the crowded Chinese restaurant, bombarded by raucous laughter, a moment of quiet separated us from the crowd.

'You should tell people,' said this raggedy queen in her paper crown, who still contrived to be beautiful. By now, Irene was a forlorn figure. Her hair had long since been taken by the chemotherapy treatment, and her face was thin and sallow.

'Tell people what?' I asked, laughing.

'Everything,' she said.

And I have.

No more silence.

Help and Support for Victims of Abuse

BRITISH SUPPORT AND SURVIVOR GROUPS

FORMER BOYS AND GIRLS ABUSED OF QUARRIERS HOMES (FBGA)
Supports individuals and families from Quarriers and other
  institutions.
www.fbga.co.uk
Email: fbga1@aol.com

SCOTTISH HUMAN RIGHTS COMMISSION (SHRC)
Promotes and protects the human rights of everyone in
  Scotland.
www.scottishhumanrights.com

SIBLINGS TOGETHER
Promotes positive contact between siblings separated by care.
It aims to provide opportunities for planned, enjoyable,
high quality contact for those siblings separated.
www.siblingstogether.org.uk

SPEAKUP
Run by and for people with learning disabilities and their
supporters.
www.speakup.org.uk

THE MEDIAWISE TRUST
Helps victims of media abuse.
www.mediawise.org.uk

THE SALVATION ARMY
Offers a Family Tracing Service.
www.salvationarmy.org.uk

VICTIM SUPPORT
Helps people cope with the effects of crime.
www.victimsupport.org.uk
Helpline: 0845 30 30 900

INTERNATIONAL SURVIVOR GROUPS

AUSTRALIA
CARE LEAVERS AUSTRALIA NETWORK (CLAN)
Support and advocacy group for children brought up in care
in Australia.
www.clan.org.au

CANADA

THE CANADIAN CHILD ABUSE SURVIVOR MONUMENT-
RESIDENTIAL INSTITUTIONS AND REACHING OUT
AWARENESS CAMPAIGN

www.irvingstudios.com

IRELAND

ONE IN FOUR

Supports women and men who have experienced sexual
abuse and or sexual violence.

www.oneinfour.org